Fodor's
BEIJING

WELCOME TO BEIJING

China's capital city is a vibrant jumble of neighborhoods and districts. Home to such ancient treasures as the Forbidden City and the Summer Palace, Beijing is constantly transforming itself with a building boom that never seems to end. Colorful markets stand toe-to-toe with ritzy shopping malls, and lively old *hutongs* (alleyway neighborhoods) stand in the shadow of glittering towers that dwarf their surroundings. Discovering today's Beijing is a fascinating journey between an ancient civilization and a brave new world.

TOP REASONS TO GO

★ **Forbidden City:** The world's best-preserved palace housed emperors for centuries.

★ **Modern Architecture:** The world's top architects are reshaping Beijing.

★ **Great Wall:** Mankind's most impressive fortification is just a short drive away.

★ **Real Chinese Food:** Flavors from all over the country are here for the tasting.

★ **Unique Markets:** Everything from kitsch to curio, cheap handbags to grade-A pearls.

★ **Tiananmen Square:** The country's political heart is also a spectacular public square.

Fodor's BEIJING

Publisher: Amanda D'Acierno, *Senior Vice President*

Editorial: Arabella Bowen, *Editor in Chief*; Linda Cabasin, *Editorial Director*

Design: Tina Malaney, *Associate Art Director*; Chie Ushio, *Senior Designer*; Ann McBride, *Production Designer*

Photography: Jennifer Arnow, *Senior Photo Editor*; Jennifer Romains, *Photo Researcher*

Production: Linda Schmidt, *Managing Editor*; Evangelos Vasilakis, *Associate Managing Editor*; Angela L. McLean, *Senior Production Manager*

Maps: Rebecca Baer, *Senior Map Editor*; David Lindroth; Mark Stroud (Moon Street Cartography), *Cartographers*

Sales: Jacqueline Lebow, *Sales Director*

Marketing & Publicity: Heather Dalton, *Marketing Director*; Katherine Punia, *Publicity Director*

Business & Operations: Susan Livingston, *Vice President, Strategic Business Planning*; Sue Daulton, *Vice President, Operations*

Fodors.com: Megan Bell, *Executive Director, Revenue & Business Development*; Yasmin Marinaro, *Senior Director, Marketing & Partnerships*

Copyright © 2015 by Fodor's Travel, a division of Random House LLC

Editors: Stephen Brewer, John Rambow, Caroline Trefler

Editorial Contributors: Kit Gillet, Tom O'Malley, Yuan Ren, Adrian Sandiford

Production Editor: Carrie Parker

5th Edition

ISBN 978-1-101-87804-0

ISSN 1934-5518

SPECIAL SALES

This book is available at special discounts for bulk purchases for sales promotions or premiums. For more information, e-mail specialmarkets@penguinrandomhouse.com

PRINTED IN THE UNITED STATES OF AMERICA

10 9 8 7 6 5 4 3 2 1

CONTENTS

Fodor's Features

CONTENTS

MAPS

ABOUT THIS GUIDE

Fodor's Recommendations

Everything in this guide is worth doing—we don't cover what isn't—but exceptional sights, hotels, and restaurants are recognized with additional accolades. **Fodor's Choice** ★ indicates our top recommendations; and **Best Bets** call attention to notable hotels and restaurants in various categories. Care to nominate a new place? Visit Fodors.com/contact-us.

Trip Costs

We list prices wherever possible to help you budget well. Hotel and restaurant price categories from **$** to **$$$$** are noted alongside each recommendation. For hotels, we include the lowest cost of a standard double room in high season. For restaurants, we cite the average price of a main course at dinner or, if dinner isn't served, at lunch. For attractions, we always list adult admission fees; discounts are usually available for children, students, and senior citizens.

Hotels

Our local writers vet every hotel to recommend the best overnights in each price category, from budget to expensive. Unless otherwise specified, you can expect private bath, phone, and TV in your room. For expanded hotel reviews, facilities, and deals visit Fodors.com.

Top Picks		Hotels & Restaurants	
★ **Fodor's Choice**		☒	Hotel
Listings		⤴	Number of rooms
✉	Address	⌘|	Meal plans
✉	Branch address	✗	Restaurant
☎	Telephone	⌾	Reservations
🖨	Fax	⌂	Dress code
⊕	Website	▭	No credit cards
✍	E-mail	Ⓢ	Price
⛭	Admission fee		
⌚	Open/closed times	**Other**	
Ⓜ	Subway	⇨	See also
✛	Directions or Map coordinates	☞	Take note
		🏌	Golf facilities

Restaurants

Unless we state otherwise, restaurants are open for lunch and dinner daily. We mention dress code only when there's a specific requirement and reservations only when they're essential or not accepted. To make restaurant reservations, visit Fodors.com.

Credit Cards

The hotels and restaurants in this guide typically accept credit cards. If not, we'll say so.

EUGENE FODOR

Hungarian-born Eugene Fodor (1905–91) began his travel career as an interpreter on a French cruise ship. The experience inspired him to write *On the Continent* (1936), the first guidebook to receive annual updates and discuss a country's way of life as well as its sights. Fodor later joined the U.S. Army and worked for the OSS in World War II. After the war, he kept up his intelligence work while expanding his guidebook series. During the Cold War, many guides were written by fellow agents who understood the value of insider information. Today's guides continue Fodor's legacy by providing travelers with timely coverage, insider tips, and cultural context.

EXPERIENCE BEIJING

BEIJING TODAY

The air is dirty, the traffic is horrendous, and almost nobody speaks more than a word or two of English—so what makes Beijing one of the world's top destinations?

Old and new live together. The flat skyline of Beijing, punctuated only by imposing ceremonial towers and the massive gates of the city wall, is lost forever. But still, standing on Coal Hill and looking south across the Forbidden City—or listening to the strange echo of your voice atop an ancient altar at the Temple of Heaven—you can't help but feel the weight of thousands of years of history. It was here that Marco Polo supposedly dined with Kublai Khan and his Mongol hordes; that Ming and Qing emperors ruled over China from the largest and richest city in the world; and that Mao Zedong proclaimed the founding of the People's Republic in 1949. Much of Beijing's charm comes from the juxtaposition of old and new. When you're riding a taxi along the Third Ring Road it may seem that the high-rise apartments and postmodern office complexes stretch on forever. They do, almost, but tucked in among the glass and steel are elaborate temples exuding wafts of incense, and tiny alleyways where old

folks still gather in their pajamas every evening to play cards and drink warm beer. Savoring these small moments is the key to appreciating today's Beijing.

There are interesting things to eat. If you really love General Tso's chicken back at your local Chinese take-out place, you may want to skip Beijing altogether. Many a returned visitor has complained of being unable to enjoy the bland stuff back home after experiencing the myriad flavors and textures of China's regional cuisines. From the mouth-numbing spices of Sichuan, to the delicate presentation of an imperial banquet, or the cumin-sprinkled kebabs of China's Muslim west, Beijing has it all. If you're looking for the ultimate in authenticity, dine at a restaurant attached to one of the city's provincial representative offices, where the chefs and ingredients are imported to satisfy the taste buds of bureaucrats working far from home. The crispy skin and tender flesh of the capital's signature dish, Peking duck, is on everyone's must-eat list. But don't worry if you tire of eating Chinese food three times a day. As Beijing has grown rich in recent years, Western and fusion cuisine offerings have improved greatly, with everything from French to Middle

INTERESTING FACTS ABOUT THE CAPITAL CITY

With around 20 million residents, Beijing is vying with Shanghai to become the largest city in China.

The city has existed in various forms for at least 2,500 years, but *Homo erectus* fossils prove that humans have lived here for 250,000 years.

Beijing was once surrounded by a massive city wall constructed during the Ming Dynasty. Of its 16 original gates, only three remain standing. The wall was demolished in 1965 to make way for the Second Ring Road.

At 100 acres, Tiananmen Square is the largest urban square in the world; during the Cultural Revolution, as many as 1 million people were able to stand on numbered spaces for huge rallies with Chairman Mao.

Eastern to Texas-style barbecue now available. If you're looking for a special—although somewhat expensive—night out, try Temple Restaurant Beijing, where East meets West in the grounds of a 600-year-old temple, now a dining destination for contemporary European cuisine.

This is a global city. Prestige projects such as the National Center for the Performing Arts ("The Egg"), the new CCTV building, and a massive subway expansion are clearly aimed at showing the world that China is playing with the big boys. The Chinese are fiercely patriotic, and antiforeign demonstrations occasionally break out when the country's collective pride is insulted. The official version of Chinese history taught in schools emphasizes the nation's suffering at the hands of foreign colonial powers during the 19th and 20th centuries, and the subsequent Communist "liberation." Still, you'll find most Beijingers infinitely polite and generally curious about your life back home. People here aren't quite sure what to make of their new surroundings, and they're as interested in finding out about you as you are about them. So strike up a conversation (with your hands if necessary), but be sure to go easy on the politics.

Beijing is a happening destination. Newcomers could be forgiven for seeing bustling Shanghai as China's go-to place. But anyone who has spent a little time in the capital swears that it's the soul of the country. People from all over China, and the world, are drawn here by the many opportunities the city offers, the cultural fervor, and the chance to reinvent themselves. There's an unusual freedom here that has made Beijing the creative center of the country, and this attracts the creative elite from all around the world. Art galleries have sprung up in hotels, courtyard houses, shut-down factories, and even an ancient watchtower. This is where serious Chinese musicians must come to make it or break it, and even no-nonsense businessmen see Beijing as a mecca because they believe the challenges—and rewards—are greater here.

Despite major efforts to improve Beijing's air quality, pollution levels in the city remain several times higher than World Health Organization limits. Adding to the problem, a single sandstorm (usually arriving in spring) can drop tens of thousands of tons of dust onto the city in mere hours.

Beijingers love to brew, and more than 1,000 tea shops can be found along Maliandao Tea Street in the city's southwest. Top-quality leaves can run as high as 5,000 yuan per pound.

The 798 Art District is home to China's red-hot modern art scene on an international scale; visit on a Saturday or Sunday when the area is filled with locals and visitors.

WHAT'S WHERE

1 Dongcheng District. This is where you'll find the city's top must-see attractions, including Tiananmen Square and the Forbidden City, the Buddhist grandeur of the Lama Temple, and the *hutong* (alleyway) neighborhoods that surround the Drum and Bell towers. Since 2010 the district has also included Chongwen, southeast of the imperial palace. Once upon a time, this area teemed with the activity of markets, gambling parlors, and less savory establishments. A historically accurate (but sanitized) re-creation of old Qianmen Street recaptures some of that lost glory, although it can feel stale and lifeless. The Temple of Heaven features some of China's most impressive imperial-era architecture.

2 Xicheng District. With Dongcheng, Xicheng encompasses the historically significant areas of Beijing that once lay inside the city walls; together the two make up the capital's old inner core with the Forbidden City, home to the ruling imperial family, at its center. Six small lakes west of that key landmark lie at the heart of the district, which was once an imperial playground and is now home to China's top leaders. Farther west, fashionable young Beijingers spend

their hard-earned cash in the side-by-side shopping malls at Xidan. Tea lovers won't want to miss Maliandao Tea Street.

3 Chaoyang District. This district wraps around many of the areas forming new Beijing. The skyline-altering Central Business District is in the south, the nightlife of Sanlitun is in the middle, and the 798 Art District (aka Dashanzi) and Olympic Park are in the north. This is today's China, with lots of flash and little connection to the country's 5,000 years of history.

4 Haidian District. The nation's brightest minds study at prestigious Tsinghua and Peking universities in Beijing's northwestern Haidian District. China's own budding Silicon Valley, Zhongguancun, is also here. Head for one of the former imperial retreats at the Summer Palace, Fragrant Hills Park, or the Beijing Botanical Garden for some fresh air.

5 Side Trips from Beijing. No visit to the Beijing area is complete without a side trip to the Great Wall, that ancient defensive perimeter that's just 75 km (47 miles) to the north. Those who have time for a longer excursion could also head to the old imperial retreat of Chengde, now a vibrant city 230 km (143 miles) to the northeast.

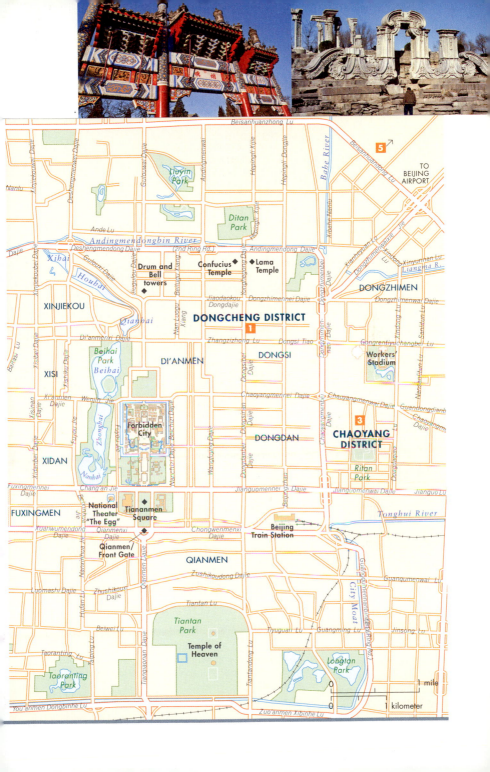

Beisanhuanzhong Lu

TO
BEIJING
AIRPORT

Bahe River

Beisanhuandong Lu

5

Nantu

Liuyin
Park

Ditan
Park

Ande Lu

Andingmendongbin River
(2nd Ring Rd.)

Deshengmendong Dajie   Andingmendong Dajie

Xihai

Houhai

Qianhai

Drum and
Bell
towers

Confucius
Temple

Lama
Temple

DONGZHIMEN

Dongzhimenwai Dajie

XINJIEKOU

Jiaodaokou
Dongdajie

Dongzhimennei Dajie

DONGCHENG DISTRICT

1

Di'anmenxi Dajie

Zhangzizhong Lu   Dongsi Tiao

Gongrentiyuchangbei Lu

Beihai
Park
Beihai

DI'ANMEN

DONGSI

Workers'
Stadium

XISI

Xi'annen
Dajie

Wenjin Jie

Chaoyangmennei Dajie

Chaoyangmenwai Dajie

Guandongdianb

Zhonghai

Forbidden
City

3

CHAOYANG
DISTRICT

XIDAN

Nanhai

DONGDAN

Ritan
Park

Fuxingmennei
Dajie

Chang'an Jie

Jianguomennei Dajie

Jianguomenwai Dajie

Jianguo Lu

FUXINGMEN

National
Theater
"The Egg"

Tiananmen
Square

Tonghui River

Xuanwumendong
Dajie

Qianmenxi
Dajie

Beijing
Train Station

Qianmen/
Front Gate

Chongwenmenxi
Dajie

Luomashi Dajie

QIANMEN

Zhushikoudong
Dajie

Zushikoudong Dajie

Tiantan Lu

Taoranting Lu

Tiantan
Park

Beiwei Lu

Longtan
Park

Guangming Lu

Jinsong Lu

Tiyuguan Lu

Taoranting
Park

Temple of
Heaven

You anmen Dongbinhe Lu

Zuo'anmen Xibinhe Lu

0   1 mile

0   1 kilometer

WELCOME TO BEIJING

When to Go

The best time to visit Beijing is spring or early fall; the weather is better and crowds are a bit thinner. Book at least one month in advance during these times of year. In winter Beijing's Forbidden City and Summer Palace can look fantastical and majestic, especially when their traditional tiled roofs are covered with a light dusting of snow and there are few tourists.

The weather in Beijing is at its best in September and October, with a good chance of sunny days and mild temperatures. Winters are very cold, but it seldom snows. Some restaurants may be poorly heated, so bring a warm sweater. Late April through June is lovely. In July the days are hot and excruciatingly humid with a good chance of rain. Spring is also the time of year for Beijing's famous dust storms. Pollution is an issue year-round but particularly in winter months.

Avoid travel during Chinese New Year and National Day. Millions of Chinese travel during these weeks, making it difficult to book hotels, tours, and transportation. If you must visit during Chinese New Year, be sure to check out the traditional temple fairs that take place at religious sites around the city.

Getting Around

On Foot: Although traffic and modernization have put a bit of a cramp in Beijing's walking style, meandering on foot remains one of the best ways to experience the capital—especially the old *hutong* neighborhoods.

By Bike: Some 1,000 new automobiles take to the streets of the capital every day, bringing the total to more than 5 million vehicles. All this competition has made biking less pleasant and more dangerous. Fortunately, most streets have wide, well-defined bike lanes often separated from other traffic by an island. Bikes can be rented at many hotels and next to some subway stations. (And the local government has said it will reduce the number of new license plates by 40 percent by 2017).

By Subway: The subway is the best way to avoid Beijing's frequent traffic jams. With the opening of new lines, Beijing's subway service is increasingly convenient. The metropolitan area is currently served by 14 lines as well as an express line to the airport. The subway runs from about 5 am to midnight daily, depending on the station. Fares are Y2 per ride for any distance and transfers are free. Stations are marked in both Chinese and English, and stops are also announced in both languages. Subways are best avoided during rush hours, when severe overcrowding is unavoidable.

By Taxi: The taxi experience in Beijing has improved significantly as the city's taxi companies gradually shift to cleaner, more comfortable new cars. In the daytime, flag-fall for taxis is Y13 for the first 3 km (2 miles) and Y2 per km thereafter. The rate rises to Y3 per km on trips over 15 km (8 miles) and after 11 pm, when the flag-fall also increases to Y14. At present, there's also a Y1 gas surcharge for any rides exceeding 3 km (2 miles). ⚠ **Be sure to check that the meter has been engaged to avoid fare negotiations at your destination.** Taxis are easy to hail during the day, but can be difficult during evening rush hour, especially when it's raining. If you're having difficulty, go to the closest hotel and wait in line there. Few taxi drivers speak English, so ask your hotel concierge to write down your destination in Chinese.

Getting Oriented

At the heart of Beijing lies the Forbidden City, home of the emperors of old, which is adjacent to the secretive and off-limits Zhongnanhai, home of China's current leadership. The rest of the city revolves around this core area, with a series of concentric rings roads reaching out into the suburbs, and most major arteries running north–south and east–west. As you explore Beijing, you'll find that taxis are often the best way to get around. However, if the subway goes where you're headed, it's often a faster option than dealing with traffic.

The city is divided into 18 municipal and suburban districts (*qu*). Only four of these districts are the central stomping grounds for most visitors; our coverage focuses on them. The most important, **Dongcheng** ("east district") encompasses the Forbidden City, Tiananmen Square, Wangfujing (a major shopping street), the Lama Temple, and many other historical sites dating back to imperial times. **Xicheng** ("west district"), directly west of Dongcheng, is a lovely lake district that includes Beihai Park, a former playground of the imperial family, and a series of connected lakes bordered by willow trees, courtyard-lined *hutong*, and lively bars. **Chaoyang** is the biggest and busiest district, occupying the areas north, east, and south of the eastern Second Ring Road. Because it lies outside the Second Ring Road, which marked the eastern demarcation of the old city wall, there's little of historical interest here, though it does have many of the city's top hotels, restaurants, and shops. Chaoyang is also home to the foreign embassies, multinational companies, the Central Business District, and the Olympic Park. **Haidian,** the district that's home to China's top universities and technology companies, is northwest of the Third Ring Road; it's packed with shops selling electronics and students cramming for their next exam.

Etiquette

It's respectful to dress modestly at religious sites: cover your shoulders and don't wear short skirts or shorts. Keep in mind that authorities are very sensitive about public behavior in Tiananmen Square, which teems with plainclothes state security officers at all times.

Street Vocabulary

Here are some terms you'll see over and over again. These words will appear on maps and street signs, and they're part of the name of just about every place you go:

Dong is east, **xi** is west, **nan** is south, **bei** is north, and **zhong** means middle. **Jie** and **lu** mean street and road respectively, and **da** means big, so dajie equals avenue.

Gongyuan means park. Jingshan Park is, therefore, also called Jingshan Gongyuan.

Nei means inside and **wai** means outside. You will often come across these terms on streets that used to pass through a gate of the old city wall. Andingmen Neidajie, for example, is the section of the street located inside the Second Ring Road (where the gate used to be); Andingmen Waidajie is the section outside the gate.

Qiao, or bridge, is part of the place name at just about every entrance and exit on the ring roads.

Men, meaning door or gate, indicates a street that once passed through an entrance in the old wall that surrounded the city until it was mostly torn down in the 1960s. The entrances to parks and some other places are also referred to as *men*.

BEIJING TOP ATTRACTIONS

Summer Palace

(A) This beautiful complex, surrounding a large lake, dates back eight centuries. Notable sights include the Long Corridor (a covered wooden walkway) and the Hall of Benevolent Longevity. At the west end of the lake is the famous Marble Boat that Cixi built with money intended to create a Chinese navy. The palace, which served as an imperial summer retreat, was ransacked by British and French soldiers in 1860 and later burned by Western soldiers seeking revenge for the Boxer Rebellion in 1900 (don't confuse this with Yuan Ming Yuan, the Old Summer Palace, which was almost completely destroyed by foreign soldiers in 1860).

Great Wall of China

(B) Touristy it may be, but make time to see it while you're in Beijing. The closest location, at Badaling, is a one-hour drive away—you may recognize some of the views and angles here from their frequent use in photo ops.

Lama Temple

(C) The smell of incense permeates one of the few functioning Buddhist temples in Beijing. When Emperor Yongzheng took the throne in 1722, his former residence was converted into this temple. During the Qianlong Period (1736–95) it became a center of the Yellow Hat sect of Tibetan Buddhism. At its high point, 1,500 lamas lived here. The Pavilion of Ten Thousand Fortunes (Wanfu Ge) has a 60-foot tall statue of the Maitreya Buddha carved from a single piece of sandalwood.

Forbidden City

(D) The Forbidden City has been home to a long line of emperors, beginning with Yongle, in 1420, and ending with Puyi (made famous by Bernardo Bertolucci's 1987 film *The Last Emperor*), who was forced out of the complex by a warlord in 1924, over a decade after he abdicated his throne. This is the largest palace in the world, as well as the best preserved,

and offers the most complete collection of imperial architecture in China.

Tiananmen Square

(E) Walking beneath the red flags of Tiananmen Square is a quintessential Beijing experience. The political heart of modern China, the square covers 100 acres, making it the world's largest public square. It was here, from the Gate of Heavenly Peace, that Mao Zedong proclaimed the founding of the People's Republic of China on October 1, 1949, and it is here that he remains, embalmed in a mausoleum constructed in the square's center. Many Westerners think only of the massive student demonstrations here in 1989, but it has been the site of protests, rallies, and marches for close to 100 years.

Temple of Heaven

(F) The 15th-century Temple of Heaven is one of the best examples of religious architecture in China. The complex contains three main buildings where the emperor, as the "Son of Heaven," offered semiannual prayers. The sprawling, tree-filled complex is a pleasant place for wandering: watch locals practicing martial arts, playing traditional instruments, and enjoying ballroom dancing on the grass.

Confucius Temple

(G) This temple, with its towering cypress and pine trees, offers a serene escape from the crowds at the nearby Lama Temple. This is the second-largest Confucian temple in China, after the one in Qufu, the master's hometown in Shandong Province. First built in the 14th century, the Confucius Temple was renovated in the 18th century.

TOP EXPERIENCES

See the city by bike

Four wheels may be good for getting around, but two wheels are better. The capital demands to be discovered by bicycle. Unlock a different perspective on the city by renting a bike from Serk (⊕ *www.serk.cc*) and spending a day in the saddle. Or take a tour with Bike Beijing (⊕ *www.bikebeijing.com*).

Dance the night away

Beijing's older inhabitants love to dance wherever they can set up a sound system: parks, squares, streets, and underpasses. One of the best places to join in is outside Saint Joseph's Cathedral on Wangfujing. Hundreds of movers and groovers gather here every night. Get yourself down there and sway along to the sounds.

Train in tai chi

You'll see plenty of folk practicing this gentle Chinese martial art throughout town. Our favorite way to train is with Bespoke Beijing (⊕ *www.bespoke-beijing.com*), who can arrange a private hour-long class among the trees of the Temple of Heaven. It's led by a tai chi master who trained at the Shaolin Temple as a child.

Eat scary snacks

There's some wonderful food to be had here. There are also some truly terrifying dishes to try if you're feeling brave. The likes of scorpions on a stick are served up at Wangfujing Snack Street. To be safer, choose carts with a high turnover. For something less weird but just as savory, head to Xiaoyou Hutong, where a dozen eateries, refugees from urban renewal, serve traditional specialties inside a renovated courtyard house.

Go for gold at the Olympic Park

If you have the time, a visit to the Olympic Park, just north of the Fourth Ring Road, is a chance to see the starkly modern side of China—the face it wants the world to see. The Bird's Nest stadium dominates the landscape, while the Water Cube, the venue for Michael Phelps's extraordinary eight gold medals, has been turned into a thrilling water park, complete with a lazy river and slides and rides for all ages.

Meditate with monks

If a visit to the downtown Lama Temple awakens your spiritual side, then a weekend away staying with monks at Chaoyang Temple—an hour or two outside the city in Huairou District—may be the key to reaching real enlightenment. A crash course in Zen Buddhism awaits the curious (⊕ *www.90travel.com*).

Enjoy a night at the opera

Peking opera is regarded as one of the country's cultural treasures. If you want to check out this unique form of traditional Chinese theater then you won't get a better opportunity than in its birthplace (⇨ *see Chapter 6 for more*). Be warned: the sonic style may not be music to all ears, but finding out is all part of the fun.

Hike the Great Wall

There's more than one way to see the world's most famous wall. Abandon the tourist trail and escape the crowds with Beijing Hikers (⊕ *www.beijinghikers.com*). This walking group runs regular trips to some of the more interesting areas of the Great Wall. Join them to explore unrestored sections most tourists don't even know exist.

Rock out

Beijing is the beating heart of China's burgeoning rock scene. Join the city's hipsters and rock kids at one of the many gigs on the local circuit. MAO Live House (⊕ *www.mao-music.com*) and Yugong Yishan (⊕ *www.yugongyishan.com*) are

two of the best venues to crash if you're out cool hunting.

Have a Beijing tea party

Fans of a nice cup of *cha* won't want to miss Maliandao—the largest tea market in north China. For a more personal experience you should head to Fangjia Hutong, where you'll find Tranquil Tuesdays (⊕ *www.tranquiltuesdays.com*), a local social enterprise dedicated to China's tea culture. Its founder, Charlene Wang, personally sources the nation's best natural leaves for sale. Call ahead for an appointment.

Check out the stunning stunts

China's acrobats train harder than any others. The results, as seen in many of the shows across town, are guaranteed to elicit oohs and aahs. Take your pick of the bunch *listed in Chapter 6*, although the show at the Chaoyang Theater is the most conveniently located, and has an excellent Japanese whisky bar attached.

Take a look down the lanes

The capital's ancient alleys are there for all to explore. Walk or cycle, it's up to you. But for a completely different view of things we recommend booking a tour with Beijing Sideways (⊕ *www.beijing-sideways.com*) who will whiz you off to hard-to-find places deep in the *hutong* network while riding aboard the sidecar of a vintage motorbike.

Hone your haggling skills

It's hard to resist: so much to bargain for in Beijing markets, and so little time! Visit outdoor Panjiayuan (aka the Dirt Market), where some 3,000 vendors sell antiques (both legitimate and otherwise), Cultural Revolution memorabilia, and handicrafts from across China. Looking for knockoffs? The Silk Market is popular with tourists, but local expats prefer Yashow Market, which generally has better prices.

Let the games begin

Basketball is so popular in China that it's practically the national sport. Cheer on the Beijing Ducks (led to their first title in 2012 by ex-NBA star Stephon Marbury) at their nest in Shijingshan District. It is, however, quite the trek. For an easier sporting fix, go support the soccer team, Beijing Guoan, at the Workers' Stadium in Sanlitun.

Get suited up

London's got Savile Row. Beijing's got top tailoring for a fraction of the dough. Where you go depends on how much cash you want to splash, but you can't go wrong at Wendy's (on the third floor of Yashow Market). There's no way you'll get made-to-measure shirts of this quality for such a low price back home.

Get cooking

If you dine right (with our help, we hope), you'll eat so well that you'll want to take the secrets of these tasty Chinese treats home. Hurry down to The Hutong (⊕ *www.thehutongkitchen.com*) for its packed calendar of cooking classes, which cover everything from making dumplings to creating sizzling Sichuan dishes.

GREAT ITINERARIES

The Italian priest Matteo Ricci arrived in Beijing in 1598. His efforts to understand the capital led him to stay until his death, 12 years later. You, on the other hand, have to get back home before the week's out. But while you may not have the luxury of time on your side, you do have the advantage of something Ricci could only dream of: our handy guide to the best one-, three- and five-day tours. Hit the best; forget the rest.

Beijing in One Day

It's impossible to see everything Beijing has to offer in a single day. Still, if that's all you've got, you can cover a lot of the key sights if you go full steam. The geographical center of **Tiananmen Square** is on most people's must-do list. Fundamentally, however, it's just a big square. Make the trip worthwhile by being first in line for the **Mao Zedong Memorial Hall** at 8 am (early birds may want to take in the pomp of the flag-raising ceremony held each dawn, which takes place around 7 am during winter months). Within this stern-looking building, which dominates the center of the square, you'll find the Chairman's embalmed remains. Remember to take your passport (and deposit any bags at the designated storage facility before lining up).

Follow this curious experience by heading to the north side of the square to the **Gate of Heavenly Peace**, which marks the entrance to the **Forbidden City**, a sight that needs no introduction. This may be the home of the emperors, but the mark of Mao remains. You'll have to pass under his portrait to make your way in. Exploring this imperial palace takes hours. The peripheral courtyards provide a welcome escape if the crowds become too trying. Save some energy for the gentle hike to the top of the hill in **Jingshan Park** opposite the north exit of the Forbidden City. Too many run out of gas and skip the stunning views.

Reward yourself with a cracking good lunch deal at **Temple Restaurant Beijing**: fine dining in a 600-year-old temple. Take it easy in the afternoon with a stroll around Beihai Park—a former imperial garden—before renting a boat for a lazy time on its large lake. It's then a half-hour walk (or short cab ride) to **Wangfujing**, a street made for shopping. The snack stalls here are particularly fun, especially if you're brave enough to try the likes of starfish or scorpion on a stick.

Ride the subway two stops from Wangfujing to Tiananmen West to round off the night with some world-class classical music at the architectural wonder that is the **National Center for Performing Arts** (also known as the Egg).

Beijing in Three Days

Start with our one-day tour as above. But then what to do with your other two days? Well, it'd be foolish to come all the way to China and not visit the **Great Wall**. There's no getting around the fact, however, that this requires a full day. The Badaling section is closest; the wall at Mutianyu is better—both are somewhat "touristy." If that bothers you then you may want to hike one of the "wilder" sections of the Great Wall. It's possible, although not recommended, to do this independently. You're better off hiring a guide. Our favorite is Tony Chen at Stretch-a-leg Travel (⊕ *www.stretchalegtravel.com*). Once you're back in town, dine on Peking duck for dinner. Take your pick from **Da Dong Roast Duck**, **Made in China**, or **Duck de Chine**—three of the best places in town to try Beijing's signature dish.

For your final day get ready to explore the capital's historical *hutong*—the fast-disappearing network of ancient alleyways that were the lifeblood of old Peking. Start at the atmospheric **Lama Temple** (easily reached via Line 2). This is the most important functioning Buddhist temple in Beijing and it remains full of life. Drop by the nearby **Confucius Temple**, dedicated to China's great sage, before wandering through the area's atmospheric *hutong*—Wudaoying and Guozijian are of particular interest. Wind your way through the area's alleys en route to the **Drum** and **Bell towers**, which provided the city's official means of timekeeping up until 1924. It should be a half-hour walk. But don't worry if you get lost in the lanes, as that's all part of the adventure. Climb either tower for a fabulous view. You'll see the nearby **Houhai** lakes to the west—a good spot to rent a boat in summer or go ice-skating in winter. If you want to explore the area on foot, then head to the **Silver Ingot Bridge** instead, before finishing your day in the buzzing *hutong* around Nanluoguxiang (1 km [½ mile] east of Houhai), packed with boutiques, bars, and restaurants.

Beijing in Five Days

Lucky enough to have five days in the capital? Follow our three-day tour, then spend your remaining time taking in Beijing's glorious mix of old and new, from temples and palaces to contemporary art and shopping galore. Kick off day four with an early start down south at the beautiful **Temple of Heaven**. This is where the emperors used to pray for prosperity. Today you'll find it populated with the city's older residents, who can often be found practicing tai chi or singing songs here.

Once done with this impressive imperial sight, hop into a cab for the 5-km (3-mile) journey east to the **Panjiayuan Antiques Market**, which is a great place to pick up presents and mementos. Traders here sell everything from Chinese chess sets and delicate porcelain to Mao alarm clocks and traditional instruments. Another cab ride will take you to the **798 Art District** up in the northeast part of the city (a half-hour drive in good traffic; an hour in bad), which is a wonderful way to spend an afternoon—avoid Monday, however, when most galleries here are shut. Formerly a factory complex, the area is now a thriving arts hub. The best gallery to visit is the UCCA, but the proliferation of little shops, cafés, and bars make this a great place to hang out even if you're not into art.

Head back to downtown **Sanlitun** for sundown. Shopaholics can squeeze in some last-minute spending at **Yashow**, an indoor market full of cheap clothes, bags, and such; bargain harder than you ever have before. Spend the evening soaking up Sanlitun's bustling nightlife. Avoid the main "bar street" and check out the watering holes and eateries in **Village Sanlitun** instead. Get out of the city on your final day. Spend the morning back in imperial China at the striking **Summer Palace** up in Beijing's northwest corner. Combine the trip with the ruins of nearby Yuan Ming Yuan, the **Old Summer Palace**. You may want to spend the afternoon at the **Fragrant Hills Park**—popular among residents escaping the urban grind—or the **Beijing Botanical Garden**. Both are even farther west than the Summer Palace and visiting just one will take the rest of the day.

BEIJING THEN AND NOW

In the beginning

Since the birth of Chinese civilization, different towns of varying size and import have stood at or near the site of today's Beijing. For example, a popular local beer, Yanjing, is named for a city-kingdom based here 3,000 years ago. With this in mind, it's not unreasonable to describe Beijing's modern history as beginning with the Jin Dynasty, approximately 800 years ago. Led by nine generations of the Jurchen tribe, the Jin Dynasty eventually fell into a war against the Mongol hordes.

The Mongols

Few armies had been able to withstand the wild onslaught of the armed Mongol cavalry under the command of the legendary warrior Genghis Khan. The Jurchen tribe proved no exception, and the magnificent city of the Jin was almost completely destroyed. A few decades later, in 1260, when Kublai Khan, the grandson of Genghis Khan, returned to use the city as an operational base for his conquest of southern China, reconstruction was the order of the day. By 1271 Kublai Khan had achieved his goal, declaring himself emperor of China under the Yuan Dynasty (1271–1368), with Beijing (or Dadu, as it was then known) as its capital.

The new capital was built on a scale befitting the world's then superpower. Its palaces were founded around Zhonghai and Beihai lakes. Beijing's current layout still reflects the Mongolian design.

The Mings

About 100 years after the Mongolians settled Beijing they suffered a devastating attack by rebels from the south. The southern roots of the quickly unified Ming Dynasty (1368–1644) deprived Beijing of its capital status for half a century. But in 1405, the third Ming emperor, Yongle, began construction on a magnificent new palace in Beijing: an enormous maze of interlinking halls, gates, and courtyard homes, known as the Forbidden City.

The Ming also contributed mightily to China's grandest public works project: the Great Wall. The Ming Great Wall linked or reinforced several existing walls, especially near the capital, and traversed seemingly impassable mountains. The majority of the most spectacular stretches of the wall that can be visited near Beijing were built during the Ming Dynasty. But wall building drained Ming coffers and, in the end, failed to prevent Manchu horsemen from taking the capital and the rest of China in 1644.

And finally, the Qings

This foreign dynasty, the Qing, inherited the Ming palaces, built their own retreats (most notably, the "old" and "new" summer palaces), and perpetuated feudalism in China for another 267 years. In its decline, the Qing proved impotent to stop humiliating foreign encroachment. It lost the first Opium War to Great Britain in 1842 and was forced to cede Hong Kong "in perpetuity" as a result. In 1860 a combined British and French force stormed Beijing and razed the Old Summer Palace.

Mao takes the reins

After the Qing crumbled in 1911, its successor, Sun Yat-sen's Nationalist Party, struggled to consolidate power. Beijing became a cauldron of social activism. On May 4, 1919, students marched on Tiananmen Square to protest humiliations in Versailles, where Allied commanders negotiating an end to World War I gave Germany's extraterritorial holdings in China to Japan. Patriotism intensified, and in 1937 Japanese imperial armies stormed across Beijing's Marco

Polo Bridge to launch a brutal eight-year occupation. Civil war followed close on the heels of Tokyo's 1945 surrender and raged until the Communist victory. Chairman Mao himself declared the founding of a new nation from the rostrum atop the Gate of Heavenly Peace on October 1, 1949.

Like Emperor Yongle, Mao built a capital that conformed to his own vision. Soviet-inspired structures rose up around Tiananmen Square. Beijing's historic city wall was demolished to make way for a ring road. Temples and churches were torn down, closed, or turned into factories during the brutal upheaval of the Cultural Revolution, which began in 1966 and lasted until Mao's death, in 1976.

Economic growth and the city

In more recent years the city has suffered most, ironically, from prosperity. Many ancient neighborhoods have been bulldozed to make room for glitzy commercial developments. A growing commitment to preservation has very slowly begun to take hold, but *chai* (to pull down) and *qian* (to move elsewhere) remain common threats across the capital.

Today Beijing's some 20 million residents—including 7 million migrant workers—enjoy a fascinating mix of old and new. Early morning tai chi enthusiasts, ballroom and disco dancers, old men with caged songbirds, and amateur Beijing opera crooners frequent the city's many parks. Cyclists clog the roadways, competing with cars on the city's thoroughfares. Beijing traffic has gone from nonexistent to nightmarish in less than a decade.

As the seat of China's immense national bureaucracy, Beijing carries a political charge. The Communist Party, whose self-described goal is "a dictatorship of the proletariat," has yet to relinquish its political monopoly.

Communism today

In 1989 student protesters in Tiananmen Square dared to challenge the party. The government's harsh response remains etched in global memory, although younger Chinese people are likely never to have heard of that seismic moment due to the taboo nature of the subject and the country's strict censorship laws. More than 25 years later, secret police still mingle with tourists on the square. Mao-style propaganda persists. Slogans that preach unity among China's national minorities and patriotism still festoon the city on occasion. Yet as Beijing's robust economy—now the second largest in the world—is boosted even further by the government's continuing embrace of "a socialist market economy" (read: state-sanctioned capitalism) and the massive influx of foreign investment, such campaigns appear increasingly out of touch with the iPhone-wielding generation. And so there is now a more modern side to the city to consider, one perhaps best encapsulated by the drastic changes continually being made to both skyline and streets. The result is an incongruous mixture of new prosperity and throwback politics: socialist slogans adorn shopping centers selling everything from Big Macs to Louis Vuitton. In modern Beijing the ancient and the sparkling new are constantly colliding.

A CITY IN TRANSITION

The 2008 Summer Olympics changed the look of the Chinese capital like never before. Whole city blocks were razed to make way for modern buildings, new hotels, and state-of-the-art sports facilities. The subway system has expanded from just two to 16 lines, with four more under construction. Just about everywhere you look you'll find signs of the feverish development boom that didn't end when the games left off. But the focus has switched from iconic Olympic venues and government-initiated state buildings—such as the extraordinary headquarters for the state-run TV network—to more commercially minded projects looking to mix architectural innovation with office space and shopping malls. Yes, China is rightly proud of its 5,000 years of history, but in terms of looking forward and not back, Beijing's 21st-century projects—many designed by top international architects—are impressive to say the least.

Beijing Capital International Airport, Terminal 3

With its lantern-red roof shaped like a dragon, Beijing's airport expansion embraces traditional Chinese motifs with a 21st-century twist: its architect calls it "the world's largest and most advanced airport building." This single terminal contains more floor space than all the terminals at London's Heathrow Airport combined. Construction started in 2004 with a team of 50,000 workers and was completed a few months before the Olympic Games.

Architect: Norman Foster, the preeminent British architect responsible for global icons such as Hong Kong's widely respected airport, London's "Gherkin" skyscraper, and the Reichstag dome in Berlin.

Beijing Linked Hybrid

With 700 apartments in eight bridge-linked towers surrounding a plethora of shopping and cultural options, including Beijing's best art-house cinema, the Linked Hybrid has been applauded for parting from the sterility of typical Chinese housing. The elegant complex also features an impressive set of green credentials such as geothermal heating and a wastewater recycling system. ⊠ *Adjacent to the northeast corner of the 2nd Ring Rd.*

Architects: New York–based Steven Holl—who has won awards for his contemporary art museum in Helsinki, Finland, and innovative "horizontal skyscraper" in Shenzhen—and Li Hu, who helped design China's first contemporary museum in Nanjing.

CCTV (China Central Television) Headquarters

Perhaps the most remarkable of China's new structures, the central television headquarters twists the idea of a skyscraper quite literally into a 40-story-tall gravity-defying loop. What some have called the world's most complex building (and what locals have nicknamed "The Big Pants") is also, with a $1.3 billion price tag, one of the world's priciest. An accompanying building that was to include a hotel, a visitor center, and a public theater was destroyed after it caught on fire during the Chinese New Year fireworks display in 2009. Due to the complex engineering involved. the secondary building remains under reconstruction. ⊠ *32 Dong San Huanzhonglu (32 E. 3rd Ring Middle Rd.).*

Architects: Rem Koolhaas (a Dutch mastermind known for his daring ideas and successful Seattle Public Library) and Ole Scheeren (Koolhaas's German protégé).

National Stadium ("the Bird's Nest")

Despite the heft of 42,000 tons of steel bending around its center, this 80,000-seat stadium somehow manages to appear delicate rather than clunky, with its exterior lattice structure resembling the twigs of an elegant nest—hence the nickname. Now used occasionally for events such as visiting soccer games and concerts, it's an absolutely massive structure, and must be seen to be believed. ⊠ *Beijing Olympic Park at Bei Si Huanlu (N. 4th Ring Rd.).*

Architects: The Herzog & de Meuron firm of Switzerland, which won the prestigious Pritzker Prize for converting London's Bankside Power Station into the much-loved Tate Modern art gallery. The stadium also saw the involvement of leading Chinese artist Ai Weiwei as artistic consultant.

National Aquatics Center ("the Water Cube")

The translucent skin and hexagonal high-tech "pillows" that define this 17,000-seat indoor swimming stadium create the impression of a building fashioned entirely out of bubbles. The structure is based on the premise that bubbles are the most effective way to divide a three-dimensional space—and they help save energy and keep the building earthquake-proof. The center has now been turned into a public aquatics center and water park. ⊠ *Beijing Olympic Park.*

Architects: PTW Architects, the Australian firm that cut its teeth on venues for the 2000 Olympic Games in Sydney.

National Center for the Performing Arts ("the Egg")

Located near Tiananmen Square, and completely surrounded by water, this bulbous opera house—a spectacular dome of titanium and glass known locally as "The Egg"—might cause passersby to think that some sort of spaceship has landed in the capital. Its close proximity to the Forbidden City, and its soaring costs (more than $400 million), earned it a hostile welcome among some Chinese architects, although it has now been embraced by the city thanks to its excellent program of classical music and refreshingly unconventional appearance. ⊠ *Xi Chang'an Jie (just west of Tiananmen Sq.).*

Architect: French-born Paul Andreu, who designed the groundbreaking Terminal 1 of Paris's Charles de Gaulle airport in 1974, as well as working on the French capital's La Grande Arche.

Galaxy SOHO

Consisting of four huge amorphous globes, wrapped in curved white panels and flowing glass curtain walls, this mixed-use complex from one of the country's largest property developers (SOHO China) continues the futuristic theme of The Egg. Opened at the end of 2012, it's quite the statement: a bold continuation of the architectural ambition initiated by the Games, now transferred to the more functional world of office and retail space. Welcome to Beijing's next chapter. ⊠ *E. 2nd Ring Rd. (next to Chaoyangmen subway station).*

Architect: Iraqi-British starchitect Zaha Hadid—the first woman to win the Pritzker Prize—who made a splash in China prior to this with her opera house in the southern city of Guangzhou.

BEIJING WITH KIDS

Education Without Yawns

Learning doesn't have to boring! There are excellent ways to teach the kids a few things about history while they have a good time. You can't miss with the **Forbidden City**, the largest surviving palace complex in the world. There are plenty of wide-open spaces here for kids to run amok in, so that while you're appreciating the finest collection of imperial architecture in China, your little ones can imagine what it was like to have thousands of mandarins catering to their every whim. Sort of like having parents.

For museums, the **Military Museum of the People's Republic of China** is a toy soldier–lover's dream come true. It has endless collections of AK-47s, captured tanks, missile launchers, and other war toys. Your kids will love every minute of China's 5,000-year military history. Easy access by subway ensures they won't have to ask, "Are we there yet?" And the **China Science & Technology Museum** is a paradise for curious kids, this museum features hands-on interactive displays with a strong focus on Chinese inventions like the compass, gunpowder, and paper. The on-site "Fundazzle" playground will keep your little one entertained even when the robot performance is finished.

Performances

Take the kids out to see amazing acrobats and they'll see that hand-eye coordination doesn't only come from playing video games. To really inspire, look for a performance featuring child acrobats who dedicate every day to perfecting their awe-inspiring craft. Another great entertainment option is the **China Puppet Theater,** where actors manipulate huge puppets through performances of Western classics like *The Nutcracker* and Chinese classics like *The Monkey King*. There's a playground at the theater, too, for kids who just won't sit still.

Activities

China's love affair with kites goes back nearly 3,000 years. Head for the open spaces of Tiananmen Square, Ditan Park, or the Temple of Heaven **to fly a kite**. Older folks with decades of flying experience will help send your child's kite soaring into the air.

Kids love to climb, so **climbing the Great Wall i**s a win-win. After climbing hundreds (or thousands) of steps, your little one will sleep soundly while dreaming of turning back the marauding Mongol hordes.

Head to **Ritan Park** (Altar of the Sun). Little tykes can ride the merry-go-round, older kids can try their luck on the climbing wall, and you can stop in for a drink at the outdoor Stone Boat, a particularly kid-friendly bar.

Who doesn't love a **boat ride**? Cruise the imperial lakes at Houhai in a paddleboat, and take the family for a rectangular pie at Hutong Pizza when you get back to shore. In winter the lakes freeze over, and kids in ice chairs gleefully glide across the surface.

FREE (OR ALMOST FREE)

Although Beijing isn't as inexpensive as it once was, it's still a fabulous bargain compared to travel in Europe, North America, and more developed Asian nations such as Japan and South Korea. While expats have complained more and more of rising prices in the post-Olympics era, visitors from Western countries are often overwhelmed by a feeling that life in the city is practically free. Bottled water, snacks, subway and bus rides, or some steamed dumplings from a street stall, will all cost well under the equivalent of 50 cents. Average-length cab rides, a dish at a decent restaurant, or museum admission tickets will set you back only two or three dollars. And the capital is filled with acceptable hotels for about 50 bucks per night. Little is free in Beijing, but there's also very little to make much of a dent in your wallet.

Art

The modern art scene in China has exploded onto the world stage over the past decade. Beijing's 798 Art District, located northeast of the city center along the road to the airport, is the country's artistic nucleus. The complex was built under East German supervision in the 1950s to house sprawling electronics factories, but artists took over after state subsidies dried up in the late 1990s. The district is now home to at least 100 top-notch galleries, and almost all of them are free.

Offbeat Experiences

Beijing's urban sprawl is interrupted by a number of lovely parks designed in traditional Chinese style. Of particular historical significance are the four parks built around altars used for imperial sacrifice: the **Altar of the Sun** (Ritan), **Altar of Heaven** (Tiantan), **Altar of the Earth** (Ditan), and **Altar of the Moon** (Yuetan).

If you happen to be in Beijing for Spring Festival (Chinese New Year), you literally won't be able to avoid the party atmosphere that overtakes the city. You may have seen a display of fireworks before, but have you ever been *inside* a fireworks show? It's a good idea to bring earplugs, as the explosions go on at all hours for days on end.

Cheap Sightseeing

Don't be afraid to hop on one of Beijing's municipal buses and see where it takes you! Just remember the number of the line you took so you can get back to where you started—and grab a business card from your hotel just in case you get lost and need to flag down a taxi. Here's a hint: bus lines with only one or two digits stay more or less within the city center, so you won't have to worry about ending up in a farming village near Hebei.

Bus 4: Runs east–west along Chang'an Jie, the city's main horizontal axis. Stops include the Military Museum, Xidan, Tiananmen Square, Wangfujing, and Jianguomen. **Bus 5:** Starts near the Di'anmen intersection south of the Drum and Bell towers and runs past Beihai Park and Tiananmen Square toward Qianmen (Front Gate). **Bus 44:** This loop line more or less follows the same route as Line 2 on the subway—a chance to travel along the path where the ancient city walls once stood, and you can get off at the same place you got on.

Museums

The city's most famous museums aren't exactly charging an arm and a leg for admission, and some ask only for donations or charge less than Y10.

BEIJING MADE EASY

Do I need any special documents to get into the country?

Aside from a passport that's valid for at least six months after date of entry, and a valid visa, you don't need anything else to enter the country. In theory, you're required to have your passport with you at all times during your trip, but it's safer to carry a photocopy and store your passport in a safe at your hotel (if they have one).

How difficult is it to travel around the city?

It's extremely easy (traffic aside). Taxis are plentiful and cheap, and Beijing also has a good subway system that has expanded rapidly and now reaches more places. Stops are announced in both English and Chinese. Public buses can be a challenge because street signs are not often written in English and bus drivers are unlikely to be conversational in any foreign languages. Renting a car can be difficult and traffic and roads can be quite challenging, so driving on your own isn't recommended. However, hiring a car and driver isn't very expensive and is a good alternative for getting around. Beijing, with its many bike lanes, is a cycle lover's city, so consider renting some wheels for part of your stay.

Should I consider a package tour?

If the thought of traveling unescorted to Beijing absolutely terrifies you, then sign up for a tour. But Beijing is such an easy place to get around in that there's really no need. Discovery is a big part of the fun—exploring an ancient temple, walking down a narrow *hutong* or alleyway, stumbling upon a great craft shop or small restaurant—and that's just not going to happen on a tour. If you're more comfortable with a package tour, pick one with a specific focus, like a pedicab *hutong* ride or an afternoon of food shopping and cooking, so that you're less likely to get a generic package.

Do I need a local guide?

Guides are really not necessary in a city like Beijing, where it's easy to get around by taxi and public transportation, and where most of the important tourist destinations are easy to reach. An added plus is that the local people are friendly and always willing to give a hand. It's much more gratifying to tell the folks back home that you discovered that wonderful backstreet or interesting restaurant all by yourself.

Will I have trouble if I don't speak Chinese?

Not really. Most people in businesses catering to travelers speak at least a little English. If you encounter someone who doesn't speak English, they'll probably point you to a coworker who does. Even if you're in a far-flung destination, locals will go out of their way to find somebody who speaks your language. Or you can make use of travel services such as Bespoke Beijing, which will arm you with a mobile phone, plus a stylish and personalized guide to the best sights, restaurants, bars, and nightlife, as well as access to a Chinese translator or English-speaking expert (⊕ *www.bespoke-beijing.com*).

Can I drink the water?

No, you can't. All drinking water must be boiled. Bottled water is easily available all over the city and in outlying areas, such as the Great Wall. Most hotels provide two free bottles of drinking water each day. To be on the safe side, you may also want to avoid ice.

Are there any worries about the food?

China has suffered from some major national food scandals in recent years, from tainted milk to exploding water-

melons, but there's no need to be afraid in Beijing. Even the humblest roadside establishment is likely to be clean. If you have any doubts about a place, just move on to the next one. There's no problem enjoying fruit or other local products sold from street stands, but any fruit that can't be peeled should perhaps be cleaned with bottled water before eating.

Do I need to get any shots?

You probably don't have to get any special vaccinations or take any serious medications if you're not planning on venturing outside the capital. The U.S. Centers for Disease Control and Prevention warn that there's some concern about malaria in some of the rural provinces much farther south of Beijing, such as Anhui, Yunnan, and Hainan. Immunizations for hepatitis A and B are recommended for all visitors to China.

Should I bring any medications?

It can be difficult to readily find some medications in Beijing, and while the city has several international clinics, prices for even over-the-counter remedies can be quite expensive. So make sure you have all your medications with you.

Can I use my ATM card?

Most ATMs in Beijing accept both MasterCard and Visa cards, but each bank may charge a different fee for each transaction. There are Citibank ATM machines located at several places around the city. Check the exchange rate before you use an ATM for the first time so that you know exactly how much local currency you want to withdraw.

Do most places take credit cards?

Almost all traveler-oriented businesses accept credit cards. You may encounter smaller restaurants and hotels that don't accept them at all, but these are pretty rare. Some businesses don't like to accept credit cards because their banks charge them exorbitant fees for credit-card transactions. They will usually relent and charge you a small fee for the privilege.

What if I don't know how to use chopsticks?

Chopsticks are the utensils of choice, but cutlery is available in many restaurants. That said, it's a good idea to brush up on your chopstick chops. The standard eating procedure is to hold the bowl close to your mouth and eat the food. Noisily slurping up soup and noodles is also the norm. It's considered bad manners to point or play with your chopsticks, or to place them on top of your rice bowl when you're finished eating (place the chopsticks horizontally on the table or plate). Don't leave your chopsticks standing up in a bowl of rice—it makes them look like the two incense sticks burned at funerals, and is seriously frowned upon.

How should I dress?

Most Chinese people dress for comfort and you can do the same. There's very little risk of offending people with your dress; Westerners tend to attract attention regardless of attire. Although miniskirts are best left at home, pretty much anything else goes.

Should I tip?

For a long time, tipping was officially forbidden by the government; as a result, locals simply don't do it. In general, you can follow their lead without any qualms. Nevertheless, the practice is now beginning to catch on, especially among tour guides. You don't need to tip in restaurants or in taxis.

A GOOD WALK

Check out what remains of West's 19th-century fingerhold in Beijing. The Old Legation Quarter, a walled area where foreign businesses and government offices were once housed, was heavily vandalized during the Cultural Revolution and altered again during the '80s boom. That said, a surprising number of early-20th-century European structures can still be found here.

The Old Legation Quarter

This walk begins on Dong Jiao Min Xiang. It can easily be reached via the lobby of the Novotel Xinqiao hotel. Exit through the back door right to the street. We'll first take you down the north side of the street and then along its south side. The most prominent structure that remains of the quarter is **St. Michael's Catholic Church.** Built by French Vincentian priests in 1902, this Gothic church is still crowded during Mass every Sunday.

Foreign Emissaries

The red building opposite the church started out as the **Belgian Embassy** and later became the **Burmese (now Myanmar) Embassy** following Burma's liberation.

On the north side of the street at No. 15 is the former location of the **French Legation**. The former Cambodian leader Prince Sihanouk stayed here during his many visits to China. The old **French Post Office** is now a Sichuan restaurant. **Hongdu Tailors** (No. 28) was once tailor to the top Communist officials who came here to have their revolutionary Mao jackets custom-made.

At the northeast corner of Zhengyi Lu, the former Rue Meiji, is a grand-looking building that was once the **Yokohama Specie Bank**; peek in for a look at the early-20th-century interior and ceilings. The pleasant patch of greenery you see running down the center of Zhengyi Lu was created in 1925, when the old rice-transport canal was filled in with earth.

Continue west on Dong Jiao Min Xiang. In the middle of the next block on your right are the gleaming headquarters of **China's Supreme People's Court** (27 *Dong Jiao Min Xiang*), which sits on the site of the former Russian Legation. A gate remains here from the original Russian complex.

Financial Street

Walking up the south side of the street, you'll see a building with thick Roman columns; this was first the **Russia Asiatic Bank**, and afterwards the **National City Bank of New York**—the fading letters NCB can still be seen in a concrete shield at the top of the building. This is now the **Beijing Police Museum**. Down a bit farther on the north side of the street, just before Tiananmen Square, is the old **French Hospital**. Opposite the hospital is the former **American Legation** (this is the last complex just before the steps leading to Tiananmen Square). It was rebuilt in 1901 after being destroyed by the Boxers. More than a century later, it has become home to some particularly high-end restaurants and retail spaces.

Highlights:	Excellent examples of the types of colonial buildings that served as Western legations, shops, and financial institutions around the turn of the 20th century
Where to Start:	Dong Jiao Min Xiang (east end)
Length:	One hour if you're walking at a leisurely pace (just over a mile)
Where to Stop:	At the former American Legation next to Tiananmen Square (or you can walk back down the street to where you started)
Best Time to Go:	Early morning or late afternoon when the weather is better
Worst Time to Go:	In the afternoon during the heat of the day
For lunch:	Lost Heaven, 23 Qian Men Dong Dajie

MAJOR FESTIVALS

Most of China's holidays and festivals are calculated according to the lunar calendar and can vary by as much as a few weeks from year to year. Check online for more specific dates.

Chinese New Year. China's most celebrated and important holiday, Chinese New Year follows the lunar calendar and falls between mid-January and mid-February. Also called Spring Festival (Chunjie), it gives the Chinese an official week-long holiday to visit their relatives, eat special meals, and set off firecrackers to celebrate the New Year and its respective Chinese zodiac animal. Students and teachers get up to four weeks off. Most offices and services reduce their hours or close altogether. ⚠ **Avoid visiting during Spring Festival, as Beijing tends to shut down; many of the sights you'll want to see may be closed.**

Dragon Boat Festival. The Dragon Boat Festival, on the fifth day of the fifth moon (usually in June), celebrates the national hero Qu Yuan, an honest politician who drowned himself during the Warring States Period of ancient China in despair over his inability to save his state (it was a time of great corruption). Legend has it that the fishermen who unsuccessfully attempted to rescue Qu by boat tried to distract fish from eating his body by throwing rice dumplings wrapped in bamboo leaves into the river. Today, crews in narrow dragon boats race to the beat of heavy drums, while balls of rice wrapped in bamboo leaves (*zongzi*) are consumed by the population en masse.

Labor Day. Labor Day falls on May 1, and is another busy travel time. In 2008 the government reduced the length of this holiday from five days to two, but the length of the holiday now changes from year to year.

Mid-Autumn Festival. Mid-Autumn Festival is celebrated on the 15th day of the eighth moon, which usually falls between mid-September and early October. The Chinese spend this time (trying to) gaze at the full moon and exchanging edible "mooncakes": moon-shaped pastries filled with meat, red-bean paste, lotus paste, salted egg, or date paste, or other delicacies.

National Day. Every October 1, China celebrates National Day, in honor of the founding of the People's Republic of China back in 1949. Tiananmen Square fills up with a hefty crowd of visitors on this official holiday, with people granted the entire week off work and school. Domestic tourists from around the country flock to the capital during this time. Steer clear of Beijing during national week if you don't want to battle endless crowds at all the main sights.

Qing Ming. Not so much a holiday as a day of worship, Qing Ming (literally, "clean and bright"), or Tomb Sweeping Day, gathers relatives at the graves of the deceased on the 15th day from the spring equinox—April 4th, 5th, or 6th, depending on the year—to clean the surfaces and leave fresh flowers. In 1997 the staunchly atheist Communist party passed a law stating that cremation is compulsory in cities and other densely populated areas. Accordingly, this festival has since lost much of its original meaning.

Spring Lantern Festival. The Spring Lantern Festival marks the end of the Chinese New Year, and is celebrated on the 15th day of the first lunar month (sometime in February or March, depending on the year). Residents flock to local parks for a display of Chinese lanterns and fireworks.

Continued on page 40

Terracotta warriors

THE AGE OF EMPIRES

When asked his opinion on the historical impact of the French Revolution, Zhou Enlai, the first Premier of Communist China, quipped, "It's too early to tell." Though a bit tongue in cheek, China does measure its history in millennia, and in its grand timeline, interactions with the West have been mere blips.

According to historical records, Chinese civilization stretches back to the 15th century BC—markings found on turtle shells carbon dated to around 1500 BC bear some similarity to modern Chinese script. China then resembled city-states rather than a unified nation. Iconic figures such as Laozi (the father of Taoism), Sun Tzu (author of the Art of War), and Confucius lived during this period. Generally, 221 BC is accepted as the beginning of Imperial China, when the city-states united under various banners.

Over the next 2,200 years (give or take a few), China alternated between periods of harmony and political upheaval. Its armies conquered new territory and were in turn conquered by external invaders (most of whom wound up themselves being assimilated).

By the early 18th century, the long, slow decline of the Qing—the last of China's Imperial dynasties—was already in progress, making the ancient nation ripe for exploitation by rising European powers. The Imperial era ended with the forced abdication of child Emperor Puyi (whose life is chronicled in Bernardo Bertolucci's The Last Emperor), and it's here that the history of modern China, first with the founding of the republic under Sun Yat-sen and then with the establishment of the People's Republic under Mao Zedong, truly begins.

(left) Oracle shell with early Chinese characters. (top, right) The Great Wall stretches 4,163 miles from east to west. (bottom, right) Confucius, Lao-tzu, and a Buddhist Arhat.

Writing Appears

circa 1500 BC

The earliest accounts of Chinese history are still shrouded in myth and legend, and it wasn't until 1959 that stories were verified by archaeological findings. For millennia, people formed communities in the fertile lands of what is now central China. The first recorded Chinese characters are said to have been developed 3,500 years ago. Though sometimes referred to as the Shang Dynasty, this period was more of a precursor to modern Chinese dynasties than a truly unified kingdom.

The Warring States Period

475–221 BC

China was so far from unified that these centuries are collectively remembered as the Warring States Period. As befitting such a contentious time, military science progressed, iron replaced bronze, and weapons material improved. Some of China's greatest luminaries lived during this period, including the father of Taoism, Laozi, Confucius, and Sun-Tzu, one of the greatest military tacticians and the author of the infamous *Art of War*, which is still studied in military academies around the world.

The First Dynasty

221–207 BC

The Qin Dynasty eventually defeated all of the other warring factions thanks to their cutting-edge military technology, namely the cavalry. The Qin were also called Ch'in, which may be where the word China first originated. The first Emperor, Qin Shi Huang, unified much of the lands and established a legal code and vast bureaucracy to hold it together. The Qin dynasty also standardized the written and spoken language and introduced a common currency.

(left) Terracotta warrior.
(top right) Temple of Xichan in Fuzhou

In order to protect his newly unified country, Qin Shi Huang ordered the creation of the massive Great Wall of China, which was built and rebuilt over the next 1,000 years. He was also a sculpture enthusiast and commissioned a massive army of stone soldiers to follow him into the afterlife. Buried with him, these terracotta warriors would remain hidden from the eyes of the world for two thousand years, until they were found by a farmer digging in a field just outside of Xian. These warriors are among the most important archaeological finds of the 20th century.

Buddhism Arrives

220–265 BC

Emperor Qin's dreams of a unified China fell apart, and eventually the kingdom split into three warring factions. But what was bad for stability turned out to be good for literature. The Three Kingdoms Period is still remembered in song and story. *The Romance of the Three Kingdoms* is as popular among Asian bookworms as the *Legend of King Arthur* is among Western readers. It's still widely read and has been translated into almost every language. Variations of the story have been adapted for manga, television series, and video games.

The Three Kingdoms period was filled with court intrigue, murder, and massive battles that, while exciting to read about centuries later, weren't much fun at the time. Armies ravaged the countryside, and most people lived and died in misery. Perhaps it was the carnage and disunity of the time that turned the country into a magnet for forces of harmony; it was during this period that Buddhism took hold in China, traveling over the Himalayas from India, via the Silk Road.

(left) Statue of Genghis Khan. (top right) Dongguan Mosque in Xining, Qinghai. (bottom right) Empress Shengshen

Religion Diversifies

618–845

Chinese spiritual life continued to diversify. Nestorian Monks from Asia Minor arrived bearing news of Christianity, and Saad ibn Abi Waqqas (a companion of the Prophet Muhammad) supposedly visited the Middle Kingdom to spread the word of Islam. During this era, Wu Zetian, onetime concubine, seized power from the Tang Dynasty and became the first (and only) woman to assume the title of emperor. She ruled for 25 years through puppet emperors and finally, for 15 years, as Emperor Shengshen.

Ghengis Invades

1271–1368

In Xanadu did Kublai Khan a stately pleasure dome decree…

Or so goes the famed Coleridge poem. But Kublai's grandfather Temujin (better known as Ghengis Khan) had bigger things in mind. One of the greatest war tacticians in history, he united the restive nomads of Mongolia's grassy plains and eventually sacked, looted, and pillaged much of the known west and most of the Chinese landmass. By the time Ghengis died in 1227, his grandson was well-tutored and ready to take on the rest of China.

By 1271, Kublai had established a capital in a land-locked city that would only much later become known as Beijing. This marks the beginning of the first (but not last) non-Han dynasty. Kublai Khan kept fighting southward and by 1279, Guangzhou fell to the Mongols, and Khan became the ultimate monarch of China. Though barbarians at heart, the Mongols must be credited for encouraging the arts and a number of early public works projects, including extending the highways and grand canals.

(left) Emperor Chengzu of the Ming Dynasty. (top right) Forbidden City in Beijing (bottom right) Child emperor Puyi.

Ming Dynasty

1368–1644

Many scholars believe that the Mongols' inability to relate with the Han is what ultimately pushed the Han to rise up and overthrow them. The reign of the Ming Dynasty was the last ethnically Han Dynasty to rule over a unified China. At its apex, the Bright Empire encompassed a landmass easily recognized as China, even by today's mapmakers. The Ming Emperors built a huge army and navy, refurbished the agricultural system, and printed many books using movable type long before Gutenberg. In the 15th century, Emperor Yongle began construction of the famous Forbidden City in Beijing, a veritable icon of China.

Also during the Ming Dynasty, China's best known explorer, Zheng He, plied the seven seas in massive treasure fleets that dwarfed in size and range the ships of Christopher Columbus. A giant both in stature and persona, Admiral Zheng (who was also a eunuch) spent two decades expanding China's knowledge of the world outside of its already impressive borders. He traveled as far as India, Africa, and (some say) even the coast of the New World.

Qing Dynasty

1644–1911

The final dynasty represented a serious case of minority rule. They were Manchus from the northeast. The early Qing dynasty was a brutal period as forces loyal to the new emperor crushed those loyal to the old. The Qing Dynasty peaked in the mid-to-late 18th century but soon after, its military powers began to wane. In the 19th century, Qing control weakened and prosperity diminished. By 1910 China was fractured, a baby sat on the Imperial throne, and the Qing Dynasty was on its deathbed.

(top left) A depiction of the Second Opium War. (bottom left) Chiang Kai-shek (top, right) Mao Zedong on December 6, 1944. (bottom, right) Sun Yat-sen.

The Opium Wars

1834–1860

European powers were hungry to open new territories up for trade, but the Qing weren't buying. The British East India Company, strapped for cash, realized they could sell opium in China at huge profits. The Chinese government quickly banned the nefarious trade and in response, a technologically superior Britain declared war. After a humiliating defeat in the first Opium War, China was forced to cede Hong Kong. Other foreign powers soon followed with territorial demands of their own.

Republican Era

1912–1949

China's Republican period was chaotic and unstable. The revolutionary Dr. Sun Yat-sen—revered by most Chinese as the father of modern China—was unable to build a cohesive government without the aid of regional warlords and urban gangsters. When he died of cancer in 1925, power passed to Chiang Kai-shek, who set about unifying China under the Kuomintang. What began as a unified group of both left- and right-wingers quickly deteriorated, and by the mid-1920s, civil war between the Communists and Nationalists was brewing.

The '30s and '40s were bleak decades for the Chinese people, caught between a vicious war with Japan and periodic clashes between Kuomintang and Communist forces. After Japan's defeat in 1945, China's civil war kicked into high gear. Though the Kuomintang were armed with superior weapons and backed by American money, the majority of Chinese people rallied behind the Communists. Within four years, the Kuomintang were driven off the mainland to Taiwan, where the Republic of China exists to the present day.

(top left) 1950s
Chinese stamp with
Mao and Stalin.
(top right) Shenzhen
(bottom left) Poster of
Mao's slogans.

1949–Present

The People's Republic

On October 1, 1949, Mao Zedong declared from atop Beijing's Gate of Heavenly Peace that "The Chinese People have stood up." And so the People's Republic of China was born. The Communist party set out to overhaul China's ancient feudal system, emphasizing class struggle, redistribution of wealth, and elimination of foreign dominance. The next three decades would see a massive, often painful transformation of Chinese society from feudalism into the modern age.

The Great Leap Forward was a disaster—Chinese peasants were encouraged to cram 100 years of industrial development into as many weeks. Untenable decisions led to industrial and agricultural ruin, widespread famine, and an estimated 30 million deaths. The trauma of this period, however, pales in comparison to The Great Proletarian Cultural Revolution. From 1966–1976, fear and zealotry gripped the nation as young revolutionaries heeded Chairman Mao's call to root out class enemies. During this decade, millions died, millions were imprisoned, and much of China's accumulated religious,

historical, and cultural heritage literally went up in smoke.

Like a phoenix rising from its own ashes, China rose from its own self-inflicted destruction. In the early 1980s, Deng Xiao-ping took the first steps in reforming China's stagnant economy. With the maxim "To Get Rich is Glorious," Deng loosened central control on the economy and declared Special Economic Zones where the seeds of capitalism could be incubated. Three decades later, the nation is one of the world's most vibrant economic engines. Though China's history is measured in millennia, her brightest years may well have only just begun.

EXPLORING

Updated by Adrian Sandiford

There's nowhere else in the world quite like Beijing. It's a modern-day megalopolis at the very core of the world's second-greatest economy, but it's also a gateway into China's imperial past and 5,000 years of history. This is a city where you can stand at the crossroads of time.

In Beijing the march to modernity may seem unrelenting at times, but the city still clings to parts of the past, including a heritage perhaps best encapsulated by the extraordinary Forbidden City. Once home to the emperors of old, it still dominates the city's center. And then, just an hour or two from downtown, stands one of the great wonders of the world: the Great Wall. Built during the Ming Dynasty to keep out the world, it's a telling contrast to the China of today.

Despite the proliferation of shiny office towers, high-rise residences, and shopping centers, there are still plenty of world-class historic sites to be discovered, including the famous rapidly disappearing *hutong*, neighborhoods formed from alleyways. Scores of the city's imperial palaces, mansions, and temples built under the Mongols during the Yuan Dynasty (1271–1368) were rebuilt during the later Ming and Qing dynasties. Despite the ravages of time and the Cultural Revolution, many of these refurbished sites are still in excellent condition.

On a seemingly superhuman scale that matches its status as the capital city of the world's most populous nation, Beijing is laid out with vast expanses of wide avenues and roadways organized in an orderly pattern. There are four key districts to note. Within the Second Ring Road (which replaced Beijing's now-forgotten city walls) are **Dongcheng** (the east half of the old center) and **Xicheng** (the west half). Dongcheng is home to many notable imperial sights; Xicheng is more relaxed and laid-back, thanks to a combination of charming alleyways, parks, and lakes. The **Chaoyang** District, east of the Old City, is where the full force of contemporary China can be felt, among the skyscrapers of the Guomao business district and the main shopping and nightlife hub of Sanlitun. To the northwest is **Haidian**, the city's university and tech district, as well as the location of some of Beijing's more far-flung sights, such as the Summer Palace.

Continued on page 50

BEIJING'S SUBWAY

Although Beijing's subway system has grown to 17 lines, the original two lines provide access to the most popular areas of the capital. **Line 1** runs east and west along Chang'an Jie past the China World Trade Center, Jianguomen (one of the embassy districts), the Wangfujing shopping area, Tiananmen Square and the Forbidden City, Xidan (another major shopping location), and the Military Museum, before heading out to the far western suburbs. **Line 2** (the inner loop line) runs along a sort of circular route around the center of the city shadowing the Second Ring Road. Important destinations include the Drum and Bell towers, Lama Temple, Dongzhimen (with a connection to the airport express), Dongsishitiao (near Sanlitun and the Workers' Stadium), Beijing Train Station, and Qianmen (Front Gate), south of Tiananmen Square. Free transfers between Line 1 and 2 can be made at either Fuxingmen or Jianguomen stations. Line 10, which forms a rough loop following the Third Ring Road, runs through the Central Business District at Guomao station (where a transfer is possible to Line 1), up toward the Sanlitun area at Tuanjiehu, and connects with the airport express line at Sanyuanqiao.

If both you and your final destination are near the Second Ring Road, on Chang'an Jie, or on the northern or eastern sides of the Third Ring Road, the best way to get there is probably by subway. It stops just about every kilometer (half mile), and you'll easily spot the entrances (with blue subway logos) dotting the streets. Each stop is announced in both English and Chinese, and there are clearly marked signs in English

or pinyin at each station. Transferring between lines is easy and free, with the standard Y2 ticket including travel between any two destinations.

Subway tickets can be purchased from electronic kiosks and ticket windows in every station. Start off by finding the button that says "English," insert your money, and press another button to print. Single-ride tickets cost Y2, and you'll want to pay with exact change; the machines don't accept Y1 bills, only Y1 coins. It's also possible to buy a stored-value subway card with a Y20 deposit and a purchase of Y10–Y100.

In the middle of each subway platform you'll find a map of the Beijing subway system along with a local map showing the position of exits. Subway cars also have a simplified diagram of the line you're riding above the doors.

Trains can be very crowded, especially during rush hour, and it's not uncommon for people to push onto the train before exiting passengers can get off. Prepare to get off by making your way to the door before you arrive at your station. Be especially wary of pickpockets.

■ **TIP→ Unfortunately, the subway system is not convenient for disabled people. In some stations there are no escalators, and sometimes the only entrance or exit is via steep steps.**

THE FORBIDDEN CITY

Undeniably sumptuous, the Forbidden City, once home to a long line of emperors, is Beijing's most enduring emblem. Magnificent halls, winding lanes, and stately courtyards await you—welcome to the world's largest palace complex.

As you gaze up at roofs of glazed-yellow tiles—a symbol of royalty—try to imagine a time when only the emperor ("the son of God") was permitted to enter this palace, accompanied by select family members, concubines, and eunuch-servants. Now, with its doors flung open, the Forbidden City's mysteries beckon.

The sheer grandeur of the site—with 800 buildings and more than 8,000 rooms—conveys the pomp and circumstance of Imperial China. The shady palaces, musty with age, recall life at court, where corrupt eunuchs and palace officials schemed and bored concubines gossiped.

BUILDING TO GLORY

Under the third Ming emperor, Yongle, 200,000 laborers built this complex over the course of 14 years, finishing in 1420. Yongle relocated the Ming capital to Beijing (from Nanjing in the south) to strengthen China's northern frontier. After Yongle, the palace was home to 23 Ming and Qing emperors, until the dynastic system crumbled in 1911.

In imperial times, no buildings were allowed to exceed the height of the palace. Moats and massive timber doors protected the emperor. Gleaming yellow roof tiles marked the vast complex as the royal court's exclusive dominion. Ornate interiors displayed China's most exquisite artisanship, including ceilings covered with turquoise-and-blue dragons, walls draped with priceless scrolls, intricate cloisonné screens, sandalwood thrones padded in delicate silks, and floors of golden-hued bricks. Miraculously, the palace survived fire, war, and imperial China's collapse.

MORE THAN FENG SHUI

The Forbidden City embodies Feng Shui, architectural principles used for thousands of years throughout China. Each main hall faces south, opening to a courtyard flanked by lesser buildings. This symmetry repeats itself along a north–south axis that bisects the imperial palace, with a broad walkway paved in marble. This path was reserved exclusively for the emperor's sedan chair.

The entire complex follows the principles of Feng Shui.

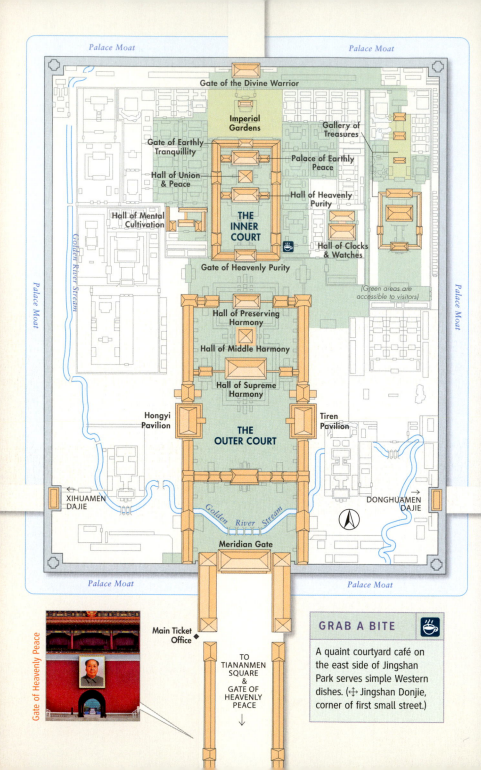

Palace Moat

Palace Moat

Gate of the Divine Warrior

Imperial Gardens

Gallery of Treasures

Gate of Earthly Tranquillity

Palace of Earthly Peace

Hall of Union & Peace

Hall of Heavenly Purity

Hall of Mental Cultivation

THE INNER COURT

Gate of Heavenly Purity

Hall of Clocks & Watches

(Green areas are accessible to visitors)

Golden River Stream

Palace Moat

Palace Moat

Hall of Preserving Harmony

Hall of Middle Harmony

Hall of Supreme Harmony

Hongyi Pavilion

Tiren Pavilion

THE OUTER COURT

← XIHUAMEN DAJIE

DONGHUAMEN DAJIE →

Golden River Stream

Meridian Gate

Palace Moat

Palace Moat

Gate of Heavenly Peace

Main Ticket Office ◆

TO TIANANMEN SQUARE & GATE OF HEAVENLY PEACE ↓

GRAB A BITE

A quaint courtyard café on the east side of Jingshan Park serves simple Western dishes. (⊕ Jingshan Donjie, corner of first small street.)

WHAT TO SEE

The most impressive way to reach the Forbidden City is through the **Gate of Heavenly Peace** (Tiananmen), connected to Tiananmen Square. The Great Helmsman himself stood here to establish the People's Republic of China on October 1, 1949.

The **Meridian Gate** (Wumen), sometimes called Five Phoenix Tower, is the main southern entrance to the palace. Here, the emperor announced yearly planting schedules according to the lunar calendar; it's also where errant officials were flogged. The main ticket office and audio-guide rentals are just west of this gate.

The central entrance of the Meridian was reserved for the emperor. The one day the empress was allowed to walk through it was her wedding day.

THE OUTER COURT

The **Hall of Supreme Harmony** (Taihedian) was used for coronations, royal birthdays, and weddings. Bronze vats, once kept brimming with water to fight fires, ring this vast expanse. The hall sits atop three stone tiers with an elaborate drainage system with 1,000 carved dragons. On the top tier, bronze cranes symbolize longevity. Inside, cloisonné cranes flank the imperial throne, above which hangs a heavy bronze ball—placed there to crush any pretender to the throne.

Take a close look at the bronze vats and you'll see the telltale scratch marks of greedy foreign soldiers who scraped the gold with their bayonets.

Emperors greeted audiences in the **Hall of Middle Harmony** (Zhonghedian). It also housed the royal plow, with which the emperor would turn a furrow to commence spring planting.

The highest civil service examinations, which were personally conducted by the emperor, were once administered in the **Hall of Preserving Harmony** (Baohedian). Behind the hall, a 200-ton marble relief of dragons, the palace's most treasured stone carving, adorns the staircase.

The Hall of Supreme Harmony was the site of many imperial weddings.

A short jaunt to the right is **Hall of Clocks and Watches** (Zhongbiaoguan), where you'll find a collection of early timepieces. It's pure opulence, with jeweled, enameled, and lacquered timepieces (some astride elephants, others implanted in ceramic trees). Our favorites? Those crafted from red sandalwood. *(additional admission cost)*

You'll see that lions in the palace live in pairs. A female lion playing with a cub symbolizes imperial fertility. A male lion, sitting majestically with a sphere beneath his paw, represents power.

Marble dragons will greet you behind the Hall of Preserving Harmony.

Emperors Throne in the Palace of Heavenly Purity

THE INNER COURT

Now you're approaching the very core of the palace. Several emperors chose to live in the Inner Palace with their families. The **Hall of Heavenly Purity** (Qianqinggong) holds another imperial throne; the **Hall of Union and Peace** (Jiaotaidian) was the venue for the empress's annual birthday party; and the **Palace of Earthly Peace** (Kunninggong) was where royal couples consummated their marriages. The banner above the throne bizarrely reads DOING NOTHING.

On either side of the Inner Palace are six western and six eastern palaces—the former living quarters of concubines, eunuchs, and servants. The last building on the western side, the **Hall of Mental Cultivation** (Yangxindian), is the most important of these; starting with Emperor Yongzheng, all Qing Dynasty emperors attended to daily state business in this hall.

AN EMPEROR CHEAT SHEET

JIAJING (1507–1567)

Ming Emperor Jiajing was obsessed with Taoism, which he hoped would give him longevity, but which also led him to ignore state affairs for 25 years. His other fixation was the pursuit of girls: his 18 concubines conspired to strangle him in his sleep, but their plot was uncovered. Nearly all of the girls, and their families, were killed.

YONGZHENG (1678–1735)

The third emperor of the Qing Dynasty, Yongzheng was tyrannical but efficient. He became emperor amid rumors that he had forged his father's will. He appeased his brothers by promoting them, but then proceeded to murder and imprison anyone who posed a challenge, including his own brothers, two of whom died in prison.

Pagoda in the Imperial Garden

The Gallery of Treasures (Zhenbaoguan), actually a series of halls, has breathtaking examples of imperial ornamentation. The first room displays candleholders, wine vessels, tea sets, and a golden pagoda commissioned by Qing emperor Qian Long in honor of his mother. A cabinet on one wall contains the 25 imperial seals. Jade bracelets, golden hair pins, and coral fill the second hall; carved jade landscapes a third. *(Admission: Y10)*

HEAD FOR THE GREEN

North of the Forbidden City's private palaces, beyond the **Gate of Earthly Tranquillity**, lie the most pleasant parts of the Forbidden City: the **Imperial Gardens** (Yuhuayuan), composed of ancient cypress trees and stone mosaic pathways. During festivals, palace inhabitants climbed the Hill of Accumulated Elegance. You can exit the palace at the back of the gardens through the park's **Gate of the Divine Warrior** (Shenwumen).

FAST FACTS

Address: The main entrance is just north of the Gate of Heavenly Peace, which faces Tiananmen Square on Chang'an Jie.

Web site: www.dpm.org.cn

Open: Tues.–Sun.

UNESCO Status: Declared a World Heritage Site in 1987. You must check your bags prior to entry and also pass through a metal detector.

■ The palace is always packed with visitors, but it's impossibly crowded on national holidays.

■ Allow 2–4 hours to explore the palace. There are souvenir shops and restaurants inside.

■ You can rent audio guides at the Meridian Gate.

2

IN FOCUS THE FORBIDDEN CITY

CIXI (1835–1908)

The Empress Dowager served as de facto ruler of China from 1861 until 1908. She was a concubine at 16 and soon became Emperor Xianfeng's favorite. She gave birth to his only son to survive: the heir apparent. Ruthless and ambitious, she learned the workings of the imperial court and used every means to gain power.

PUYI (1906–1967)

Puyi, whose life was depicted in Bertolucci's classic *The Last Emperor*, took the throne at age two. The Qing dynasty's last emperor, he was forced to abdicate after the dynasty fell. During an attempted restoration in 1917, he held the throne for 12 days. Puyi was forced out of the Imperial City in 1924 by a warlord.

DONGCHENG DISTRICT 东城区

Sightseeing
★★★★☆

Dining
★★★☆☆

Lodging
★★★★☆

Shopping
★★★☆☆

Nightlife
★★★☆☆

Feeling the weight and the power of China's history is inevitable as you stand on the Avenue of Eternal Peace, Chang'an Jie, at the crossroads of ancient and modern China. The pale expanse of Tiananmen Square, built by Mao Zedong to fit up to a million revolutionary souls, leaves even mobs of tourists looking tiny and scattered. An iconic portrait of Mao sits upon the scarlet wall of Tiananmen Gate, the serenity of his gaze belying the tumult of his reign. And beyond, the splendors of the Forbidden City await.

The soul of old Beijing lives on throughout Dongcheng District, where you'll find the city's top historic sites and idyllic hutong worth getting lost in. A day or two exploring the district will leave you feeling as if you've been introduced to the complicated character of the capital. Dongcheng is also one of the smaller districts in the city, which makes it ideal for tackling on foot or by bicycle.

Start with the imposing majesty of Tiananmen Square and the Forbidden City for a view of official China at its peak, past and present. Nearby, witness the rise of China's middle class firsthand on Wangfujing, where you'll find familiar brands (McDonald's, Nike) amid a dwindling number of large stores, relics from the days of central planning. Then take a detour deeper into the past-meets-present dichotomy with a visit to the hutong surrounding the Confucius Temple. Wudaoying Hutong and Fangjia Hutong currently feature the best array of restaurants, boutiques, and cafés in the neighborhood. From the old men playing chess in the hutong to the sleek, chauffeured Audis driving down Chang'an Jie, to the colorful shopping on Wangfujing, the Dongcheng District offers a thousand little tastes of what makes Beijing such a fascinating city.

TOP ATTRACTIONS

Fodor's Choice
★

Confucius Temple (孔庙 *Kǒngmiào*). This tranquil temple to China's great sage has endured close to eight centuries of additions and restorations. The Hall of Great Accomplishment in the temple houses Confucius's funeral tablet and shrine, flanked by copper-colored statues depicting China's wisest Confucian scholars. As in Buddhist and Taoist temples, worshippers can offer sacrifices (in this case to a mortal, not a deity). The 198 tablets lining the courtyard outside the Hall of Great Accomplishment contain 51,624 names belonging to advanced Confucian scholars from the Yuan, Ming, and Qing dynasties. Flanking the Gate of Great Accomplishment are two carved stone drums dating to the Qianlong period (1735–96). In the Hall of Great Perfection you'll find the central shrine to Confucius. Check out the huge collection of ancient musical instruments.

In the front and main courtyards of the temple you'll find a cemetery of stone tablets. These tablets, or stelae, stand like rows of crypts. On the front stelae you can barely make out the names of thousands of scholars who passed imperial exams. Another batch of stelae, carved in the mid-1700s to record the *Thirteen Classics*, which are philosophical works attributed to Confucius, line the west side of the grounds.

■**TIP→** We recommend combining a tour of the Confucius Temple with the nearby Lama Temple. Access to both is convenient from the Yonghegong subway stop at the intersection of Line 2 and Line 5. You can also easily get to the Temple of Heaven by taking Line 5 south to Tiantandongmen.

The complex is now combined with the Imperial Academy next door, once the highest educational institution in the country. Established in 1306 as a rigorous training ground for high-level government officials, the academy was notorious, especially during the early Ming Dynasty era, for the harsh discipline imposed on scholars perfecting their knowledge of the Confucian classics. The Riyong Emperors Lecture Hall is surrounded by a circular moat (although the building is rectangular in shape). Emperors would come here to lecture on the classics. This ancient campus would be a glorious place to study today with its washed red walls, gold-tiled roofs, and towering cypresses (some as old as 700 years). ⊠ *13 Guozijian Lu, off Yonghegong Lu near Lama Temple, Dongcheng District* ☎ *010/8401–1977* ⊕ *www.kmgzj.com* ⊠ *Y30* ⊙ *Daily 8:30–5* Ⓜ *Yonghegong.*

Dongbianmen Watchtower (东便门角楼 *Dōngbiànmén jiǎolóu*). This is Beijing's last remaining Ming watchtower. Be sure to check out the Red Gate Gallery inside, which shows works by well-known contemporary Chinese artists. The gallery was set up in 1991 by Brian Wallace, an Australian who studied art history at China's Central Academy of Fine Arts. The second and third floors are devoted to the history of the Chongwen District. ⊠ *Dongbianmen Watchtower, Chongwen District* ☎ *010/6525–1005* ⊕ *www.redgategallery.com* ⊠ *Free* ⊙ *Daily 9–5.*

Fodor's Choice
★

Forbidden City. *See the highlighted feature in this chapter for more about the Forbidden City.* ⊠ *Main entrance just north of the Gate of Heavenly Peace, which faces Tiananmen Square on Chang'an Jie, Dongcheng*

GETTING ORIENTED

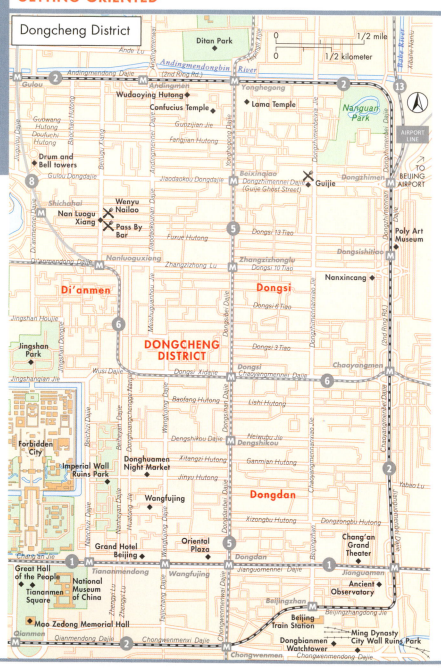

Dongcheng District

Ditan Park

Ande Lu

Andingmendong Dajie
Andingmendongbin River
(2nd Ring Rd.)

Hepingli Xijie

Yonghegong

M Gulou
2 Andingmen

Wudaoying Hutong ◆
Confucius Temple ◆

Lama Temple ◆

Nanguan Park

M
2

13

AIRPORT LINE

Guowang Hutong
Doufuchi Hutong

Guozijian Jie
Fangjian Hutong

Dongzhimennei Dajie
(Guijie Ghost Street)
Beixinqiao ✕ Guijie

Dongzhimen

TO BEIJING AIRPORT

Drum and Bell towers

Jiaodaokou Dongdajie
M

Baochao Hutong
Beilou Xiang
Andingmennei Dajie
Yonghegong Dajie
Dongzhimennei Dajie

8
Gulou Dongdajie

Wenyu Nailao ✕
Nan Luogu Xiang ◆ ✕ Pass By Bar

Fuxue Hutong

Dongsi 13 Tiao

Nanxincang ◆

Poly Art Museum
M

Dongsishitiao
M

Shichahai

Di'anmennei Dajie

Nanluoguxiang

Zhangzizhong Lu

Zhangzizhonglu
M
Dongsi 10 Tiao

M
Di'anmendong Dajie

5

Di'anmen

Meishuguanhou Jie
Dongsibei Dajie

Dongsi
Dongsi 6 Tiao

Dongzhimennannaxiao Jie
(2nd Ring Rd.)

Jingshan Houjie

6

DONGCHENG DISTRICT

Dongsi 3 Tiao

Chaoyangmen

Jingshan Park ◆

Jingshan Dongjie

Wusi Dajie
Dongsi Xidajie
Dongsi
Chaoyangmennei Dajie

6

Jingshangian Jie

Wangfujing Dajie
Dongsinan Dajie
M

Baofang Hutong
Lishi Hutong

Chaoyangmennanxiao Jie
Chaoyangmennei Dajie

Beichizi Dajie
Beiheyan Dajie
Dongdanchengge Nanjie

Dengshikou Dajie
M
Dengshikou
Neiwubu Jie

Forbidden City

Imperial Wall Ruins Park ◆
Donghuamen Night Market ◆

Xitangzi Hutong
Ganmian Hutong

Nanheyan Dajie
Huatong Jie
Wangfujing Dajie

Jinyu Hutong

Dongdan
Wangfujing ◆
Dongdanbei Dajie

Xizongbu Hutong
Dongzongbu Hutong

Chang'an Grand Theater ◆

Nanchizi Dajie

Grand Hotel Beijing ◆

Oriental Plaza ◆

M
5
Dongdan
Beijingzhan

Yabao Lu

M
2
Jianguomenbei Dajie

Chang'an Jie
1
M
Tiananmendong
Great Hall of the People ◆

Zhengyi Lu
Zhengyi Lu
Tailichang Dajie
Wangfujing Dajie

M
Wangfujing
Chongwenmenwai Dajie

Jianguomennei Dajie
1
Jianguomen
Ancient Observatory ◆

National Museum of China
Tiananmen Square ◆

Beijingzhan
Beijingzhangdong Jie

◆ Mao Zedong Memorial Hall

Qianmen

M
Qianmendong Dajie
2

Chongwenmenxi Dajie

Beijing Train Station ◆

Dongbianmen ◆ Watchtower

Ming Dynasty City Wall Ruins Park

M
Chongwenmen
Chongwenmennei Dajie

0   1/2 mile
0   1/2 kilometer

QUICK BITES

Wenyu Nailao. Have a cup of fresh yogurt at Wenyu Nailao, which makes its yogurt the traditional Chinese way. ✉ *49 Nan Luogu Xiang* ☎ *010/6405–7621.*

Pass By Bar. The Pass By Bar offers good drinks, food, and wireless Internet access. ✉ *108 Nan Luogu Xiang* ☎ *010/8403—8004.*

Guijie (簋街 *Guǐjiē*). For a nighttime-munchies cure, head to Guijie, also known as Ghost Street, which is full of restaurants serving up noodles, hotpot, and fried delights. One of the most popular dishes here is *malaxia,* or spicy crawfish. ✉ *Dongzhimennei Dajie.*

TOP REASONS TO GO

Explore the wonders of the **Forbidden City** and **Tiananmen Square.** Then climb the hill in **Jingshan Park** for a timeless view of the golden rooftops of the Forbidden City.

Visit the **Lama Temple,** Beijing's most famous Tibetan Buddhist temple, then the **Confucius Temple;** finally, stroll down nearby Wudaoying Hutong to take in the trendy shops and cafés.

Have dinner in the renovated courtyard of **The Source** (⇨ *Chapter 3*), then walk through **Nan Luogu Xiang,** the city's hippest hutong area.

Walk up **Wangfujing,** Beijing's premier shopping spot, and try some local delicacies (scorpion on a stick, perhaps) from the vendors at Wangfujing Snack Street or at the Donghuamen Night Market.

Walk along the well-landscaped **Imperial Wall Ruins Park,** which begins one block north of Chang'an Jie on Nan Heyandajie.

GETTING HERE

Dongcheng is easily accessible by subway, with stops along most of its perimeter: Tiananmen East station to Jianguomen on Line 1 forms the south side of this district; Jianguomen to Gulou Dajie on Line 2 forms the district's north and east sides. Line 2 stops at the Lama Temple, the Ancient Observatory, Wangfujing, and Tiananmen Square. Taxi travel during peak hours (7 to 9 am and 5 to 8 pm) is difficult. At other times traveling by taxi is affordable, convenient, and the fastest option (especially at noon, when much of the city is at lunch, and after 10 pm). Renting a bike to see the sites is also a good option. Bus travel within the city is only Y1 for shorter distances and can be very convenient, but requires reading knowledge of Chinese to find the correct bus to take. Once on the bus, stops are announced in Chinese and English.

MAKING THE MOST OF YOUR TIME

Most of Dongcheng can be seen in a day, but it's best to set aside two, because the **Forbidden City** and **Tiananmen Square** will likely take the better part of one day. The climb up Coal Hill (also called Prospect Hill) in **Jingshan Park** will take about 30 minutes for an average walker. From there, take a taxi to the **Lama Temple,** which is worth a good two hours, then visit the nearby **Confucius Temple.**

Though many sights were damaged during the Cultural Revolution, Confucian temples can still be seen.

District ☎010/6404–4071 ✍Y40 Nov. 1–Mar. 31; Y60 Apr. 1–Oct. 31; the Hall of Clocks and Watches and the Gallery of Treasures are an additional Y10 each ⊙ Nov. 1–Mar. 31, daily 8:30 am–4:30; Apr. 1–Oct. 31, daily 8:30–5. Closed Mon. throughout the year

Jingshan Park (景山公园 *Jǐngshān gōngyuán*). This park, also known as Coal Hill Park, was built around a small peak formed from earth excavated for the Forbidden City's moats. Ming rulers ordered the hill's construction to improve the feng shui of their new palace to the south. You can climb a winding stone staircase past peach and apple trees to Wanchun Pavilion, the park's highest point. On a clear day it offers unparalleled views of the Forbidden City and the Bell and Drum towers. Chongzhen, the last Ming emperor, is said to have hanged himself at the foot of Coal Hill as his dynasty collapsed in 1644. ✉*Jingshanqian Dajie, opposite the north gate of the Forbidden City, Xicheng and Dongcheng districts* ☎010/6404–4071 ✍Y2 ⊙ *Daily 6 am–7 pm.*

Lama Temple (雍和宫 *Yōnghégōng*). One of the most important functioning Buddhist temples in Beijing, this much-visited Tibetan Buddhist masterpiece has five main halls and numerous galleries hung with finely detailed *thangkhas* (Tibetan religious scroll paintings). The entire temple is decorated with Buddha images—all guarded by somber lamas dressed in brown robes. Originally a palace for Prince Yongzheng, it was transformed into a temple once he became the Qing's third emperor in 1723. The temple flourished under Emperor Qianlong, housing some 500 resident monks. This was once the official "embassy" of Tibetan Buddhism in Beijing, but today only about two dozen monks live in this complex.

2

TIPS FOR TOURING WITH KIDS

Although incense-filled temples and ancient buildings may not, at first glance, seem child-friendly, Beijing's historic sites do offer some unique and special activities for the young. The Summer Palace is a great place for kids to run around and go splashing in paddleboats; the old Summer Palace has a fun maze; Tiananmen Square is a popular spot to fly kites; the Drum Tower holds percussion performances; and the Temple of Heaven's Echo Wall offers up some unusual acoustical fun. Budding astronomers might also be intrigued by the Ancient Observatory, with its Ming Dynasty star map and early heaven-gazing devices built by early Jesuit missionaries who worked for the imperial court. Wherever you go, remember this: Chinese kids are generally allowed to run around and act like children, so don't worry that your own tyke's behavior will be disapproved of.

Don't miss the **The Hall of Heavenly Kings**, with statues of Maitreya, the future Buddha, and Weitou, China's guardian of Buddhism. This hall is worth a slow stroll. In the courtyard beyond, a pond with a bronze mandala represents paradise. The Statues of Buddhas of the Past, Present, and Future hold court in **The Hall of Harmony**. Look on the west wall where an exquisite silk thangkha of White Tara—the embodiment of compassion—hangs. Images of the Medicine and Longevity Buddhas line **The Hall of Eternal Blessing**. In **The Pavilion of Ten Thousand Fortunes** you see the breathtaking 26-meter (85-foot) Maitreya Buddha carved from a single block of sandalwood. ■TIP➜ Combine a visit to the Lama Temple with the Confucius Temple and the Imperial Academy, which are a five-minute walk away, within the hutong neighborhood opposite the main entrance. ✉ *12 Yonghegong Dajie, Beixinqiao, Dongcheng District* ☎ *010/6404–4499* 💰 *Y25* 🕐 *Daily 9–4:30* Ⓜ *Yonghegong, Line 2.*

NEED A BREAK?

Lao She Teahouse. The area just south of Qianmen was once the nightlife hub of imperial China. Visit this old teahouse for a taste of Chinese performing arts along with your cuppa. ✉ *Building 3, 3 Qianmenxi Dajie, Xicheng District* ☎ *010/6303–6830.*

Ming Dynasty City Wall Ruins Park (明城墙遗址公园 *Míng chéngqiáng yízhǐ gōngyuán*). This rebuilt section of Beijing's old inner-city wall is a nicely landscaped area with paths full of Chinese walking their dogs, flying kites, practicing martial arts, and playing with their children. It was made using original bricks that had been snatched decades earlier, after the city wall had been torn down. At the eastern end of the park is the grand Dongbianmen Watchtower, home to the popular Red Gate Gallery. ✉ *Dongbianmen, Dongdajie Street, Chongwen District* 💰 *Free* 🕐 *Daily, park open 24 hrs* Ⓜ *Jiandemen.*

National Museum of China (中國國家博物館 *Zhōngguó guójiā bówùguǎn*). This monumental edifice on the eastern side of Tiananmen Square showcases 5,000 years of history in immaculate surroundings. With 2 million square feet of exhibition space, it's impossible to

DID YOU KNOW?

The Lama Temple (Yonghe Temple) is one of the largest and most important Tibetan Buddhist monasteries in the world. The building originally served as an official residence for court eunuchs but was later turned into a lamasery. In addition to many other works of art, in the center of the hall you'll find the Temple's 55-foot-tall golden statue of Maitreya Buddha. The temple is rumored to have survived the Cultural Revolution thanks to the intervention of Premier Zhou Enlai.

2

see everything. The propaganda-heavy history sections can be safely skipped; focus instead on the ancient China section on the lower level, which houses magnificent displays of bronzes and jade artifacts. The museum also features strong shows of visiting works from abroad, such as Renaissance art from Florence and ceramics from the British Museum and the Victoria and Albert Museum. ✉ *16 Dong Chang An Jie, Dongcheng District* ☏ *010/6511–6400* ⊕ *en.chnmuseum.cn* 💳 *Free with passport* ⏱ *Tues.–Sun. 9–5, ticket booth closes at 3:30* Ⓜ *Tiananmen East.*

Fodor's Choice
★

Red Gate Gallery (红门画廊 *Hóngmén huàláng*). This gallery, one of the first to open in Beijing, displays and sells contemporary Chinese art in the extraordinary location of the old Dongbianmen Watchtower, which dates back to the 16th century. The venue is worth a visit even if you're not interested in the art. Be aware that the subway stop listed here is about a 25-minute walk from the gallery. ✉ *1/F & 4/F, Dongbianmen Watchtower, Chongwenmen Dongdajie, Dongcheng District* ☏ *010/6525–1005* ⊕ *www.redgategallery.com* Ⓜ *Jianguomen.*

Fodor's Choice
★

Tiananmen Square (天安门广场 *Tiānānmén guǎngchǎng*). The world's largest public square, and the very heart of modern China, Tiananmen Square owes little to grand imperial designs and everything to Mao Zedong. At the height of the Cultural Revolution, hundreds of thousands of Red Guards crowded the square; in June 1989 the square was the scene of tragedy when student demonstrators were killed.

Today the square is packed with sightseers, families, and undercover policemen. Although formidable, the square is a little bleak, with no shade, benches, or trees. Come here at night for an eerie experience—it's a little like being on a film set. Beijing's ancient central axis runs right through the center of Mao's mausoleum, the Forbidden City, the Drum and Bell towers, and the Olympic Green. The square is sandwiched between two grand gates: the Gate of Heavenly Peace (Tiananmen) to the north and the Front Gate (Qianmen) in the south. Along the western edge is the Great Hall of the People. The National Museum of China lies along the eastern side. The 125-foot granite obelisk you see is the Monument to the People's Heroes; it commemorates those who died for the revolutionary cause of the Chinese people. ✉ *Bounded by Chang'an Jie to the north and Qianmen Dajie to the south, Dongcheng District* 💳 *Free* ⏱ *5 am–10 pm* Ⓜ *Qianmen.*

DID YOU KNOW?

A network of tunnels lies beneath Tiananmen Square. Mao Zedong is said to have ordered them dug in the late 1960s after Sino-Soviet relations soured. They extend across Beijing and many have been sealed up or fallen into disrepair, though migrant workers inhabit some.

Wangfujing (王府井 *Wángfǔjǐng*). Wangfujing, one of the city's oldest and busiest shopping districts, is still lined with a handful of *laozihao*, old brand-name shops, some dating back a century, and 1950s-era state-run stores. This short walking street is a pleasant place for window-shopping. Also on Wangfujing is the gleaming Oriental Plaza, with its expensive high-end shops (Tiffany's, Burberry, Ermenegildo Zegna, and Audi among them), interspersed with Levi Jeans, Esprit,

MAO ZEDONG (1893–1976)

Some three decades after his passing, Mao continues to evoke radically different feelings. Born into a relatively affluent farming family in Hunan, Mao became active in politics at a young age; he was one of the founding members of the Chinese Communist Party in 1921. When the People's Republic of China was established in 1949, Mao served as chairman. After a good start in improving the economy, he launched radical programs in the mid-1950s. The party's official assessment is that Mao was 70% correct and 30% incorrect. His critics reverse this ratio.

Starbucks, Pizza Hut, KFC, Häagen-Dazs, and a modern movie multiplex. ⊠ *Wangfujing, Dongcheng District.*

WORTH NOTING

Ditan Park (地坛公园 *Dìtán gōngyuán*). In "Temple of Earth Park," 105 acres of 16th-century green space, are the square altar where emperors once made sacrifices to the earth god, and the Hall of Deities. This is a lovely place for a stroll, especially if you're already near the Drum Tower or Lama Temple. ⊠ *Hepingli Xilu, just north of Second Ring Rd., Dongcheng District* ☎ *010/6421–4657* ☒ *Y2* ☉ *Daily 6 am–9 pm.*

Guijie (簋街 *Guǐjiē*). This nearly mile-long stretch, also known as Ghost Street, is lined with more than 100 restaurants, many open 24 hours a day and attracting the spillover from nightclubs. Although the restaurants here are generally just average, the lively atmosphere is enticing, with red lanterns often strung across the sidewalks (these are taken down from time to time on the whim of the local authorities). There are a wide number of cuisines on the menus here, though night owls tend to favor spicy dishes such as fiery Sichuan hotpot, crayfish in chili oil, and barbecued fish. ⊠ *Dongzhimennei Dajie, Dongcheng District.*

Mao Zedong Memorial Hall (毛主席纪念堂 *Máozhǔxí jìniàntáng*). Sentries here will assure that your communion with the Great Helmsman is brief. First, check your bag and camera at the designated point to the east of the hall. Then, join the long and winding line that leads first to a spacious lobby dominated by a marble Mao statue and then to the Hall of Reverence, where his embalmed body lies in state, wrapped in the red flag of the Communist Party of China and inside a crystal coffin that's lowered each night into a subterranean freezer. In a bid to limit Mao's deification, a second-story museum was added in 1983; it's dedicated to the former Premier Zhou Enlai, former general Zhu De, and China's president before the Cultural Revolution, Liu Shaoqi (who was persecuted to death during the Cultural Revolution). The hall's builders willfully ignored Tiananmen Square's geomancy: the mausoleum faces north, contradicting centuries of imperial ritual. Note that the hall is open only in the mornings. ⊠ *Tiananmen Sq., Dongcheng District* ☎ *010/6513–2277* ☒ *Free* ☉ *Sept.–June, Tues.–Sun. 8 am–noon; July and Aug., Tues.–Sun. 7 am–11 am.*

Nan Luogu Xiang (南锣鼓巷 *Nánluógǔxiàng*). The narrow Nan Luogu Xiang, or South Gong and Bell Alley, which dates back some 700 years, got a new lease on life when it was discovered by young entrepreneurs

Tiananmen Square

around 2006. They quickly began opening souvenir shops, boutiques, cafés, bars, and snack stalls in the aging but rustic structures that line the sidewalks. The narrow street is flanked by eight historic *hutongs* to the east and west that are worth exploring, especially when the crowds in the main section get overwhelming, which, as the years go by, and the street's popularity grows, they so often do. It's a great place to try some of the snacks popular with young Chinese, such as milk tea, chicken wings, and the famous custard-like yogurt at Wenyu Nailao. ⊠ *Nan Luogu Xiang, Dongcheng District* Ⓜ *Nanluoguxiang.*

Nanxincang (南新仓 *Nánxîncâng*). China's oldest existing granary, dating back to the Yongle period (1403–24), is now an entertainment hub of sorts, with couple of art galleries, a teahouse, and a changing line-up of bars and restaurants, including the most established of the bunch, a well-loved branch of the famed Dadong Roast Duck. The structures at Nanxincang—just 10 years younger than those of the Forbidden City—were just one of the more than 300 granaries that existed in this area during imperial days. ⊠ *Dongsi Shitiao, 1 block west of the Second Ring Road, Dongcheng District.*

The Poly Art Museum (保利艺术博物馆 *Bǎolì yìshù bówùguǎn*). This impressive but often overlooked museum, located in a gleaming glass office tower, was established in 1998 to promote traditional art and to protect Chinese art from being lost to foreign countries. The museum has focused on the overseas acquisition of ancient bronzes, sculpture, and painting. The space is divided into two galleries, one for the display of early Chinese bronzes, and the other for Buddhist scriptures carved in stone. Also on display here are four bronze animal heads that were once located in the Old Summer Palace. ⊠ *New Poly Plaza, 1 Chaoy-angmen Bei Dajie, next to the Dongsishitiao subway stop on Line 2, Dongcheng District* ☏ *010/6500–8117* 🎟 *Y20* ⊘ *Mon.–Sat. 9:30–4:30* Ⓜ *Dongsishitiao.*

NEED A BREAK?

Donghuamen Night Market (东华门夜市 *Dōnghuâmén yèshì*). Crunchy deep-fried scorpions and other critters are sold at the Donghuamen Night Market, at the northern end of Wangfujing's wide walking boulevard. We'll admit: this is more of a place to look at and perhaps photograph food rather than devour it. In addition to standard street foods, hawkers here also serve up deep-fried starfish, plus a variety of insects and other hard-to-identify food items. Most street-market food is usually safe to eat as long as it's hot. The row of stalls makes for an intriguing walk with great photo ops. ⊠ *Donganmen Dajie, on the northern side of Wangfujing, Dongcheng District.*

XICHENG DISTRICT 西城区

Sightseeing
★★★☆☆

Dining
★★☆☆☆

Lodging
★☆☆☆☆

Shopping
★★☆☆☆

Nightlife
★★★☆☆

Xicheng District is home to a charming combination of some of the most distinctive things that the city has to offer: cozy *hutongs*, palatial courtyard houses, charming lakes, and fine restaurants. For many visitors, this is one of the best areas in which to fall in love with Beijing.

The best way to do that is to take a walk or bicycle tour of the hutongs here: there's no better way to scratch the surface of this sprawling city (before it disappears) than by exploring these courtyard houses as you wander in and out of historic sites in the area.

This is also a great area for people-watching, especially along the shores of Houhai. As you wander, sample the local snacks sold from shop windows. Treats abound on Huguosi Jie (just west of Mei Lanfang's house). In the evening, relax at a restaurant or bar with a view of the lake. The lakes at Shichahai are hopping day and night.

A GOOD WALK

Start just north of the Forbidden City at **Jingshan Park.** From here you can walk several blocks west to the south gate of **Beihai Park,** which is beautiful in August's lotus season. Exit at the north gate. After crossing Di'anmen Xidajie, you'll arrive at **Qianhai,** or "front lake."

Walk on the right, or east, side of the lake for about 10 minutes until you reach the famous Ming Dynasty **Silver Ingot Bridge.** Take a side trip to the **Bell Tower,** which is a short walk northeast of the bridge (and which straddles the border with the Dongcheng District). To get here, head down Yandai Xiejie, turn left at the end and you'll see the tower. Directly behind it is the Drum Tower. Return to the Silver Ingot Bridge and follow the lake's northern shore until you arrive at **Soong Ching-ling's Former Residence.** Next, walk or take a short cab ride to **Prince Gong's Palace** behind the opposite side of the lake, to see how imperial relatives once lived. An alternative to those lavish interiors is the **Museum of Antique Currency,** where you can feast your eyes on rare Chinese coins.

GETTING ORIENTED

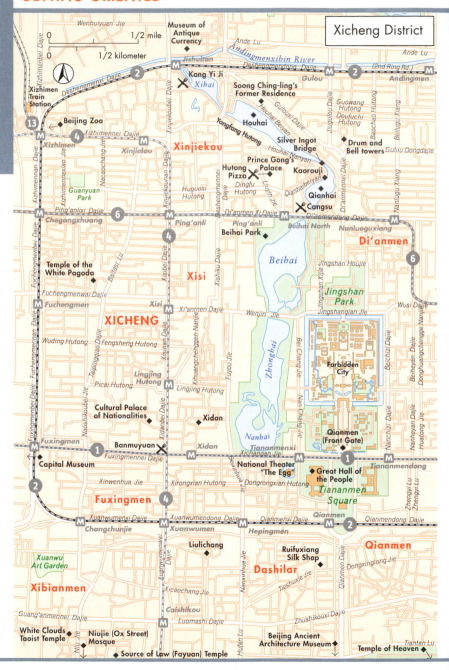

Xicheng District

MAKING THE MOST OF YOUR TIME

Xicheng's must-see sites are few in number but all special. Walk around **Beihai Park** in the early afternoon. If you come to Beijing in the winter, **Qianhai** will be frozen and you can rent skates, runner-equipped bicycles, or the local favorite, a chair with runners welded to the bottom and a pair of metal sticks with which to propel yourself across the ice. Dinner along the shores of **Houhai** is a good option. Head toward the northern section for a more tranquil setting or join the crowds for a booming bar scene farther south. Plan to spend a few hours shopping at **Xidan**; this can be a great place to pick up funky, cheap gifts.

QUICK BITES

Banmuyuan. For a simple meal in the Xidan area, try Banmuyuan, a Taiwanese-owned restaurant that serves chewy *zhajiang* noodles, beef dishes, and vegetarian pies. It's located directly behind the Bank of China headquarters, which was designed by I.M. Pei. ⊠ *45 Fuxingmen Nei Dajie* ☎ *010/5851–8208* Ⓜ *Xidan.*

Hutong Pizza. This is a great spot to take a break from Houhai and the hutongs. It's in a renovated courtyard house just west of the Silver Ingot Bridge. ⊠ *9 Yindingqiao Hutong, Xicheng District* ☎ *010/8322–8916.*

Kaorouji. Romantics, take note: you'll be serenaded by your own personal *pipa* (four-stringed lute) musician at this old lakeside restaurant, which specializes in Chinese-style barbecue. ⊠ *14 Qianhai Dongyan, just southeast of the Silver Ingot Bridge, Xicheng District* ☎ *010/6404–2554.*

Kong Yi Ji. On the northwestern edge of Houhai, Kong Yi Ji is named after a story by the famous writer Lu Xun—it serves some of the dishes mentioned in the story. ⊠ *Houhai South Bank, 2A Deshengmennei Dajie, Xicheng District* ☎ *010/6618–4915.*

2

GETTING HERE

Houhai and Beihai Park are conveniently reached by taxi. Line 1 subway stops include Tiananmen West, Xidan, and Fuxingmen. Line 2 makes stops from Fuxingmen to the Drum Tower (Gulou), following Xicheng's perimeter.

TOP REASONS TO GO

Sip coffee or an evening cocktail lakeside at **Houhai** or on one of the rooftop restaurants or bars overlooking the lake.

Explore Houhai's well-preserved hutong and historical sites by pedicab or bicycle.

Skate on **Houhai Lake** in winter, or, in the warmer months, take an evening boat tour of the lake. Dine onboard on barbecued lamb provided by Kaorouji.

Wander the hills and temples of historic Beihai Park.

Shop for great gifts and snazzy clothes on the cheap at **Xidan.**

Beihai Park

TOP ATTRACTIONS

Beihai Park (北海公园 *Běihǎi gōngyuán*). A white stupa is perched on a small island just north of the south gate of this park. Also at the south entrance is **Round City,** which contains a white-jade Buddha and an enormous jade bowl given to Kublai Khan. Nearby, the well-restored **Temple of Eternal Peace** houses a variety of Buddhas. Climb to the stupa from Yongan Temple. Once there, you can pay an extra Y1 to ascend the Buddha-bedecked **Shanyin Hall.**

The lake is Beijing's largest and most beautiful public waterway. On summer weekends the lake teems with paddleboats. The **Five Dragon Pavilion,** on Beihai's northwest shore, was built in 1602 by a Ming Dynasty emperor who liked to fish under the moon. ⊠ *Weijin Jie, Xicheng District* ☏ *010/6403–1102* ⊕ *www.beihaipark.com. cn* ☏ *Y10; extra fees for some sites* ⊗ *Apr.–May and Sept.–Oct., daily 6.30 am–8:30 pm; Nov.–Mar., daily 6.30 am–8 pm; June–Aug., daily 6.30 am–10 pm.*

Capital Museum (首都博物馆 *Shǒudū bówùguǎn*). Moved to an architecturally striking new home west of Tiananmen Square in 2005, this is one of China's finest cultural museums. Artifacts are housed in a multistoried bronze cylinder that dominates the building's facade, while paintings, calligraphy, and photographs of historic Beijing fill the remaining exhibition halls. The museum gets extra points for clear English descriptions and modern, informative displays. Entry is free, but tickets must be booked (via the website) in advance. ⊠ *16 Fuxingmenwai Dajie, Xicheng District* ☏ *010/6337–0491* ⊕ *www.capitalmuseum.org.cn/en* ☏ *Free* ⊗ *Tues.–Sun. 9–4.*

2

Drum Tower (鼓楼 *Gǔlóu*). Until the late 1920s, the 24 drums once housed in this tower were Beijing's timepiece. Sadly, all but one of these huge drums have been destroyed. Kublai Khan built the first drum tower on this site in 1272. You can climb to the top of the present tower, which dates from the Ming Dynasty. Old photos of *hutong* neighborhoods line the walls beyond the drum; there's also a scale model of a traditional courtyard house. The nearby **Bell Tower**, renovated after a fire in 1747, offers fabulous views of the *hutong* from the top of a long, narrow staircase. The huge 63-ton bronze bell, supported by lacquered wood stanchions, is also worth seeing. In recent years the authorities have demolished a number of historic *hutongs* in this area, so don't be surprised if you come across serious signs of reconstruction around here. ✉ *North end of Dianmen Dajie, Xicheng District* ☎ *010/6404–1710* 🎫 *Drum Tower Y20, Bell Tower Y20; ticket for both Y30* 🕐 *Daily 9–5* Ⓜ *Guloudajie.*

Niujie (Ox Street) Mosque (牛街清真寺 *Niújiē qīngzhēnsì*). Originally built during the Liao Dynasty in 996, Niujie is Beijing's oldest and largest mosque. It sits at the center of the Muslim quarter and mimics a Chinese temple from the outside, with its hexagonal wooden structure. When the mosque was built, only traditional Chinese architecture was allowed in the capital. An exception was made for the Arabic calligraphy that decorates many of the mosque's walls and inner sanctums. The interior arches and posts are inscribed with Koranic verse, and a special moon tower helps with determining the lunar calendar. The Spirit Wall stands opposite the main entrance and is meant to prevent ghosts from entering the mosque. This wall is covered with carved mural works on the premise that ghosts can't turn sharp corners. Two dark tombs with Chinese and Arabic inscriptions are kept in one of the small courtyards. They belong to two Persian imams (the prayer leaders of a mosque) who came to preach at the mosque in the 13th and 14th centuries. Because Muslims must pray in the direction of Mecca, which is westward, the main prayer hall opens onto the east. At the rear of the complex is a minaret from which a muezzin calls the faithful to prayer. From this very tower, imams measure the beginning and end of Ramadan, Islam's month of fasting and prayer. Ramadan begins when the imam sights the new moon, which appears as a slight crescent.

The hall, which is open only to Muslims, can fit up to 1,000 worshippers. All visitors must wear long trousers or skirts and keep their shoulders covered. It's most convenient to get to the mosque by taxi. If you want to take the subway, it's about a 10-minute walk from Line 4's Caishikou station. ✉ *18 Niu Jie, Xuanwu District* ☎ *010/6353–2564* 🎫 *Y10* 🕐 *Daily 8–4* Ⓜ *Caishikou.*

Qianhai and Houhai (前海后海 *Qiánhǎi, Hòuhǎi*). Most people come to these lakes, along with Xihai to the northwest, to stroll and enjoy the shoreside bars and restaurants. In summer you can boat or fish. In winter, sections of the frozen lakes are fenced off for skating. This daytrip is easily combined with a visit to Beihai Park or the Bell and Drum towers. ✉ *North of Beihai Lake, Xicheng District.*

DID YOU KNOW?

The Temple of Heaven's overall layout symbolizes the relationship between Heaven and Earth. Earth is represented by a square and Heaven by a circle. The temple complex is surrounded by two cordons of walls; the taller outer wall is semicircular at the northern end (Heaven) and shorter and rectangular at the southern end (Earth). Both the Hall of Prayer for Good Harvests and the Circular Mound Altar are round structures on a square yard.

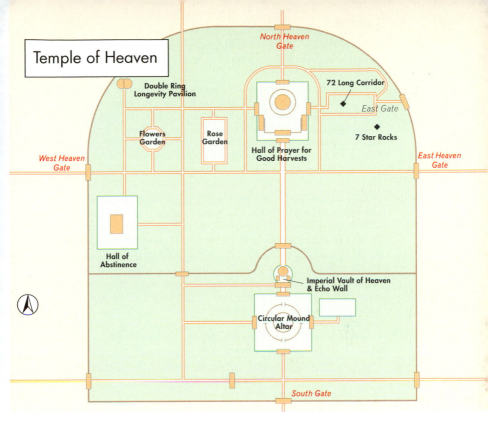

Temple of Heaven

- North Heaven Gate
- Double Ring Longevity Pavilion
- 72 Long Corridor
- East Gate
- Flowers Garden
- Rose Garden
- 7 Star Rocks
- West Heaven Gate
- East Heaven Gate
- Hall of Prayer for Good Harvests
- Hall of Abstinence
- Imperial Vault of Heaven & Echo Wall
- Circular Mound Altar
- South Gate

Temple of Heaven (天坛 *Tiântán gôngyuán*). A prime example of Chinese religious architecture, this is where emperors once performed important rites. It was a site for imperial sacrifices, meant to please the gods so they would generate bumper harvests. Set in a huge, serene, mushroom-shaped park southeast of the Forbidden City, the Temple of Heaven is surrounded by splendid examples of Ming Dynasty architecture, including curved cobalt blue roofs layered with yellow and green tiles. Construction began in the early 15th century under Yongle, whom many call the "architect of Beijing." Shaped like a semicircle on the northern rim to represent heaven and square on the south for the earth, the grounds were once believed to be the meeting point of the two. The area is double the size of the Forbidden City and is still laid out to divine rule: buildings and paths are positioned to represent the right directions for heaven and earth. This means, for example, that the northern part is higher than the south.

The temple's hallmark structure is a magnificent **blue-roofed wooden tower** built in 1420. It burned to the ground in 1889 and was immediately rebuilt using Ming architectural methods (and timber imported from Oregon). The building's design is based on the calendar: 4 center pillars represent the seasons, the next 12 pillars represent months, and 12 outer pillars signify the parts of a day. Together these 28 poles, which also correspond to the 28 constellations of heaven, support the structure without nails. A carved dragon swirling down from the ceiling represents the emperor.

Across the Danbi Bridge you'll find the **Hall of Prayer for Good Harvests**. The middle section was once reserved for the Emperor of Heaven, who was the only one allowed to set foot on the eastern side, while aristocrats and high-ranking officials walked on the western strip. ■ TIP➜ **If you're coming by taxi, enter the park through the southern entrance (Tiantan Nanmen). This way you approach the beautiful Hall of Prayer for Good Harvests via the Danbi Bridge—the same route the emperor favored.**

Directly east of this hall is a long, twisting platform, which once enclosed the animal-killing pavilion. The Long Corridor was traditionally hung with lanterns on the eve of sacrifices. Today it plays host to scores of Beijingers singing opera, playing cards and chess, and fan dancing.

Be sure to whisper into the echo wall encircling the **Imperial Vault of Heaven**. This structure allows anyone to eavesdrop. It takes a minute to get the hang of it, but with a friend on one side and you on the other it's possible to hold a conversation by speaking into the wall. Tilt your head in the direction you want your voice to travel for best results. Just inside the south gate is the **Round Altar**, a three-tiered, white-marble structure where the emperor worshipped the winter solstice; it's based around the divine number nine. Nine was regarded as a symbol of the power of the emperor, as it's the biggest single-digit odd number, and odd numbers are considered masculine and therefore more powerful.

The Hall of Abstinence, on the western edge of the grounds, is where the emperor would retreat three days before the ritual sacrifice. To understand the significance of the harvest sacrifice at the Temple of Heaven, it's important to keep in mind that the legitimacy of a Chinese emperor's rule depended on what is known as the *tian ming*, or the mandate of heaven, essentially the emperor's relationship with the gods.

A succession of bad harvests, for example, could be interpreted as the emperor's losing the favor of heaven and could be used to justify a change in emperor or even in dynasty. When the emperor came to the Temple of Heaven to pray for good harvests and to pay homage to his ancestors, there may have been a good measure of self-interest to his fervor.

The sacrifices consisted mainly of animals and fruit placed on altars surrounded by candles. Many Chinese still offer sacrifices of fruit and incense on special occasions, such as births, deaths, and weddings.

■ TIP➜ **We recommend buying an all-inclusive ticket. If you only buy a ticket into the park, you'll need to pay an additional Y20 to get into each building.**

Beijing's subway Line 5 (purple line) makes getting to the Temple of Heaven particularly simple. Get off at the Tiantandongmen (Temple of Heaven East Gate) stop. This line also runs direct to the Lama Temple (Yonghegong), so combining the two sites in a day makes a lot of sense.

Shoppers enjoy a sunny day in the Xidan neighborhood.

Automatic audio guides (Y40) are available at stalls inside all four entrances. ✉ *Yongdingmen Dajie (South Gate), Xuanwu District* ☎ *010/6702–8866* ⊕ *en.tiantanpark.com* 🎦 *All-inclusive ticket Y35; entrance to park only Y15* ⊙ *Daily 6 am–10 pm; ticket booth closes at 4:30* Ⓜ *Tiantandongmen.*

Xidan (西单 *Xîdân*). This area teems with shopping malls and small stores selling clothing and accessories, and upwardly mobile Chinese coming to browse and buy. The glitzy 13-story Joy City mall, full of local and international brands, is a major sign of commerce's grip here. Ⓜ *Xidan.*

WORTH NOTING

Beijing Ancient Architecture Museum (北京古代建筑博物馆 *Běijîng gǔdài jiànzhù bówùguǎn*). This little-known museum, located inside a Ming Dynasty temple, exhibits photos, objects, and elaborate models of ancient Chinese architecture—from ancient huts and mud houses to Ming and Qing Dynasty palaces. The sand-table model of old Beijing is fascinating. ✉ *21 Dongjing Lu, Xicheng District* ☎ *010/6317–2150* 🎦 *Y15* ⊙ *Tues.–Sun. 9–4.*

Beijing Zoo (北京动物园 *Běijîng dòngwù yuán*). Though visitors usually go straight to see the giant pandas, don't miss the other interesting animals, like tigers from the northeast, yaks from Tibet, enormous sea turtles from China's seas, and red pandas from Sichuan. The zoo started out as a garden belonging to one of the sons of Shunzhi, the first emperor of the Qing dynasty. In 1747 the Qianlong emperor had it refurbished (along with other imperial properties, including the summer palaces) and turned it into a park in honor of his mother's 60th birthday. In 1901, the Empress Dowager gave it another extensive facelift and used it to house a collection of animals given to her as a gift by a Chinese minister who had bought them during a trip to Germany. By the 1930s most of the animals had died and were stuffed and put on display in a museum on the grounds. ⊠ *137 Xizhimenwai Dajie, Xicheng District* ☎ *010/6839–0274* ⊕ *www.bjzoo. com* ⊠ *Apr.–Oct. Y15; Nov.–Mar. Y10; plus Y5 for the pandas* ⊗ *Apr.– Oct. 7:30–6; Nov.–Mar. 7:30–5.*

WORD OF MOUTH

"I love the hutong areas, and they are made for walking. You can get a bit lost, but eventually you end up on a main street and can reorient yourself. Lots of little restaurants and shops there."

—JPDeM

Cultural Palace of Nationalities (民族文化宫 *Mínzú wénhuà gōng*). Dedicated to the 56 official ethnic groups that make up China's modern population, this museum houses traditional clothing and artifacts from the country's remote border regions. Exhibits on topics like the "peaceful liberation of Tibet" are as interesting for the official government line as for what's left out. Entrance is free, but you'll need to show your passport to get in. ⊠ *49 Fuxingmennei Dajie, next to the Minzu Hotel, Xicheng District* ☎ *010/6602–4433* ⊠ *Free* ⊗ *Daily 9–5.*

Great Hall of the People (人民大会堂 *Rénmín dàhuìtáng*). This solid edifice owes its Stalinist weight to the last years of the Sino-Soviet pact. Its gargantuan dimensions (205,712 square yards of floor space) exceed that of the Forbidden City. It was built by 14,000 laborers, who worked around the clock for eight months. China's legislature meets in the aptly named Ten Thousand People Assembly Hall, beneath a panoply of 500 star lights revolving around a giant red star. Thirty-one reception rooms are distinguished by the arts and crafts of the provinces they represent. Have someone who speaks Chinese call a day ahead to confirm that it's open, as the hall often closes for political events and concerts. ⊠ *West side of Tiananmen Sq., Xicheng District* ☎ *010/6309–6156* ⊠ *Y30* ⊗ *Dec.–Mar., daily 9–2; Apr.–June, daily 8:15–3; Jul.–Aug., daily 7:30–4; Sept.–Nov., daily 8:30–3.*

Liulichang (琉璃厂 *Liúlíchǎng*). This quaint old street is best known for its antiques, books, and paintings. The street has been completely restored and a multitude of small shops, many privately owned, make it a fun place to explore, even if you're just window-shopping. Liulichang, often referred to as "Antiques Street," was built more than 500 years ago during the Ming Dynasty. It was the site of a large factory that made glazed tiles for the Imperial Palace. Gradually other smaller tradesmen began to cluster around, and at the beginning of the Qing Dynasty booksellers began to move in. The area became a meeting place for intellectuals and a prime shopping district for art objects, books, handicrafts, and antiques. In 1949 Liulichang still had over 170 shops, but many were taken over by the state; the street was badly ransacked during the Cultural Revolution. Following large-scale renovation of the traditional architecture, the street reopened in 1984 under the policy that shops could only sell arts, crafts, and cultural objects. Today the

Liulichang (Antiques Street)

street is a mixture of state-run and privately owned stores. ✉ *Liulichang, Xuanwu District.*

Museum of Antique Currency (北京古代钱币博物馆 *Běijîng gǔdài qiánbì bówùguǎn*). This museum in a tiny courtyard house (within the Deshengmen tower complex) showcases a small but impressive selection of rare Chinese coins. Explanations are in Chinese only. Also in the courtyard are coin and curio dealers. ✉ *Deshengmen Jianlou, Bei'erhuan Zhonglu, Xicheng District* ☎ *010/6602–4178* ✉ *Y10* ⏱ *Tues.–Sun. 9–4.*

Prince Gong's Palace (恭王府 *Gōngwángfǔ*). This grand compound sits in a neighborhood once reserved for imperial relatives. Built in 1777 during the Qing Dynasty, it fell to Prince Gong—brother of Qing emperor Xianfeng and later an adviser to Empress Dowager Cixi—after the original inhabitant was executed for corruption. With nine courtyards joined by covered walkways, it was once one of Beijing's most lavish residences. The museum offers Beijing opera and tea to visitors who pay the higher ticket price. Some literary scholars believe this was the setting for *Dream of the Red Chamber,* one of China's best-known classical novels. ✉ *17 Qianhai Xijie, Xicheng District* ☎ *010/8328–8149* ⊕ *www.pgm.org.cn* ✉ *Y40–Y70* ⏱ *Mid-Mar.–mid.-Nov., daily 8–4; mid.-Nov.–mid.-Mar., daily 7:30–4:30.*

Qianmen (Front Gate) (前门大街 *Qiánmén dàjiě*). From its top, looking south, you can see that Qianmen (Front Gate) is actually two gates: the Sun-Facing Gate (Zhengyangmen) and the Arrow Tower (Jian Lou), which were, until 1915, connected by a defensive half-moon wall. The central gates of both structures opened only for the emperor's biannual ceremonial trips to the Temple of Heaven. The gate now defines the southern edge of Tiananmen Square. ✉ *Xuanwumen Jie, Dongcheng District* ☎ *010/6522–9382* 🚇 *Y10* ⊘ *8:30–4* Ⓜ *Qianmen.*

Ruifuxiang Silk Shop (瑞蚨祥绸布店 *Ruìfúxiáng chóubù diàn*). Established in 1893, this shop has thick bolts of silk, cotton, cashmere, and wool piled high, in more colors than you'll find in a box of crayons: chartreuse, candy-pink, chocolate-brown, fresh-cut-grass-green—you name it. Clerks deftly cut yards of cloth while tailors take measurements for colorful *qipao* (traditional gowns). Even though you might not be shopping for fabric, it's interesting to browse: in this corner of Beijing life seems to continue much as it did a century ago. ✉ *5 Dazhalan Dajie, Xuanwu District* ☎ *010/6303–5313.*

Soong Ching-ling's Former Residence (宋庆龄故居 *Sòng Qìnglíng gùjū*). Soong Ching-ling (1893–1981) was the youngest daughter of Charles Soong, a wealthy, American-educated Bible publisher. At the age of 18, disregarding her family's strong opposition, she eloped to marry the much older Sun Yat-sen. When her husband founded the Republic of China in 1911, Soong Ching-ling became a significant political figure. In 1924 she headed the Women's Department of the Nationalist Party. Then in 1949 she became the vice president of the People's Republic of China. Throughout her career she campaigned tirelessly for the emancipation of women, and she helped lay the foundations for many of the rights that modern-day Chinese women enjoy today. This former palace was her residence and workplace and now houses a small museum, which documents her life and work. ✉ *46 Houhai Beiyan, Xicheng District* ☎ *010/6404–4205* 🚇 *Y20* ⊘ *Daily 9–4.*

Source of Law Temple (法源寺 *Fǎyuánsì*). This quiet temple is also a school for monks—the Chinese Buddhist Theoretical Institute houses and trains them here. Of course, the temple functions within the boundaries of current regime policy. You can observe both elderly practitioners chanting mantras in the main prayer halls, as well as robed students kicking soccer balls in a side courtyard. Before lunch the smells of a vegetarian stir-fry tease the nose. The dining hall has simple wooden tables set with cloth-wrapped bowls and chopsticks. Dating from the 7th century, but last rebuilt in 1442, the temple holds a fine collection of Ming and Qing statues, including a sleeping Buddha and an unusual grouping of copper-cast Buddhas seated on a 1,000-petal lotus. ✉ *7 Fayuan Si Qianjie, Xuanwu District* ☎ *010/6353–4171* 🚇 *Y5* ⊘ *Daily 8:30–3.30.*

Temple of the White Pagoda (白塔 *Báitǎ*). This 13th-century Tibetan stupa, the largest of its kind in China, dates from Kublai Khan's reign and owes its beauty to an unnamed Nepalese architect who built it to honor Shakyamuni Buddha (the historical Buddha). It stands bright and white against the Beijing skyline. Once hidden within the structure were Buddha statues, sacred texts, and other holy relics. Many of the statues are now on display in glass cases in the **Miaoying** temple, at the foot of the stupa. ✉ *171 Fuchengmennei Dajie, Xicheng District* ☎ *010/6616–6099* 🚇 *Y20* ⊘ *Tues.–Sun. 9–4.*

White Clouds Taoist Temple (白云观 *Báiyúnguān*). This lively Taoist temple founded in the 8th century serves as a center for China's only indigenous

DID YOU KNOW?

This statue of Avalokitesvara is in the Capital Museum. It was made by the porcelain master He Chaozong during the Ming Dynasty. Avalokitesvara is a bodhisattva who embodies the compassion of all Buddhas. He (sometimes she) is one of the more widely revered bodhisattvas in mainstream Mahayana Buddhism.

religion. Monks wearing blue-cotton coats and black-satin hats roam the grounds in silence. Thirty of them now live at the monastery, which also houses the official All-China Taoist Association. Visitors bow and burn incense to their favorite deities, wander the back gardens in search of a master of qigong (a series of exercises that involve slow movements and meditative breathing techniques), and rub the bellies of the temple's three monkey statues for good fortune.

In the first courtyard, under the span of an arched bridge, hang two large brass bells. Ringing them with a well-tossed coin is said to bring wealth. In the main courtyards, the **Shrine Hall for Seven Perfect Beings** is lined with meditation cushions and low desks. Nearby is a museum of Taoist history (explanations in Chinese). In the western courtyard the temple's oldest structure is a shrine housing the **60-Year Protector.** Here the faithful locate the deity that corresponds to their birth year, bow to it, light incense, then scribble their names, or even a poem, on the wooden statue's red-cloth cloak as a reminder of their dedication. A trinket stall in the front courtyard sells pictures of each protector deity. Also in the west courtyard is a shrine to Taoist sage Wen Ceng, depicted in a 3-meter- (10-foot-) tall bronze statue just outside the shrine's main entrance. Students flock here to rub Wen Ceng's belly for good luck on their college entrance exams. The area around the temple is packed with fortune-tellers. ⊠ *Lianhuachi Donglu, near Xibianmen Bridge, Xicheng District* ☎ *010/6344–3666* ✉ *Y10* ☺ *Daily 8–4:30.*

CHAOYANG DISTRICT 朝阳区

Sightseeing
★☆☆☆☆
Dining
★★★★☆
Lodging
★★★★☆
Shopping
★★★★☆
Nightlife
★★★★☆

There's precious little of Beijing's ancient history found in Chaoyang District, where much of the old has been razed to make way for the blingy new. Impeccably dressed Chinese women shop the afternoons away at gleaming new malls, young tycoons and princelings park their Ferraris on the sidewalks, and everyone who's anyone congregates at the booming nightclubs filled with hip-hop music and VIP bottle service.

Sitting outside the Second Ring Road, which marks the boundary of the old walled imperial capital, Chaoyang represents a rapidly modernizing China at its peak. Here's where you'll find the Central Business District, with the city's tallest towers and the architecturally impressive CCTV Building; Sanlitun, the longtime playground of expats, filled with swanky bars and restaurants that could just as well be in New York City or London; shopping centers filled with just about every major global brand, from Apple to Zegna; and almost all of Beijing's embassies, lending the area a distinctly international vibe.

For dining and nightlife, you can't beat Sanlitun, which was once a sleepy farming village. In the middle of it all is Sanlitun Lu, popularly known as Bar Street, and wreathed in twinkling lights year-round. On one side of this stretch is the luxurious open-air Taikoo Li shopping center (once known as the Village Sanlitun), a destination in and of itself. On the other side is a row of dive bars, which are best avoided. There's also great shopping to be found around here.

TOP ATTRACTIONS

798 Art District (798艺术区 *Qījiǔbā yìshù qū*). Chinese contemporary art has exploded in the past decade, and to see some of the finest examples of the scene look no further than 798 Art District, located in the northeast corner of the city. This was once the site of several

GETTING ORIENTED

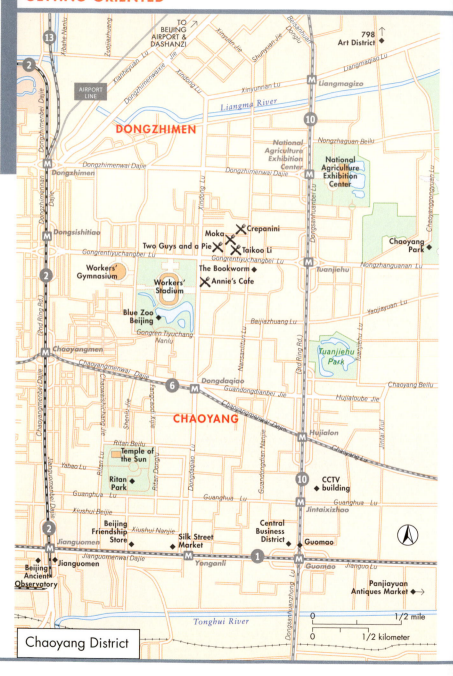

TO
BEIJING
AIRPORT &
DASHANZI

798
Art District

AIRPORT
LINE

Liangmagizo

Liangma River

DONGZHIMEN

National
Agriculture
Exhibition
Center

Nongzhaguan Beilu

National
Agriculture
Exhibition
Center

Dongzhimen

Dongzhimenwai Dajie

Dongzhimenwai Dajie

Chaoyang
Park

Dongsishitiao

Crepanini
Moka
Two Guys and a Pie
Taikoo Li
Gongrentiyuchangbei Lu
Gongrentiyuchangbei Lu

Tuanjiehu

Nongzhanguanan Lu

Workers'
Gymnasium

The Bookworm
Annie's Cafe

Workers'
Stadium

Baijiazhuang Lu

Yaojiayuan Lu

Blue Zoo
Beijing

Gongren Tiyuchang
Nanlu

Tuanjiehu
Park

Chaoyangmen

Chaoyangmenwai Dajie

Chaoyang Beilu

Dongdaqiao

Guandongdianbei Jie

Hujialoube Jie

CHAOYANG

Chaoyangmenwai Dajie

Hujialon

Ritan Beilu
Temple of
the Sun

Yabao Lu

Ritan
Park

CCTV
building

Guanghua Lu

Guanghua Lu

Guanghua Lu

Jintaixizhao

Xiushui Beijie

Beijing
Friendship
Store

Xiushui Nanjie

Silk Street
Market

Central
Business
District

Guomao

Jianguomen

Jianguomenwai Dajie

Yonganli

Guomao

Jianguo Lu

Beijing
Ancient
Observatory

Jianguomen

Panjiayuan
Antiques Market

Tonghui River

0   1/2 mile

0   1/2 kilometer

Chaoyang District

2

QUICK BITES

Annie's Café. The various branches of Annie's Café serve great pizza and Italian-American style specialties in a family-friendly atmosphere. ✉ *Chaoyang Park West Gate, Chaoyang District* ☎ *010/6591–1931* ⊕ *en.annies.com.cn* ✉ *88 Jianguo Lu, west side of SOHO New Town.*

Crepanini. Crepes + panini = Crepanini, a great spot for sweet and savory snacks right in the middle of the Sanlitun action. It's open late, too. ✉ *Nali Patio, 81 Sanlitun Lu, Chaoyang District.*

Two Guys And A Pie. Terrific savory pies, with combos such as beef brisket and onion, with mashed potatoes and gravy toppings. Plus Australian beer. ✉ *Behind Sanlitun Houjie, west of the Sanlitun Police Station, Chaoyang District* ☎ *186/1105–3912.*

Taikoo Li. If you're looking for Western food, Taikoo Li (formerly known as the Village Sanlitun) has lots of options. ✉ *Sanlitun Lu, Chaoyang District.*

TOP REASONS TO GO

Have dinner in Sanlitun and check out one of the bars or nightclubs surrounding the Workers' Stadium.

See what's going on in Chinese art today in the **798 Art District.** After strolling through the galleries, browse the vast selection of art books at Timezone 8.

Do some shopping at **Yashow Market,** where you can buy anything from knockoff jeans to a custom-tailored suit. Then take a half-hour walk north on **Sanlitun North Street** and pick a place to grab an espresso or some top-quality Western food. The Nali Patio complex has a number of worthwhile options.

Go for an early-morning stroll in **Chaoyang Park** and watch the traditional Chinese exercises.

GETTING HERE

The heart of Chaoyang District is accessible via Lines 1, 2, and 10 on the subway, but the district is huge and the sites are broadly distributed. Taking taxis between sites is usually the easiest way to get around. The 798 Art District is especially far away from central Beijing, so a taxi is also the best bet (about Y30–Y50 from the center of town). Buses go everywhere, but they're slow.

MAKING THE MOST OF YOUR TIME

You can spend years lost in Chaoyang District and never get bored. There's plenty to do, but there are very few historic sights. Spend a morning shopping at **Silk Alley Market** or **Panjiayuan Antiques Market** (best on weekend mornings) and the afternoon cooling off at **Ritan Park** or **Chaoyang Park,** the latter a large and pleasant park with a lot of activities for kids. Next, head to one of the numerous bar streets for refreshments. If you like contemporary art, browse the galleries at **798 Art District.** There are a number of nice cafés here as well.

798 Art District Dashanzi in the Chaoyang District

state-owned factories, including Factory 798, that produced electronics. Beginning in 2002, artists and cultural organizations began to move into the area, gradually developing the old buildings into galleries, art centers, artists' studios, design companies, restaurants, and bars. Note that most if not all of the galleries here are closed on Mondays.

Experimenting with classical mediums such as paint and printmaking as well as forays into new and digital media, installation, and performance art, young Chinese artists are caught between old and new, Communism and capitalism, urban and rural, rich and poor, and East and West. These conflicts set the stage and color their artistic output, with varying results. Although more and more Chinese artists are achieving international recognition, 798 still abounds with knockoffs of bad Western art and tacky Socialist Realist portraits. Nevertheless the area remains the hub of contemporary creative arts in Beijing and is definitely worth a visit if you're at all interested in the state of the arts in China.

Built in the 1950s, this factory district was a major industrial project by East German architects backed by Soviet aid. All but abandoned by the 1980s, the complex was rediscovered in the late 1990s by a small group of Beijing artists who had just been evicted from their previous haunts and were looking for a new place to set up working and living spaces. Although the scene was at first a completely DIY affair, the quality of art produced and international media attention starting from the early 2000s meant that the district government took notice. Eventually the area was declared a protected arts district, paving the way for commercial galleries, cafés, and souvenir shops. Priced out of their original studios, many working artists have decamped further

2

afield to the Caochangdi and Songzhuang neighborhoods. Both of these smaller areas are worth visiting, though neither is easily accessible except via taxi. Ask your hotel concierge for a detailed map or, better yet, call ahead to the galleries you're interested in visiting and get driving instructions.

798 is more accessible, however, and eminently walkable. Keep in mind that cabs are prohibited from driving into the complex, and much of the area is pedestrianized. Though it's also open Tuesday through Friday, most people visit on the weekend, when throngs of locals and foreigners congregate to see what's on display.

Many of the galleries there now are hit or miss, but establishments such as the **Ullens Center for Contemporary Arts (UCCA)** always put on informative, challenging exhibitions. If you need to refuel, stop by At Cafe, billed as the first café in 798 and still co-owned by Huang Rui, one of the district's cofounders. ✉ *798 Art District, 2–4 Jiuxianqiao Rd., Dashanzi, Chaoyang District* ⊕ *www.798district.com.*

Ancient Observatory (北京古观象台 *Běijīng gǔguānxiàng tái*). This squat tower of primitive stargazing equipment peeks out next to the elevated highways of the Second Ring Road. It dates to the time of Genghis Khan, who believed that his fortunes could be read in the stars. Many of the bronze devices on display were gifts from Jesuit missionaries who arrived in Beijing and shortly thereafter ensconced themselves as the Ming court's resident stargazers. To China's imperial rulers, interpreting the heavens was key to holding onto power; a ruler knew when, say, an eclipse would occur, or he could predict the best time to plant crops. Celestial phenomena like eclipses and comets were believed to portend change; if left unheeded they might cost an emperor his legitimacy—his mandate of heaven. Records of celestial observations at or near this site go back more than 500 years, making this the longest documented astronomical viewing site in the world.

The main astronomical devices are arranged on the roof. Writhing bronze dragon sculptures adorn some of the astronomy pieces at Jianguo Tower, the main building that houses the observatory. Among the sculptures are an armillary sphere to pinpoint the position of heavenly bodies and a sextant to measure angular distances between stars, along with a celestial globe. Inside, the dusty exhibition rooms shelter ancient star maps with information dating back to the Tang Dynasty. A Ming Dynasty star map and ancient charts are also on display. Most of the ancient instruments were looted by the Allied Forces in 1900, during the Boxer Rebellion, only to be returned to China at the end of World War I. ✉ *2 Dongbiaobei Hutong, Jianguomenwai Dajie, Chaoyang District* ☎ *010/6524–2202* 🎫 *Y20* ⊙ *Tues.-Sun. 9–4* Ⓜ *Jianguomen.*

NEED A BREAK?

Moka Bros. Healthy, light dishes served in modern, hip surroundings make Moka Bros a surefire winner if you're in downtown Sanlitun and time is tight. But not everyone here is in a rush: this is also where Beijing's cool crowd comes to hang out over laptops and lattes. Trendy but not pretentious, this excellent café is the perfect place for a pit stop, especially if you're after a nutritious salad and smoothie, a tasty wrap and filling rice

Ritan Park in the morning

bowl, or something similar. ✉ *Nali Patio, 81 Sanlitun Lu, Chaoyang District* ☎ *010/5208–6079.*

Central Business District (CBD) (商业中心区 *Shângyè zhôngxîn qû*). The fast-rising CBD encompasses the **China World Trade Center** (the third tower, completed in 2010, is the tallest building in Beijing) and a slew of new and impressive skyscrapers, some designed by internationally known architects. One example is the CCTV Tower, by Rem Koolhaas and Ole Scheeren. The multimillion-dollar complex employs a continuous loop of horizontal and vertical sections, and its distinctive shape has earned it the moniker "big pants." Nearby is The Place, a shopping mall best known for its massive canopy-style LED screen. ✉ *Chaoyang District.*

Ritan Park (日坛公园 *Rìtán gôngyuán*). A cool oasis of water, paths, and trees just west of the Central Business District, Ritan Park (also known as "Temple of the Sun Park") is a popular place to go for some peace and quiet, and is where many locals head to stretch their legs. Stop in at the Stone Boat café if you're in need of refreshment. ✉ *Ritan Lu, northeast of Jianguomen, Dongcheng District* ☎ *010/8563–5038* ✉ *Free* ⏲ *Daily 6am–9pm.*

Sanlitun (三里屯 *Sânlĭtún*). The famous Sanlitun Bar Street, several blocks east of the Workers' Stadium, is known for its nightlife offerings catering to foreigners, expats, and young Chinese. Avoid the dive bars on the east side of Bar Street, however. Vics and Mix at the north gate of the Workers' Stadium are two clubs always packed with people looking for a big night out, while the bars at The Opposite House hotel are a swank respite. Taikoo Li, Beijing's hottest shopping complex, can be credited with changing the face of what was once a fairly seedy area. The Japanese-designed open-air center includes a number of international shops as well as a movie theater and some of Beijing's best restaurants and cafés, and has become the city's major hangout for the in-crowd, both local and foreign. ⊠ *Chaoyang District.*

WORTH NOTING

Chambers Fine Art (前波画廊 *Qián bō huàláng*). Named after the noted British architect Sir William Chambers, Chambers Fine Art Beijing opened in 2007 in the art village of Caochangdi. Situated in a redbrick gallery complex designed by the internationally famous Chinese artist Ai Weiwei, Chambers puts on exhibitions of young native Chinese artists worth paying attention to. ⊠ *Red No. 1-D, Caochangdi, Chaoyang District* ☎ *010/5127–3298* ⊕ *www.chambersfineart.com.*

Chaoyang Park (朝阳公园 *Cháoyáng gōngyuán*). The sprawling, modern Chaoyang Park lacks the imperial aura that marks other Beijing parks, but it has quite a bit to offer in terms of recreation. About one-fourth of the park is water, and there are several kinds of boating available, primarily pedal-powered paddleboats. There's a swimming pool with an artificial beach, tennis courts, beach volleyball grounds, a gymnasium, and a small amusement park. You can hire a slow-going electromobile for easy mobility around this sprawling park on your own, or hail a ride on a group trolley. There are many snack stands serving simple dishes, but if you're looking for something more substantive, walk around to the west gate of the park, where you'll find a street lined with popular Western and Chinese eateries, or check out the Solana mall at the northwest corner of the park. ⊠ *Nongzhanguan Road South, Chaoyang District* 🚇 *Y5* ⏲ *Mid-Mar.–mid-Nov., daily 6 am–10 pm; mid-Nov.–mid-Mar., daily 6 am–9 pm.*

Jianguomen (建国门 *Jiànguómén*). The embassy area has some good foreign restaurants, but is mostly quiet blocks of gated embassy compounds; in the center there's lovely Ritan Park with its winding paths, lotus-flower ponds, a climbing wall, and a few upmarket restaurants. The area is close to the heart of Beijing's new Central Business District, aka CBD, which has some of the city's most impressive modern architecture, including the CCTV Tower, the Park Hyatt Hotel, and Tower III of the China World Trade Center, which at 81 stories is Beijing's tallest skyscraper. ⊠ *Chaoyang District.*

Pace Beijing (佩斯北京 *Pèisīběijīng*). This Beijing branch of the famed Pace Gallery operates with an independent program focusing on Chinese contemporary artists. ⊠ *No. 2 Jiuxianqiao Lu, 798 Art District, Chaoyang District* ☎ *010/5978–9781* ⊕ *www.pacegallery.com/beijing.*

Pékin Fine Arts (北京艺门 *Běijīng yì mén*). Founded by the expatriate Bostonian Meg Maggio, who has lived in Beijing for more than 20 years, Pékin Fine Arts focuses on contemporary artists from around Asia who have both international and domestic exhibition experience. ⊠ *No. 241 Caochangdi, Cuigezhuang Village, Chaoyang District* ☎ *010/5127–3220* ⊕ *pekinfinearts.com.*

Workers' Stadium (工人体育场 *Gôngrén tǐyùcháng*). North of Ritan Park is the Workers' Stadium complex, where many of the biggest visiting acts perform. The main stadium here is also home to Beijing's top-division soccer team. Running north–south, the famous Sanlitun Bar Street is several blocks east of the Workers' Stadium; it's known for its nightlife catering to foreigners, expats, and young Chinese. ⊠ *Gongti Rd., Chaoyang District* Ⓜ *Dongsishitiao.*

2

HAIDIAN DISTRICT 海淀区

Sightseeing
★★★☆☆

Dining
★☆☆☆☆

Lodging
★★☆☆☆

Shopping
★☆☆☆☆

Nightlife
★★☆☆☆

In the last decade or so Haidian has become Beijing's educational and technological center, although there's still a lot of Old Beijing left here, including the wonderful Summer Palace, with its lakes and ancient pavilions.

The major IT players, including Microsoft, Siemens, NEC, and Sun, all have offices in this area, and in the Wudaokou and Zhongguancun neighborhoods you'll find kids geeking out over the latest gadgets at electronics superstores, studying in one of the many cafés, or blowing off steam at some of the area's dance clubs.

The campuses of China's most elite educational institutions, Peking University and Tsinghua, are large by Chinese standards and provide a tranquil respite from the busy surrounding area, with wide lawns and Chinese gardens complete with scenic bridges and pagodas. A large number of foreign students attend Chinese universities, with South Koreans the most numerous, so restaurants and shops catering to their needs are easy to find, especially around Wudaokou station.

TOP ATTRACTIONS

Beijing Botanical Garden (北京植物园 *Běijīng zhíwù yuán*). Sitting at the feet of the Western Hills in Beijing's northwestern suburbs, the Beijing Botanical Garden, opened in 1955, hosts China's largest plant collection: 6,000 different plant species from all over northern China, including 2,000 types of trees and bushes, more than 1,600 species of tropical and subtropical plants, 1,900 kinds of fruit trees, and 500 flower species. With its state-of-the-art greenhouse and a variety of different gardens, this is a pleasant place to explore, especially in spring, when the peach trees burst with pretty blooms. An added feature is the wonderful Temple of the Reclining Buddha, which has an enormous statue that, it's said, took 7,000 slaves to build. ⊠ *Xiangshan Wofosi, Haidian District* ☎ *010/8259–8771* ⌂ *Outdoor garden Y10; conservatory Y50* ⌚ *7–5 (outdoor garden).*

Big Bell Temple (大钟寺 *Dàzhōngsì*). This 18th-century temple shields China's biggest bell and more than 400 smaller bells and gongs from

GETTING ORIENTED

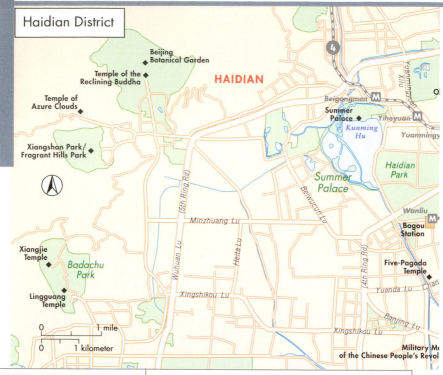

Haidian District

Beijing Botanical Garden

Temple of the Reclining Buddha

Temple of Azure Clouds

HAIDIAN

Xiangshan Park/ Fragrant Hills Park

Beigongmen

Summer Palace

Yiheyuan

Kunming Hu

Yuanmingy

Haidian Park

Summer Palace

Wanliu

Bagou Station

(5th Ring Rd)

Minzhuang Lu

Beiwucun Lu

Xiangjie Temple

Badachu Park

Wuhuan Lu

Heita Lu

(4th Ring Rd)

Five-Pagoda Temple

Yuanda Lu

Chan

Linngguang Temple

Xingshikou Lu

0   1 mile

0   1 kilometer

Xingshikou Lu

Banjing Lu

Military Mu of the Chinese People's Revol

GETTING HERE

Subway Line 13 stops at Wudaokou, the heart of Haidian. Line 4 runs far into the northwest of the city with stops at the Summer Palace and the Old Summer Palace, though Fragrant Hills Park and the Beijing Botanical Garden are farther out still and best reached by taxi. To save money, take Line 10 to Baguo station and catch a cab from there.

MAKING THE MOST OF YOUR TIME

Because the **Summer Palace** is so large, with its lovely lakes and ancient pavilions, it makes for an entire morning of great exploring. The **Old Summer Palace** is close by, so visiting the two sites together is ideal (if you've got the energy).

Fragrant Hills Park makes for a charming outing, but keep in mind that it takes at least an hour and a half to get there from the city center. The **Botanical Garden,** with some 2,000 types of orchids, bonsai, and peach and pear blossoms, along with the **Temple of the Reclining Buddha,** is also fun, especially for green thumbs. Plan to spend most of a day if you go to either of these sites.

Hailong Shopping Mall. If you want to shop for electronics, spend an afternoon wandering the five floors of the Hailong Shopping Mall. ⊠ *1 Zhongguancun Dajie.*

Evenings in Wudaokou can be fun. After dinner, visit a beer garden. A mug of Tsingtao is a great way to start a summer night off right.

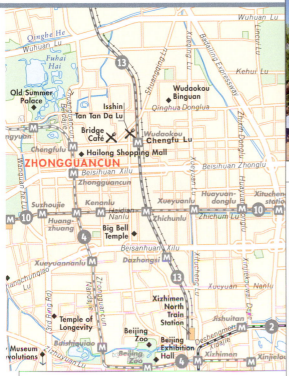

TOP REASONS TO GO

Spend a low-key day at the vast **Summer Palace** and **Old Summer Palace.** Don't miss getting out onto the water at either the Kunming Lake or the Fuhai Lake.

Eat and chat all evening at **Wudaokou Binguan** beer garden.

Browse the biggest selection of electronics and computer goods (both legitimate and pirated) this side of the Pacific at **Hailong Shopping Mall.**

Listen to China's biggest bell toll at the **Big Bell Temple.** Here you'll find bells, both large and small, from the Ming, Song, and Yuan dynasties.

Get out of town with a day trip to **Fragrant Hills Park** or **Beijing Botanical Garden.**

QUICK BITES

There are plenty of restaurants on campus and around Zhongguancun, but the coolest places to eat in Haidian are in Wudaokou.

Bridge Café. The Bridge Café, on Chengfu Lu (one block west of the subway station), serves great sandwiches, salads, and desserts. It's popular with students. ⊠ *Building 12, 35 Chengfu Lu* ☎ *010/8286–7026* Ⓜ *Wudaokou.*

Isshin. This hopping Japanese restaurant is popular with students from the surrounding campuses. ⊠ *35 Chengfu Lu, Haidian District* ☎ *010/8261–0136* Ⓜ *Wudaokou.*

Tan Tan Da Lu. Try the excellent and innovative Korean barbecue here. ⊠ *Fourth Floor, 35 Chengfu Lu, Haidian District* ☎ *010/6256–0471* Ⓜ *Wudaokou.*

The Summer Palace

the Ming, Song, and Yuan dynasties. The Buddhist temple—originally used for rain prayers—was restored after major damage inflicted during the Cultural Revolution. Before it opened as a museum in 1985, the buildings were used as Beijing No. 2 Food Factory. The bells here range from a giant 7 meters (23 feet) high to hand-sized chimes, many of them corroded to a pale green by time.

The giant, two-story bell, inscribed with the texts of more than 100 Buddhist scriptures (230,000 Chinese characters), is also said to be China's loudest. Believed to have been cast during Emperor Yongle's reign, the sound of this 46-ton relic can carry more than 15 km (10 miles) when struck forcibly. The bell rings 108 times on special occasions like Spring Festival, one strike for each of the 108 personal worries defined in Buddhism. People used to throw coins into a hole in the top of the bell for luck. The money was swept up by the monks and used to buy food. Enough money was collected in a month to buy provisions that would last for a year. ■ TIP➜ **You can ride the subway to the temple: transfer from Dongzhimen on Line 2 to the above-ground Line 13 and go one stop north to Dazhong Si station.** ⊠ *1A Beisanhuanxi Lu, Haidian District* ☎ *010/8213–2630* ✉ *Y20* ⊙ *Tues.–Sun. 9–4:30* Ⓜ *Dazhong Si.*

Fodor's Choice
★

Old Summer Palace (圆明园 *Yuánmíngyuán*). About the size of New York's Central Park, this ruin was once a grand collection of palaces—the emperor's summer retreat from the 15th century to 1860, when it was looted and blown up by British and French soldiers. More than 90% of the original structures were Chinese-style wooden buildings, but only the European-style stone architecture (designed after Versailles by Jesuits and added during the Qing Dynasty) survived the fires. Many of the priceless relics that were looted are still on display in European museums, and China's efforts to recover them have been mostly unsuccessful. Beijing has chosen to preserve the vast ruin as a "monument to China's national humiliation," though the patriotic slogans that were once scrawled on the rubble have now been cleaned off.

The palace is made up of three idyllic parks: Yuanmingyuan (Garden of Perfection and Light) in the west, Wanchunyuan (Garden of 10,000 Springs) in the south, and Changchunyuan (Garden of Everlasting Spring), where the ruins are like a surreal graveyard to European architecture. Here you'll find ornately carved columns, squat lion statues, and crumbling stone blocks that lie like fallen dominoes. An engraved concrete wall maze, known as Huanghuazhen (Yellow Flower), twists and turns around a European-style pavilion. Recently restored and located just to the left of the west gate of Changchunyuan, it was once the site of lantern parties during midautumn festivals. Palace maids would race each other to the pavilion carrying lotus lanterns. The park costs an extra Y15 to enter, but it's well worth it. The park and ruins take on a ghostly beauty if you come after a fresh snowfall. There's also skating on the lake when it's frozen over. ■ **TIP→ It's a long trek to the European ruins from the main gate. Electric carts buzz around the park; hop on one heading to Changchunyuan if you feel tired. Tickets are Y5.**

If you want to save money, travel there by subway; get out at Yuanmingyuan Park Station on Line 4. ✉ *28 Qinghua Xilu, northeast of the Summer Palace, Haidian District* ☎ *010/6262–8501* 🌐 *Park Y10; extra Y15 fee for sites* ⏰ *Apr.–Oct., daily 7–6:30; Nov.–Mar., daily 7–5:30.* Ⓜ *Yuanmingyuan Park.*

Fodor's Choice ★ **Summer Palace** (颐和园 *Yíhéyuán*). Emperor Qianlong commissioned this giant royal retreat for his mother's 60th birthday in 1750. Anglo-French forces plundered, then burned, many of the palaces in 1860, and funds were diverted from China's naval budget for the renovations. Empress Dowager Cixi retired here in 1889. Nine years later it was here that she imprisoned her nephew, Emperor Guangxu, after his reform movement failed. In 1903 she moved the seat of government from the Forbidden City to the Summer Palace, from which she controlled China until her death in 1908.

Nowadays the place is undoubtedly romantic. Pagodas and temples perch on hillsides; rowboats dip under arched stone bridges; and willow branches brush the water. The greenery is a relief from the loud, bustling city. It also teaches a fabulous history lesson. You can see firsthand the results of corruption: the opulence here was bought with siphoned money as China crumbled, while suffering repeated humiliations at the hands of colonialist powers. The entire gardens were for the Empress Dowager's exclusive use. UNESCO placed the Summer Palace on its World Heritage list in 1998.

The **Hall of Benevolent Longevity** is where Cixi held court and received foreign dignitaries. It's said that the first electric lights in China shone here. Just behind the hall and next to the lake is the **Hall of Jade Ripples,** where Cixi kept the hapless Guangxu under guard while she ran China in his name. Strung with pagodas and temples, including the impressive

The ruins of the Old Summer Palace

Tower of the Fragrance of Buddha, Glazed Tile Pagoda, and the Hall that Dispels Clouds, **Longevity Hill** is the place where you can escape the hordes of visitors—take your time exploring the lovely northern side of the hill.

Most of this 700-acre park is underwater. **Kunming Lake** makes up around three-fourths of the complex, and is largely man-made. The excavated dirt was used to build Longevity Hill. This giant body of water extends southward for 3 km (2 miles); it's ringed by tree-lined dikes, arched stone bridges, and numerous gazebos. In winter you can skate on the ice. The less-traveled southern shore near Humpbacked Bridge is an ideal picnic spot.

At the west end of the lake you'll find the **Marble Boat**, which doesn't actually float and was built by Dowager Empress Cixi with money meant for the navy. The **Long Corridor** is a wooden walkway that skirts the northern shoreline of Kunming Lake for about half a mile until it reaches the marble boat. The ceiling and wooden rafters of the Long Corridor are richly painted with thousands of scenes from legends and nature—be on the lookout for Sun Wukong (the Monkey King). Cixi's home, in the Hall of Joyful Longevity, is near the beginning of the Long Corridor. The residence is furnished and decorated as Cixi left it. Her private theater, called the **Grand Theater Building**, just east of the hall, was constructed for her 60th birthday and cost 700,000 taels of silver.

Subway Line 4 stops at the Summer Palace. Get off at Beigongmen and take exit C for the easiest access to the north gate of the park. Otherwise, you'll have to take a taxi. It's best to come early in the morning to get a head start before the busloads of visitors arrive. You'll need

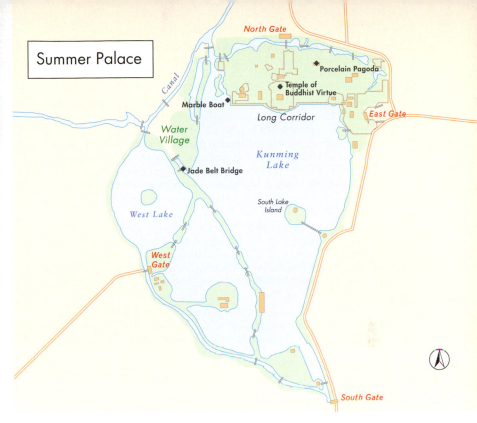

Summer Palace

Map labels:
- North Gate
- Canal
- Porcelain Pagoda
- Temple of Buddhist Virtue
- Marble Boat
- Long Corridor
- East Gate
- Water Village
- Kunming Lake
- Jade Belt Bridge
- South Lake Island
- West Lake
- West Gate
- South Gate

the better part of a day to explore the grounds. Automatic audio guides can be rented for Y40 at stalls near the ticket booth. ⊠ *Yiheyuan Lu and Kunminghu Lu, 12 km (7½ miles) northwest of downtown Beijing, Haidian District* ☎ *010/6288–1144* ⊕ *www.summerpalace-china.com* ⊠ *Y60 summer (all-inclusive), Y50 winter (all-inclusive)* ☉ *Apr.–Oct., daily 6:30–6; Nov.–Mar., daily 7–5* Ⓜ *Beigongmen.*

Fragrant Hills Park (香山公园 *Xiângshân gôngyuán*). Once an imperial retreat, Xiangshan Park is better known as Fragrant Hills Park. From the eastern gate you can hike to the summit on a trail dotted with small temples. If you're short on time, ride a cable car to the top. Note that the park becomes extremely crowded on pleasant fall weekends, when Beijingers turn out en masse to view the changing colors of the autumn leaves. ⊠ *Haidian District* ☎ *010/6259–1155* ⊠ *Y10, one-way cable car Y60* ☉ *Daily 6–6.*

WORTH NOTING

Five-Pagoda Temple (五塔寺 *Wǔ Tǎ Sì*). Hidden among trees just behind the zoo and set amid carved stones, the temple's five pagodas reveal obvious Indian influences. It was built during the Yongle years of the Ming Dynasty (1403–1424), in honor of an Indian Buddhist who came to China and presented a temple blueprint to the emperor. Elaborate carvings of curvaceous figures, floral patterns, birds, and hundreds of Buddhas decorate the pagodas. Also on the grounds is the **Beijing Art Museum of Stone Carvings,** with its collection of some 1,000 stelae and stone figures. ✉ *24 Wuta Si, Baishiqiao Lu, Haidian District* ☎ *010/6217–3543* 🎫 *Y20* ⏱ *Tues.–Sun. 9–4* Ⓜ *National Library.*

FAMILY **Military Museum of the Chinese People's Revolutions** (中国人民革命军事博物馆 *Zhōngguó rénmín gémìng jūnshì bówùguǎn*). Closed for major renovations, this museum is scheduled to reopen in 2015. Stuffed with everything from AK-47s to captured tanks to missile launchers, this is a must-see for military buffs. Five thousand years of Chinese military history are on display, and kids especially love every minute of it. It's easily accessible by taking a 10-minute subway ride west from Tiananmen Square. ✉ *9 Fuxing Road, Haidian District* ☎ *010/6686–6244* 🌐 *eng.jb.mil.cn* 🎫 *Free* ⏱ *Tues.–Sun. 8:30–5.*

Temple of Azure Clouds (碧云寺 *Bìyún sì*). Once the home of a Yuan Dynasty official, the site was converted into a Buddhist temple in 1366 and enlarged during the 16th and 17th centuries by imperial eunuchs who hoped to be buried here. The temple's five main courtyards ascend a slope in **Fragrant Hills Park.** Although severely damaged during the Cultural Revolution, the complex has been beautifully restored.

The main attraction is the Indian-influenced **Vajra Throne Pagoda.** Lining its walls and five pagodas are gracefully carved stone-relief Buddhas and bodhisattvas. The pagoda once housed the remains of Nationalist China's founding father, Dr. Sun Yat-sen, who lay in state here between March and May 1925, while his mausoleum was being constructed in Nanjing. A hall in one of the temple's western courtyards houses about 500 life-size wood and gilt statues of arhats (Buddhists who have reached enlightenment)—each displayed in a glass case. ✉ *Xiangshan Park, Haidian District* ☎ *010/6259–1155* 🎫 *Park Y10, temple Y10* ⏱ *Daily 9–5.*

Temple of Longevity (万寿寺 *Wànshòu sì*). A Ming empress built this temple to honor her son in 1578. Qing emperor Qianlong later restored it as a birthday present to his mother. From then until the fall of the Qing, it served as a rest stop for imperial processions traveling by boat to the Summer Palace and Western Hills. The site also served as a Japanese military command center during occupation. Today the temple is managed by the Beijing Art Museum and houses a small but exquisite collection of Buddha images. The statues in the main halls include dusty Ming-period Buddhas and one of Shakyamuni sitting on a 1,000-petal, 1,000-Buddha bronze throne. ✉ *Suzhou Jie, Xisanhuan Lu, on the north side of Zizhu Bridge, Haidian District* ☎ *010/6842–3565* 🎫 *Y20* ⏱ *Tues.–Sun. 9–4.*

Temple of the Reclining Buddha (卧佛寺 *Wòfó sì*). Although the temple was damaged during the Cultural Revolution and poorly renovated afterward, the Sleeping Buddha remains. Built in 627–629, during the Tang Dynasty, the temple was named after the reclining Buddha that was brought in during the Yuan Dynasty (1271–1368). An English-language description explains that the casting of the beautiful bronze, in 1321, enslaved 7,000 people. The temple is inside the **Beijing Botanical Garden;** stroll north from the entrance through the neatly manicured grounds. ✉ *Xiangshan Lu, 2 km (1 mile) northeast of Xiangshan Park, Haidian District* ☎ *010/8259–8771* 🌐 *www.beijingbg.com* 🎫 *Temple Y5, gardens Y10* ⏱ *Daily 8:00–4:30.*

WHERE TO EAT

Updated by
Tom O'Malley

Since imperial times, Beijing has drawn citizens from all corners of China, and the country's economic boom has only accelerated the culinary diversity of the capital. These days, diners can find food from the myriad cuisines of far-flung regions of China, as well as just about every kind of international food.

Highlights include rare fungi and flowers from Yunnan, chili-strewn Hunan cooking from Mao's home province, Tibetan yak and *tsampa* (barley flour), mutton kebabs and grilled flatbreads from Xinjiang, numbingly spicy Sichuan cuisine, and chewy noodles from Shaanxi. And then there are ethnic foods from all over, with some—notably Italian, Japanese and Korean—in abundance.

You can spend as little as $5 per person for a decent meal or $100 and up on a lavish banquet. The variety of venues is also part of the fun, with five-star hotel dining rooms, holes-in-the-wall, and refurbished courtyard houses all represented. Reservations are always a good idea, especially for higher-end places, so ask your hotel to book you a table.

Beijingers tend to eat dinner around 6 pm, and many local restaurants will have closed their kitchens by 9 pm, though places that stay open until the wee hours aren't hard to find. Tipping is not the custom although some larger, international restaurants will add a 15% service charge to the bill, as do five-star hotel restaurants. Be aware before you go out that small and medium venues only take cash payments or local bank cards; more established restaurants usually accept credit cards.

Yanjing, the local beer, together with the ubiquitous Tsingtao, is available everywhere in Beijing. A growing number of imported beer brands have entered the market, and Beijing has a burgeoning craft beer scene of its own. And now many Chinese restaurants now have extensive wine menus.

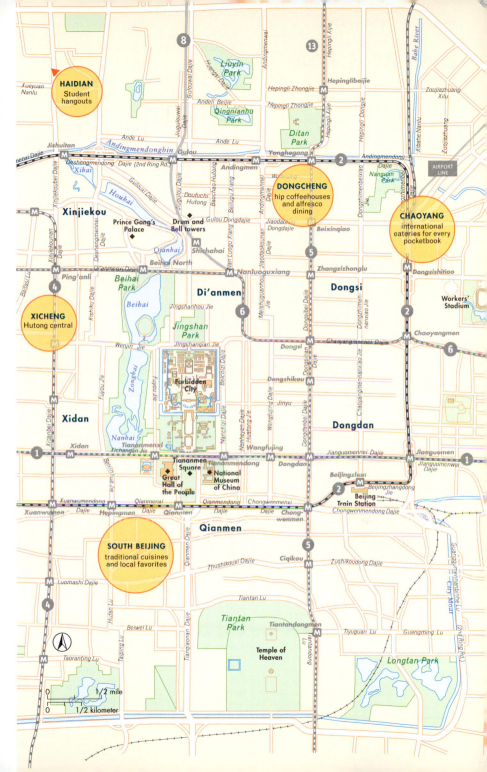

BEST BETS FOR BEIJING DINING

With thousands of restaurants to choose from, how will you decide where to eat? Fodor's writers and editors have selected their favorite restaurants by price, cuisine, and experience in the Best Bets lists here. You can also search by neighborhood in the following pages.

Fodor's Choice ★

Capital M, p. 99
Da Dong Roast Duck, p. 119
Dali Courtyard, p. 99
Din Tai Fung, p. 119
Duck de Chine, p. 119
Haidilao, p. 120
King's Joy, p. 108
Made in China, p. 111
Migas, p. 111
Najia Xiaoguan, p. 124
Opera Bombana, p. 126
Sake Manzo, p. 126
Temple Restaurant Beijing, p. 114
Transit, p. 127
Yotsuba, p. 128

Best By Price

$

Baoyuan Dumpling, p. 117
Crescent Moon, p. 99
Haidilao, p. 120
Jin Ding Xuan, p. 107
Jingzun Roast Duck Restaurant, p. 121
Kylin Private Kitchen, p. 108

Qin Tangfu, p. 112
Susu, p. 113

$$

Bellagio, p. 118
Dali Courtyard, p. 99
Din Tai Fung, p. 119
Hani Geju, p. 107
Lei Garden, p. 108
Sake Manzo, p. 126

$$$

Da Dong Roast Duck, p. 119
Hatsune, p. 121
Made in China, p. 111
Mercante, p. 111
Mosto, p. 124

$$$$

Brian McKenna @ The Courtyard, p. 95
Capital M, p. 99
Duck de Chine, p. 119
King's Joy, p. 108
Temple Restaurant Beijing, p. 114

Best By Experience

BEST PEKING DUCK

Da Dong Roast Duck, p. 119
Deyuan Roast Duck, p. 100
Duck de Chine, p. 119
Jing Yaa Tang, p. 121
Made in China, p. 111

BUSINESS DINING

Aria, p. 117
Migas, p. 111
Mosto, p. 124

GREAT VIEW

Brian McKenna @ The Courtyard, p. 95
Capital M, p. 99

HUTONG EATERIES

Café Sambal, p. 99
Dali Courtyard, p. 99
Kylin Private Kitchen, p. 108
Mercante, p. 111
Saffron, p. 112
The Source, p. 113
Susu, p. 113
Yue Bin, p. 114

Best By Cuisine

CANTONESE

Huang Ting, p. 107
Lei Garden, p. 108

GUIZHOU

Private Kitchen No. 44, p. 111

HUNAN

Karaiya Spice House, p. 121

BEIJING

Deyuan Roast Duck, p. 100
Jing Wei Lou, p. 115
Siji Minfu, p. 112

SHANGHAINESE AND JIANGZHE

Din Tai Fung, p. 119
Kong Yi Ji, p. 116

SICHUAN

Transit, p. 127
Yuxiang Renjia, p. 128

TAIWANESE

Bellagio, p. 118
Shin Yeh, p. 129

YUNNAN

Dali Courtyard, p. 99
Hani Geju, p. 107
Lost Heaven, p. 108

NORTHERN CHINESE

Dong Lai Shun, p. 100
Najia Xiaoguan, p. 124
Qin Tangfu, p. 112

WHAT IT COSTS IN YUAN			
$	$$	$$$	$$$$
At dinner	under Y100	Y101–Y150	Y151–Y200	over Y200

Prices are the average cost of a main dish at dinner or, if dinner isn't served, at lunch.

RESTAURANT REVIEWS

Listed alphabetically within neighborhoods

Use the coordinate (⊕ A1) at the end of each listing to locate a site on the corresponding map.

DONGCHENG DISTRICT 东城区

Literally "East City," Dongcheng occupies most of the center and east of the old center, from the western wall of the Forbidden City out to just beyond the East Second Ring Road, including Tiananmen Square, the popular hutong district of "Gulou," the Lama Temple, and the Temple of Heaven in the South. This is the district in which to sample Beijing's growing number of traditional courtyard eateries, where you can dine outside in the warmer months. The less-trafficked hutongs that are in and around touristy Nan Luogu Xiang are home to Western and Chinese restaurants, cafés, hip bars, and snack vendors.

$$$$
CONTEMPORARY
✕ **Brian McKenna @ The Courtyard.** With its unique perch overlooking the Forbidden City's moat, the Courtyard made a name for itself as Beijing's most romantic restaurant. Under the recent stewardship of the British chef Brian McKenna, and after a designer makeover from the team behind New York's W Hotel, it has emerged as a destination restaurant for Beijing's jet set. Prix-fixe menus of molecular-inspired cooking woo diners with kitchen tricks inspired by the likes of El Bulli and the Fat Duck. Service and execution can be hit or miss (often depending on whether Chef McKenna is at the helm or not), but some of the dishes, like the chocolate terra-cotta warrior emerging from edible "soil," are really quite special. $ *Average main: Y450* ✉ *95 Donghuamen Dajie, East Gate of Forbidden City, Dongcheng District* ☎ *010/6526–8883* ✍ *Reservations essential* ⊙ *No lunch* ⊕ *D4.*

$
FRENCH
✕ **Café de la Poste** (云游驿 *Yúnyóu yì*). In almost every French village or town there's a Café de la Poste, a humble hangout for a coffee, a beer, or a simple family meal. This haunt is just that: friendly service and a range of good-value bistro fare like steaks (including an excellent steak tartare), appetizers like grilled goat-cheese salad, free baskets of bread, and carafes of French wine. On weekend evenings it packs out with a pre-party expat crowd and leather-clad members of Beijing's affable motorcycle community; dancing on tables is not altogether uncommon. $ *Average main: Y100* ✉ *58 Yonghegong Dajie, Dongcheng District* ☎ *010/6402–7047* ⊕ *www.cafedelaposte.net* ▭ *No credit cards* Ⓜ *Yonghegong* ⊕ *E2.*

Where to Eat in Beijing

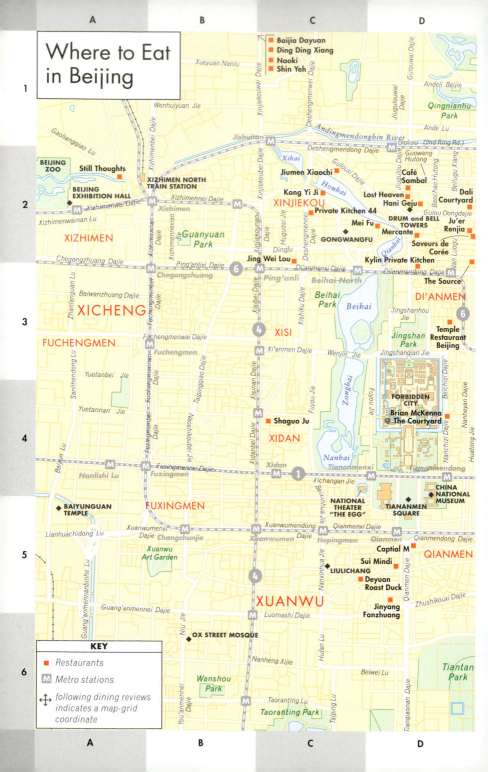

Restaurants (top right):
- Baijia Dayuan
- Ding Ding Xiang
- Naoki
- Shin Yeh

KEY
- ■ Restaurants
- Ⓜ Metro stations
- ⬦ following dining reviews indicates a map-grid coordinate

Map labels:

Xueyuan Nanlu · Wenhuiyuan Jie · Gaoliangqiao Lu · BEIJING ZOO · Still Thoughts · BEIJING EXHIBITION HALL · XIZHIMEN NORTH TRAIN STATION · Xizhimennei Dajie · Xizhimenwai Dajie · Xizhimen · Xizhimennerao · Xizhimenwainan Lu · XIZHIMEN · Guanyuan Park · Xinjiekouwai Dajie · Xinjiekounan Dajie · Deshengmenwai Dajie · Jishuitan · Andingmendongbin River · Gulou (2nd Ring Rd.) · Gulouwai Dajie · Andeli Beijie · Qingnianhu Park · Ande Lu · Gulouxi Dajie · Guowang Hutong · Jiugulou Dajie · Baochao Hutong · Beilugu Xiang · Deshengmendong Dajie · Xihai · Houhai · Deshengmennei Dajie · Jiumen Xiaochi · Kong Yi Ji · XINJIEKOU · Private Kitchen 44 · Mei Fu · GONGWANGFU · Lost Heaven · Hani Geju · Café Sambal · Dali Courtyard · DRUM and BELL TOWERS · Mercante · Ju'er Renjia · Saveurs de Corée · Kylin Private Kitchen · Qianhai · Tian Luogu · Dingfu · Jing Wei Lou · Di'anmenxi Dajie · Di'anmendong Dajie · The Source · DI'ANMEN · Chegongzhuang Dajie · Ping'anlixi Dajie · Xisibei Dajie · Xishiku Dajie · Ping'anli · Beihai North · Beihai Park · Beihai · Jingshanhou Jie · Temple Restaurant Beijing · Zhanlanguan Lu · Baiwanzhuang Dajie · XICHENG · Fuchengmennei Dajie · Xisi · Xi'anmen Dajie · Wenjin Jie · Jingshan Park · Jingshanqian Jie · Beichizi Dajie · FUCHENGMEN · Fuchengmenwai Dajie · Fuchengmen · Xisinan Dajie · Sanlihedong Lu · Yuetanbei Jie · Taipingqiao Dajie · Xidanbei Dajie · Fuyou Jie · Zonghai · FORBIDDEN CITY · Brian McKenna @ The Courtyard · Nanchizi Dajie · Huatong Jie · Yuetannan Jie · Shaguo Ju · XIDAN · Nanhai · Baiun Lu · Nanlishi Lu · Fuxingmennei Dajie · Fuxingmen · Fuxingmenwai Dajie · Nanshuncheng Jie · Xidan · Xichangan Jie · Tiananmenxi · Tiananmen · Tiananmendong · BAIYUNGUAN TEMPLE · Lianhuachidong Lu · FUXINGMEN · Xuanwumenxi Dajie · Changchunjie · Xuanwumen · NATIONAL THEATER "THE EGG" · TIANANMEN SQUARE · CHINA NATIONAL MUSEUM · Qianmenxi Dajie · Hepingmen · Qianmen · Qianmendong Dajie · Xuanwumendong Dajie · Nanxinhua Jie · Captial M · Sui Mindi · LIULICHANG · Deyuan Roast Duck · QIANMEN · Qianmen Dajie · Zhushikouxi Dajie · Guang'annennanbinhe Lu · Xuanwu Art Garden · XUANWU · Luomashi Dajie · Jinyang Fanzhuang · Guang'anmennei Dajie · Niu Jie · OX STREET MOSQUE · Hufan Lu · Beiwei Lu · Tiantan Park · Nanheng Xijie · Wanshou Park · You'anmennei Dajie · Nanheng Xijie · Taoranting Lu · Taoranting Park · Taiping Jie · Tianqiaonan Jie

Metro line numbers: ① ④ ⑥

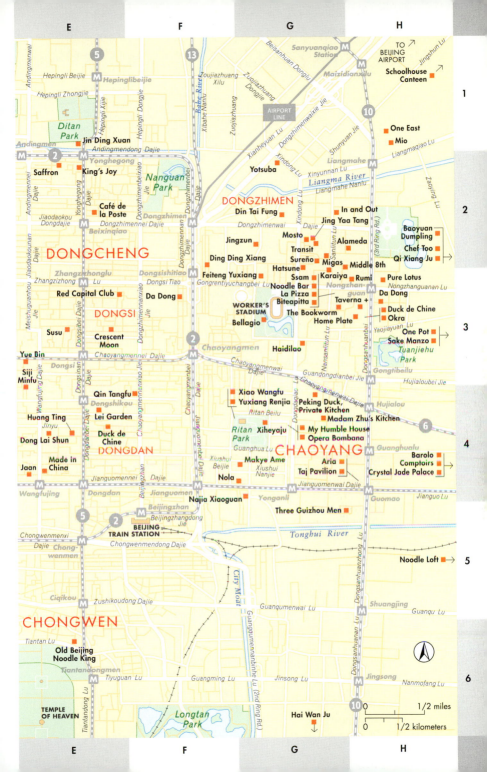

CHINESE CUISINE

We use the following regions in our restaurant reviews.

Beijing: As the seat of government for several dynasties, Beijing has evolved a cuisine that melds the culinary traditions of many regions. Specialties include Peking duck, *zhajiang* noodles, flash-boiled tripe with sesame sauce, and a wide variety of sweet snacks.

Cantonese: A diverse cuisine that roasts, fries, braises, and steams. Spices are used in moderation, and flavors are light and delicate. Dishes include wonton soup, steamed fish or scallops, barbecued pork, roasted goose and duck, and dim sum.

Chinese: Catchall term used for restaurants that serve cuisine from multiple regions of China.

Guizhou: The two key condiments in Guizhou's spicy-sour cuisine are *zao lajiao* (pounded dried peppers brined in salt) and fermented tomatoes (the latter used to make the region's hallmark sour fish soup (*suantangyu*).

Hunan: Chili peppers, ginger, garlic, dried salted black beans, and preserved vegetables are the mainstays of this "dry spicy" cuisine. Signature dishes include "red-braised" pork, steamed fish head with diced salted chilies, and cured pork with smoked bean curd.

Northern Chinese: A catch-all category encompassing the hearty stews and stuffed buns of Dongbei, the refined banquet fare of Shandong, Inner Mongolian hotpot, lamb and flat breads of Xinjiang, and the wheat noodles of Shaanxi province.

Shanghainese and Jiangzhe: Cuisine characterized by rich, sweet flavors produced by braising and stewing, and the extensive use of rice wine. Signatures include steamed hairy crabs and "drunken chicken."

Sichuan (central province): Famed for bold flavors and "*mala*" spiciness created by combining chilies and mouth-numbing Sichuan pepper-corns. Dishes include kung pao chicken, mapo doufu (tofu), *dandan* noodles, twice-cooked pork, and tea-smoked duck.

Taiwanese: This diverse cuisine centers on seafood. Specialties include oyster omelets, cuttlefish soup, and "three cups chicken," with a sauce made of soy sauce, rice wine, and sugar.

Tibetan: Cuisine reliant on foodstuffs that can grow at high altitudes, including barley flour, yak meat, milk, butter, and cheese.

Yunnan (southern province): This region is noted for its use of vegetables, fresh herbs, and mushrooms in its spicy preparations. Dishes include "crossing the bridge" rice noodle soup with chicken, pork, and fish; cured Yunnan ham with Bai-style goat cheese; and steamed or grilled fish with lemongrass.

3

$$
Café Sambal. Inside a cozy traditional courtyard house, this mainstay
of Beijing's international dining scene offers some of the city's best
MALAYSIAN
Malaysian and Southeast Asian dishes. Sambal refers to the house-made
chili sauce that gives an authentic kick to many of the dishes. Best bets
include fiery beef *rendang*, butter prawns, chili crab, and the four-sided
beans in cashew nut sauce. The antiques-furnished interior is stylish
and intimate, and a chilled-out vibe makes this a great place to linger
over a meal. $ *Average main: Y100* ⊠ *43 Doufuchi Hutong, Jiugulou
Dajie, Dongcheng District* ☎ *10/6400–4875* ⊕ *www.cafesambal.com*
Ⓜ *Guloudajie* ✛ *D2.*

$$$$ ✕ **Capital M.** This is one of the few restaurants in the capital with both
ECLECTIC stunning views and food worthy of the divine setting in front of Tianan-
Fodor's Choice men Square. Australian-influenced classics with a Mediterranean twist
★ are the order of the day here, served amid a vibrantly modern, muraled
interior. Try the crispy suckling pig or roast leg of lamb, and save room
for the famed Pavlova dessert: a cloud of meringue and whipped cream
sprinkled with fresh fruit. On weekends, hearty brunches and afternoon
high tea are served. $ *Average main: Y268* ⊠ *2 Qianmen Pedestrian
Street, Dongcheng District* ☎ *010/6702–2727* ⊕ *www.m-restaurant-
group.com* 🥢 *Reservations essential* Ⓜ *Qianmen* ✛ *D5.*

$ ✕ **Crescent Moon** (弯弯的月亮 *Wānwānde yuèliàng*). Unlike many of
ASIAN the bigger Xinjiang restaurants in town, there's no song and dance per-
formance at this Uygur family-run spot, and none needed, as the solid
cooking stands on its own merits. The heaping platters of grilled lamb
skewers, *da pan ji* (chicken, potato, and green pepper stew), homemade
yogurt, and freshly baked flatbreads are all terrific, as are the light and
dark Xinjiang beers available here. The traditional green-and-white
Islamic decor, Uygur CDs playing on the stereo, and clouds of hookah
smoke lend an authentic Central Asian atmosphere to the dining experi-
ence. $ *Average main: Y60* ⊠ *16 Dongsi Liutiao, Dongcheng District*
☎ *010/6400–5281* ▭ *No credit cards* Ⓜ *Zhangzizhonglu* ✛ *E3.*

$$$ ✕ **Crystal Jade Palace** (翡翠皇宫酒家 *Fěicuì huánggōng jiŭjiā*). At Bei-
CANTONESE jing's only outlet of a successful Singaporean restaurant brand, you'll
find some of the city's most reliable Cantonese, a cooking style not particularly well represented this far north. Weekdays see wheeler-dealers
closing deals over abalone and sea cucumber, while the weekends bustle
with families from Hong Kong and Singapore lingering over dim sum
and endless pots of tea. Plenty of pricey seafood dishes are on the menu,
but you can opt for the less expensive stir-fry dishes and dim sum. $ *Av-
erage main: Y150* ⊠ *Shin Kong Place, 87 Jianguo Lu, 6th fl., Chaoyang
District* ☎ *010/6533–1150* ⊕ *www.crystaljade.com* Ⓜ *Dawanglu* ✛ *H4.*

$$ ✕ **Dali Courtyard** (大理 *Dàlĭ*). Yunnan province's tranquillity and bohe-
YUNNAN mian spirit are captured in this enchanting traditional courtyard house,
Fodor's Choice a ten minute walk from the Drum and Bell towers. On breezy summer
★ nights the best seats are in the central courtyard with its overflowing
greenery; these are popular, so reservations are essential. The restau-
rant offers only set menus for the table, starting at Y150 per person.
Expect aromatic grilled fish, stir-fried Yunnan mushrooms, delicious
mint-infused salads, and in-season vegetable dishes. $ *Average main:*

Kebabs are a favorite street food all over China.

Y150 ✉ *67 Xiaojingchang Hutong, Gulou Dong Dajie, Dongcheng District* ☎ *010/8404–1430* Ⓜ *Guloudajie* ⚓ *D2.*

$ ✕ **Deyuan Roast Duck** (德缘烤鸭店 *Dé yuán kǎoyā diàn*). This unsung
NORTHERN Peking duck restaurant deserves a wider following. A typically lively
CHINESE dining room packs in locals for its traditional take on the capital's signature quacker, which is roasted over fruit wood, carved tableside, and
sold at a price that ought to make the bigger restaurants like Quanjude
and Bianyifang blush. Beijing's ruling triumvirate of traditional meat
(mutton, duck, donkey) comes in many tasty forms here, and there are
a wealth of appealing stir-fries and dry pot dishes that use beef, bacon,
shrimp, tofu, and country vegetables. Only about a decade old and
with no "time-honored" status to fall back on, Deyuan simply cooks
great food at great prices. $ *Average main: Y80* ✉ *57 Dashilan Xijie,
Xicheng District* ☎ *010/6308–5371* Ⓜ *Qianmen* ⚓ *C5.*

$ ✕ **Dong Lai Shun** (东来顺饭 *Dōngláishùn fàn*). Founded in 1903, this
CHINESE classic Beijing Hui (Chinese Muslim) restaurant now has branches all
over the city. Their specialty is mutton hotpot famous for three attributes: high-quality meat, sliced paper-thin, and served with delicious
sesame sauce. Dining here is by dunk and dip, cooking the meat slices
(*shuan rou*) and other accompaniments in a cauldron of bubbling soup
at the table. The best part is near the end, when the broth reaches a
tongue-tingling climax. *Zhima shaobing* (small baked sesame bread) is
the perfect accompaniment. $ *Average main: Y90* ✉ *198 Wangfujing
Dajie, Dongcheng District* ☎ *010/6513–9661* Ⓜ *Wangfujing* ⚓ *E4.*

Continued on page 107

A CULINARY TOUR OF CHINA

For centuries the collective culinary fragrances of China have drifted far beyond its borders and tantalized the entire world. Now with China's arms open to the world, a vast variety of Chinese flavors—from the North, South, East, and West—are more accessible than ever.

In dynasties gone by, a visitor to China might have to undertake a journey of a thousand li just to feel the burn of an authentic Sichuanese hotpot, and another to savor the crispy skin and juicy flesh of a genuine Beijing roast duck. Luckily for us, the vast majority of regional Chinese cuisines have made successful internal migrations. As a result, Sichuanese cuisine can be found in Guangzhou, Cantonese dim sum in Urumuqi, and the cumin-spiced lamb-on-a-stick, for which the Uigher people of Xinjiang are famous, is now grilled all over China.

Four corners of the Middle Kingdom

Before you begin your journey, remember, a true scholar of Middle Kingdom cuisine should first eliminate the very term "Chinese food" from their vocabulary. It hardly encompasses the variety of provincial cuisines and regional dishes that China has to offer, from succulent Shanghainese dumplings to fiery Sichuanese hotpots.

To guide you on your gastronomic journey, we've divided the country's gourmet map along the points of the compass—North, South, East, and West. Bon voyage and bon appétit!

Following the revolution, it was hard to find authentic Chinese cuisine.

NORTH

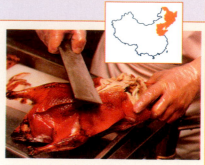

THE BASICS

Cuisine from China's Northeast is called dongbei cai, and it's more wheat than rice based. Vegetables like kale, cabbage, and potatoes are combined with robust, thick soy sauces, garlic (often raw), and scallions.

Even though many Han Chinese from southern climates find mutton too gamey, up north it's a regular staple. In many northern cities, you can't walk more than a block without coming across a small sidewalk grill with yang rou chua'r, or lamb-on-a-stick.

Peking duck sliced table-side.

NOT TO BE MISSED

The most famous of all the northern dishes is Peking duck, and if you've ever had it well prepared, you'll know why Beijingers are proud of the dish named for their city.

As far back as the 15th century it was an Imperial dish, reserved for royalty. Like many such delicacies, it's likely the recipe was smuggled out of the Forbidden City by cooks or servants, eventually finding its way into restaurants.

A bit different from the "crispy duck" eaten in Cantonese-style restaurants around the globe, proper Peking duck should have skin that's both brittle and yielding. Getting there is a meticulous, multi-day process, but the real key is the date-infused liquid poured into the duck cavity, which is sealed, and the bird is then hung over the fire. Full of fruity juice, the meat will steam gently from the inside as the flames in the oven lick and crackle the skin.

THE CAPITAL CITY'S NAMESAKE DISH

A perfectly prepared duck

Scallions

Soy based hoisin sauce

Pancakes

SOUTH

(left) Preparing for the feast. (top right) Dim sum as art. (bottom right) Place your order.

THE BASICS

The dish most associated with Southern Chinese cuisine is dim sum, which is found in great variety and abundance in Guangdong province, as well as Hong Kong and Macau. Bite-size dim sum is usually eaten early in the day. Any good dim sum place should have dozens of varieties. Some of the most popular dishes are *har gao,* a shrimp dumpling with a rice-flour skin, *siu maai,* a pork dumpling with a wrapping made of wheat flour, and *chaa-habao,* a steamed or baked bun filled with sweetened pork and onions. Adventerous eaters should order the chicken claws. Trust us, they taste better than they look.

The Cantonese saying *"fei qin zou shou"* roughly translates to "if it flies, swims or runs, it's food."

For our money, the best southern food comes from Chaozhou (Chiuchow), a coastal city only a few hours' drive north of its larger neighbors. Unlike dim sum, Chaozuo cuisine is extremely light and understated. Deep-fried bean curd is also a remarkably fresh Chaozuo dish.

NOT TO BE MISSED

One Chaozuo dish that appeals equally to the eye and the palate is the plain-sounding mashed vegetable with minced chicken soup. The dish is served in a large bowl, and resembles a green-and-white yin-yang. As befitting a dish resembling a Buddhist symbol, a vegetarian version substituting rice gruel for chicken broth is usually offered.

SOUTHWEST AND FAR WEST

Southwest

THE BASICS

When a person from the Southwest asks you if you like spicy food, consider your answer well. Natives of Sichuan and Hunan take the use of chilies, wild pepper, and garlic to blistering new heights. These two areas have been competing for the "spiciest province in China" title for centuries. The penchant for fiery food is likely due to the weather—hot and humid in the summer and harshly cold in the winter. But no matter what the temperature, if you're eating Sichuan or Hunan dishes, be prepared to sweat.

Southwest China shares some culinary traits with both Southeast Asia and India. This is likely due to the influences of travelers from both regions in centuries past. Traditional Chinese medicine also makes itself felt in the regional cuisine. Theory has it that sweating expels toxins and equalizes body temperature.

As Chairman Mao's province, Hunan has a number of dishes with revolutionary names. The most popular are red-cooked Hunan fish *(hongshao wuchangyu)* and red-cooked pork *(hongshao rou)*, which was said to have been a personal favorite of the Great Helmsman.

Sichuan pepper creates a tingly numbness.

NOT TO BE MISSED

One dish you won't want to miss out on in Sichuan is *mala zigi*, or "peppery and hot chicken." It's one part chicken meat and three parts fried chilies and a Sichuanese wild pepper called *huajiao* that's so spicy it effectively numbs the tongue. At first it feels like eating Tiger Balm, but the hot-cool-numb sensation produced by crunching on the pepper is oddly addictive.

KUNG PAO CHICKEN

One of the most famous Chinese dishes, Kung Pao chicken (or gongbao jiding), enjoys a legend of its own.

Though shrouded in myth, its origin exemplifies the improvisational skills found in any good Chinese chef. The story of Kung Pao chicken has to do with a certain Qing Dynasty era (1644–1911) provincial governor named Ding Baozhen, who arrived home unexpectedly one day with a group of friends in tow. His cook, caught in between shopping trips, had only the chicken breast and a few vegetables he was planning to cook for his own dinner. The crafty chef diced the chicken into tiny bits and fried it up with everything he could find in the cupboard—some peanuts, sugar, onion, garlic, bits of ginger, and a few handfuls of dried red peppers—and hoped for the best.

(top left) Tibetan dumplings. (center left) Uyghur-style pilaf. (bottom left) Monk stirring tsampa barley. (right) Juggling hot noodles in the Xinjiang province.

Far West

THE BASICS

Religion is the primary shaper of culinary tradition in China's Far West. Being a primarily Muslim province, chefs in Xinjiang don't use pork products of any kind. Instead, meals are likely to be heavy on spiced lamb. Baked flat breads coated in sesame seeds are a specialty. Whole lamb roasted on a spit, fine spicy tomato salads, and lightly spiced mutton and vegetable soups are also favorites.

NOT TO BE MISSED

In Tibet, climate is the major factor dictating cuisine. High and dry, the Tibetan plateau is hardly suited for rice cultivation. Whereas a Han meal might include rice, Tibetan cuisine tends to include tsampa, a ground barley usually cooked into a porridge. Another staple that's definitely an acquired taste is yak butter tea. Dumplings, known as *momo*, are wholesome and filling. Of course, if you want to go all out, order the yak penis with caterpillar fungus.

EAST

(top left) Cold tofu with pork and thousand-year-old eggs. (top right) Meaty dumplings. (bottom right) Letting off the steam of Shanghai: soup dumplings. (bottom left) Steamed Shanghai hairy crabs.

THE BASICS

The rice, seafood, and fresh vegetable-based cooking of the southern coastal provinces of Zhejiang and Jiangsu are known collectively as huiyang cai. As the area's biggest city, Shanghai has become a major center of the culinary arts. Some popular dishes in Shanghai are stir-fried freshwater eels and finely ground white pepper, and red-stewed fish—a boiled carp in sweet and sour sauce. Another Shanghai favorite are xiaolong bao, or little steamer dumplings. Similar to Cantonese dim sum, xiaolong bao tend to be more moist. The perfect steamed dumpling is meant to explode in your mouth in a juicy burst of meat.

NOT TO BE MISSED

Drunken anything! Shanghai chefs are known for their love of cooking with wine. Dishes like drunken chicken, drunken pigeon, and drunken crab are all delectable meals cooked with prodigious amounts of Shaoxing wine. People with an aversion to alcohol should definitely avoid these. Another meal not to be missed is hairy freshwater crabs, which only come into season in October. One enthusiast of the dish was 15th-century poet and essayist Li Yu, who wrote of the dish in near-erotic terms. "Meat as white as jade, golden roe . . . to use seasoning to improve its taste is like holding up a torch to brighten the sunshine."

3

$$ ✕ **Hani Geju** (哈尼个旧餐厅 *Hāní gèjiù cāntīng*). A stone's throw from
YUNNAN the Bell Tower, this cozy Yunnan restaurant boasts a trimmed down
menu of southwest Chinese fare, such as authentic Bai-minority goat
cheese with bacon (smoked in-house), fluffy-centered potato balls with
an addictively crisp coating, zingy mint salads, and delicate rice noodle
dishes. The emphasis here is on organic sourcing, moderate seasoning,
and no MSG. Innovative taster platters at lunchtime means you can
sample their best dishes in mini, single-serving portions. After your
meal, take a stroll through the surrounding warren of hutong alleyways,
some of the most atmospheric in the city. ⑤ *Average main: Y110* ✉ *48
Zhonglouwan Hutong, southeast of Bell Tower, Dongcheng District*
☎ *010/6401–3318* Ⓜ *Guloudajie* ⊕ *D2.*

$$$ ✕ **Huang Ting** (凰庭 *Huángtíng*). Beijing's traditional courtyard houses
CANTONESE provide an exquisite setting at this elegant hotel restaurant. The walls
are constructed from gray hutong bricks reclaimed from centuries-old
siheyuan that have gone the way of the wrecking ball. Pricey seafood
items like abalone and lobster are balanced by affordable and delicious
dim sum (especially the dim sum prix-fixe lunch with tea, for RMB
88). The menu is mostly Cantonese, but you can also get a traditional
Peking duck. If only the place had a little more atmosphere (and customers), it could be up there with the city's best. ⑤ *Average main: Y200*
✉ *The Peninsula, 8 Jinyu Hutong, Wangfujing, Dongcheng District*
☎ *010/6512–8899* Ⓜ *Dongdan* ⊕ *E4.*

$$$$ ✕ **Jaan** (家安 *Jiāān*). If you're looking for old-world elegance, this is the
FRENCH place. You'll be transported back to the 1920s, complete with antique
piano, graceful French windows, and a wooden dance floor on which
Mao Zedong took a turn during the building's brief tenure as the Com-
munist Party's HQ (the Great Hall of the People was still being built).
French-influenced dishes include steaks, soups, black cod, and foie gras.
The wine list is staggeringly long and befits a place that's been around
since 1917. ⑤ *Average main: Y250* ✉ *Raffles Beijing Hotel, 33 East
Chang'an Avenue, Wangfujing, Dongcheng District* ☎ *010/6526–3388*
Ⓜ *Wangfujing* ⊕ *E4.*

$ ✕ **Jin Ding Xuan** (金鼎轩酒楼 *Jīndǐngxuān jiǔlóu*). Clad in red neon
CANTONESE after dark, this jovial dim sum restaurant offers four bustling floors
of great-value dishes around the clock. Expect to wait in line at busy
periods; once inside, keep an eye out for the cold dish and drink carts
wheeling by. The menu is extensive and service is regimented—you
won't go wrong with an order of shrimp dumplings, fried turnip cake
with Cantonese sausage, and tender braised steak served in a clay pot.
A recent addition is the "pollution menu"—new dishes that claim to
counteract the effects of Beijing's smog. ⑤ *Average main: Y70* ✉ *77
Hepingli Xijie, Dongcheng District* ☎ *010/6429–6699* Ⓜ *Yonghegong*
⊕ *E1.*

$ ✕ **Ju'er Renjia** (菊儿人家 *Júér rénjiā*). A convenient pit stop when vis-
CHINESE iting Nanluoguxiang, this modest little eatery really offers only one
option: a set meal of tasty Taiwanese-style *lurou fan*—rice with an
aromatic ground pork topping complemented by a flavorful boiled egg,
mixed pickled vegetables, and a simple clear soup, for less than $4. A
vegetarian stew and rice set is also available. The home-brewed teas

and chilled custard desserts are worth a try, too. $ *Average main: Y26* ✉ *63 Xiao Ju'er Hutong, Dongcheng District* ☏ *010/6400–8117* ▭ *No credit cards* Ⓜ *Nanluoguxiang* ✛ *D2.*

$$$$
VEGETARIAN
Fodor's Choice
★

✕ **King's Joy** (京兆尹 *Jīng zhào yǐn*). The chefs at this elegantly upscale vegetarian restaurant enact miracles with tofu, mushrooms, and wheat gluten. Try the sweet and sour "ribs" made from lotus root, then the rich and earthy basil-braised eggplant, and finish with glutinous rice tarts (*ai wo wo*) filled with sweet red bean paste and crunchy walnuts. The building, designed to resemble Beijing's traditional quadrangle courtyards (*siheyuan*), is enhanced by views of the Lama Temple across the street, as well as the crisp white tablecloths, fresh orchids, and harp performances inside. $ *Average main: Y250* ✉ *2 Wudaoying Hutong, Yonghegong, Dongcheng District* ☏ *010/8404-9191* Ⓜ *Yonghegong* ✛ *E2.*

$
CHINESE FUSION

✕ **Kylin Private Kitchen** (麒麟阁私房菜 *Qílín gé sīfáng cài*). The sky-lit, plant-strewn interior of this small hidden gem is a pleasant spot to linger over the excellent contemporary Chinese food, which often blends various styles and techniques. A highlight of the compact menu is the *zhiguo* ("paper pot") dishes, featuring fragrant shrimp or green beans served in a Japanese-style paper pot over a flame. Most diners order the *zijiangyu*, an aromatic fish stew cooked with chilies, purple ginger, and fresh Sichuan peppercorns: choose from three types of fish and three levels of spiciness. The restaurant is in a narrow alley that once housed imperial midwives during the Ming Dynasty. $ *Average main: Y100* ✉ *6 Qilin Bei Hutong, Dongcheng District* ☏ *010/6407–3516* Ⓜ *Nanluoguxiang* ✛ *D2.*

$$
CANTONESE

✕ **Lei Garden** (利苑 *Lìyuàn*). Bright and bustling on any day of the week, Lei Garden really packs them in on Sunday afternoons for dim sum amid glamorous surroundings. The pan-fried turnip cake is juicy and topped with generous amounts of grated veggies, and the shrimp dumplings are bursting with sweet plump shrimp and crunchy bamboo shoots. A platter of roast pork, with bite-size pieces laced with buttery fat and capped with crisp, crunchy skin, hits the spot. Private dining rooms offer sanctuary from the crowd. $ *Average main: Y150* ✉ *Jinbao Tower, 89 Jinbao Jie, 3rd fl., Dongcheng District* ☏ *010/8522–1212* 🌐 *www.leigarden.hk* ✍ *Reservations essential* Ⓜ *Dengshikou* ✛ *E4.*

$$$
YUNNAN

✕ **Lost Heaven** (花马天堂云南餐厅 *Huā mǎ tiāntáng Yúnnán cāntīng*). The city's finest Yunnan restaurant is in an elegant compound just east of Tiananmen Square that was once used by the former U.S. legation. With impeccable service and a serious wine list, this Shanghai export, named after the vast and little-known "Mountain Mekong" region that straddles Yunnan, Burma, and Laos, is out to impress. Recommended dishes include crisp Dali-style chicken tumbled with green onions and chilies, "Miao" hot-and-sour shrimp, and steamed cod with Yunnan black truffle. Fun fact: the walls on the first and second floor are made of bricks of pu-erh tea, a kind of fermented tea from Yunnan. $ *Average main: Y180* ✉ *23 Qianmen Dongdajie, Dongcheng District* ☏ *010/8516–2698* Ⓜ *Qianmen* ✛ *D2.*

Tips for Eating out in Beijing

In China meals are a communal event, so food in a Chinese home or restaurant is always shared. Although cutlery is available in many restaurants, it won't hurt to brush up on your use of chopsticks, the utensil of choice. The standard eating procedure is to hold the bowl close to your mouth and eat the food. Noisily slurping up soup and noodles is also the norm. It's considered bad manners to point or play with your chopsticks, or to place them on top of your rice bowl when you're finished eating (put them horizontally on the table or plate). Avoid leaving your chopsticks standing up in a bowl of rice—this is said to resemble the practice of burning two incense sticks at funerals and is considered disrespectful.

The food in hotel restaurants is usually acceptable but overpriced. Restaurants frequented by locals always serve tastier fare at better prices. Don't shy from trying establishments without an English menu—a good phrase book and lots of pointing can usually get you what you want.

Beijing's most famous dish is Peking duck. The roast duck is served with thin pancakes, in which you wrap pieces of the meat, together with spring onions, vegetables, and plum sauce. Beijing-style eateries offer many little-known but excellent specialties, such as *dalian huoshao* (meat- and vegetable-filled fried dumplings) and *zhajiangmian* (thick noodles with meat sauce). If you're adventurous, sample a hearty bowl of *luzhu* (pork lung and intestines brewed in an aromatic broth mixed with bean curd, baked bread, and chopped cilantro). Hotpot is another local trademark: you order different meats and vegetables, which you cook in a pot of stock boiling on a charcoal burner. *Baozi* (small steamed buns filled with meat or vegetables) are particularly good in Beijing—sold at stalls and in small restaurants everywhere, they make a great snack or breakfast food.

MEALS AND MEALTIMES

Breakfast is not a big deal in China—congee, or rice porridge (*zhou*), is the standard dish. Most mid- and upper-end hotels do big buffet spreads, and Beijing's blooming café chains provide lattes and croissants all over town.

Snacks are a food group in themselves. There's no shortage of steaming street stalls selling baozi, spicy kebabs (called *chuan'r*), savoury pancakes (*bing*), hot sweet potatoes, and bowls of noodle soup. Pick a place where lots of locals are eating to be on the safe side.

Lunch and dinner dishes are more or less interchangeable. Meat (especially pork) or poultry tends to form the base of most Beijing dishes, together with wheat products like buns, pancakes, and noodles. Beijing food is often quite oily, with liberal amounts of vinegar; its strong flavors come from garlic, soy sauce, and bean pastes. Food can often be extremely salty and loaded with MSG. If you can manage it, try to have the waitress tell the cooks to cut back. Vegetables—especially winter cabbage and onions—and tofu play a big role in meals. As in all Chinese food, dairy products are scarce. Chinese meals usually involve a variety of dishes, which are always ordered communally in restaurants.

3

Fast Food: Beijing's Best Street Snacks

Part of the fun of exploring Beijing's lively hutong alleyways is the chance to munch on the city's traditional snacks, served by itinerant food sellers.

WHERE TO GO

Wangfujing Snack Street and nearby Donghuamen Night Market, both in Dongcheng, are fun for browsing and sampling. The two markets have an extensive lineup of cooked-food stalls, many selling food items designed to shock. Sure, it's extremely touristy, and you'll be elbow-to-elbow with wide-eyed travelers fresh off the tour buses, but they're also incredibly fun and great for photo ops. Cheerful vendors call out to potential customers, their wares glowing under red lanterns.

On the banks of Houhai, near the historical residence of Soong Ching-ling, is the entrance to Xiaoyou Hutong. Down this narrow alley you'll find Jiumen Xiaochi, a traditional courtyard house occupied by a collection of old Beijing eateries forced to relocate due to urban redevelopment. Some of these small eateries have been producing the same specialty dishes for decades. Look out for *lu dagun*, a pastry made of alternate layers of glutinous rice and red bean paste; *dalian huoshao*, northern-style pork pot stickers; and *zha guanchang*, deep-fried slices of mung bean starch dipped in a raw garlic sauce.

WHAT TO TRY

Sweet-potato sellers turn their pedicabs into restaurants on wheels. An oil drum, balanced between the two rear wheels, becomes a makeshift baking unit, with small cakes of coal at the bottom roasting sweet potatoes strung around the top. In fall and winter, sugar-coated delicacies are a popular treat. Crab apples, water chestnuts, strawberries, and yams are placed on skewers, about half a dozen to a stick; the fruit is then bathed in syrup that hardens into a shiny candy coating, providing a sugar rush for those all-day walks.

Kebabs are popular, and it seems as though anything under the sun can be skewered and fried. There are the outlandish skewers of scorpion, silkworm cocoons, and even starfish, all fried to a crisp and covered with spices. There are also the more palatable (and authentic) lamb kebabs flavored with cumin and chili flakes.

Some modern snacks are ubiquitous, such as the *jianbing*, a thin flour crepe topped with an egg and a crispy fried cracker. Briny fermented bean paste and hot chili sauce are spread thick and a sprinkling of cilantro and spring onion is added before it's rolled into a tidy package for munching on the go. Also on the streets: *baozi*, fluffy steamed buns filled with all manner of meat and vegetables, and *xianbing*, wheat flour pockets typically stuffed with chives and eggs.

COOKED TO ORDER?

The turnover at vendor carts and street-side stands is rapid, so it's unusual that anything has been sitting around long, but stick to the busier stalls. If you have any doubts, ask the vendor to cook yours to order, rather than accepting the ready-made food on display.

3

$$$
NORTHERN
CHINESE
Fodor's Choice
★

✘ **Made In China** (长安壹号 *Cháng'ān yīhào*). The glassed-in kitchens at this Grand Hyatt restaurant are like theater for foodies. White-robed chefs twirl floury noodles as beautifully bronzed Peking ducks are hooked on poles out of tall brick ovens. Tradition rules when it comes to Executive Chef Jin's famous duck, and eating it is a three-stage process: skin dipped in sugar, then breast meat with scallions, and finally pancakes stuffed with leg meat, skin, hoisin, cucumber, and minced garlic. The trick, says Jin, is to roll the pancakes small enough to eat in one mouthful. $ *Average main: Y200* ⌂ *Grand Hyatt, 1 Dong Chang An Jie, Dongcheng District* ☎ *010/8518–1234* ⌂ *Reservations essential* Ⓜ *Wangfujing* ✚ *E4.*

$$$
ITALIAN

✘ **Mercante.** Bologna-based chef Omar Maseroli and his Chinese partner are the proprietors of Mercante, a slow-food-inspired slice of Italy in a tumble-down hutong alleyway. This minuscule eatery keeps it simple, with rustic dishes like homemade pasta with an earthy ragù of duck or rabbit, plump ravioli, platters of imported cold cuts, and cheese served with fresh-baked focaccia. Rich, boozy tiramisu and a well-priced list of Italian wines makes this a fine place to linger, or you could pop around the corner for a craft-beer nightcap at Great Leap Brewing. Brunch is served on weekends. $ *Average main: Y170* ⌂ *4 Fangzhuanchang Hutong, Dianmen Wai Dajie, Dongcheng District* ☎ *010/8402-5098* ⌂ *Reservations essential* Ⓜ *Shichahai* ✚ *D2.*

$$
SPANISH
Fodor's Choice
★

✘ **Migas** (米家思 *Mǐ jiā sī*). The fact that Beijing's hottest rooftop bar and nightclub becomes a sophisticated Spanish restaurant at mealtimes is quite the Houdini act. Most heralded for its terrific three-course lunch deal, which changes weekly, Migas is a whirlwind adventure in Spanish gastronomy, starring slow-roasted suckling pig, chicken grilled on a Josper oven, creamy cod with steamed eggplant, and "liquid bombons" with deliciously sticky fillings. Throw in complimentary baskets of home-baked bread, inventive amuse-bouches, and a funky, casual environment, and you can see why Beijing's young professionals have made this place their own. $ *Average main: Y150* ⌂ *Nali Patio, 81 Sanlitun Lu, 6th fl., Chaoyang District* ☎ *010/5208–6061* Ⓜ *Tuanjiehu* ✚ *G2.*

$
NORTHERN
CHINESE

✘ **Old Beijing Noodle King** (老北京炸酱面大王 *Lǎo Běijīng zhájiàngmiàn dàwáng*). This chain of noodle houses serves hand-pulled noodles and traditional local dishes in a lively, old-time atmosphere, with waiters shouting across the room to announce customers arriving. Try the classic *zhajiang* noodle, served in a ground-meat sauce with accompaniments of celery, bean sprouts, green beans, soybeans, slivers of cucumber, and red radish. $ *Average main: Y30* ⌂ *56 Dong Xinglong Jie, Dongcheng District* ☎ *010/6701–9393* ▭ *No credit cards* Ⓜ *Chongwenmen* ✚ *E6.*

$
CHINESE

✘ **Private Kitchen No. 44** (44号私家厨房). "Farm to table" is the creed at this peaceful Guizhou-style restaurant west of Houhai Lake. Dishes like braised pork ribs and sticky rice wrapped in bamboo, stir-fried "country-style" vegetables rich with the sour-sharp tang of fermented bamboo, and even the house-made ice cream all use ingredients from the owner's own farms and small holdings on the outskirts of the city. Beyond an admirable commitment to sourcing, it's the little touches that make this eatery shine, such as complimentary tastings of homemade rice-wine tasters infused with rose petals and organic honey. ⑤ *Average main: Y100* ✉ *70 Denshengmen Nei Dajie, Xicheng District* ☎ *010/6400–1280* ▭ *No credit cards* ✛ *C2.*

$ ✗ **Qin Tangfu** (秦唐府 *Qín tángfǔ*). Pull up a tiny stool for stick-to-your-ribs goodness at this rustic haven for Shaanxi fare. Hearty wheat-based specialities include *roujia mo* (unleavened bread stuffed with tender braised pork, aka "Chinese hamburger"), and chewy hand-pulled noodles flavored with chili oil and dark vinegar. Lending a bit of charm are the framed paper cuts (a form of Chinese folk art in which red paper is cut into animal, flower, or human shapes), traditional handicrafts, and large woven baskets (you can use them to store your purse or bags while you eat). ⑤ *Average main: Y40* ✉ *69 Chaoyangmennei Nanxiaojie, Dongcheng District* ☎ *010/6559–8135* ▭ *No credit cards* ✛ *F4.*

NORTHERN
CHINESE

$$ ✗ **Saffron** (藏红花 *Cánghónghuā*). An early pioneer in the über-chic Wudaoying Hutong, Saffron is still going strong, with refined Mediterranean food served in a romantic courtyard house with outside terrace. Tapas, paella, sangria, and desserts (displayed in a glass case), served with warmth, provide the makings for a fine evening. If it's busy, head to a small place opposite called Chi. Sharing the same globe-trotting Chinese owners, it specializes in organic prix-fixe menus of European-inspired contemporary cooking. You won't go wrong. ⑤ *Average main: Y120* ✉ *64 Wudaoying Hutong, Dongcheng District* ☎ *010/8404–4909* Ⓜ *Yonghegong* ✛ *E2.*

SPANISH

$$ ✗ **Saveurs de Corée** (韩香馆 *Hán xiāng guǎn*). This longstanding Korean restaurant, which has moved with the times, remains the best contemporary option in the vicinity of Nanluogu Xiang. The redesigned central courtyard is a delightful setting in which to sample signature fragrant sliced beef with shiitake mushrooms, "seafood pizza" (a light frittata with kimchi, shrimp, and squid), and the simply divine chicken soup, made with Korean ginseng and a whole organic chicken. An adjoining bar serves Korean-inspired cocktails heavy on soju, a Korean vodka. Carnivores take note: the same owners run a Korean barbecue restaurant at nearby Xiang'er Hutong. ⑤ *Average main: Y120* ✉ *20 Juer Hutong, off Nanluoguxiang, Dongcheng District* ☎ *010/6401–6083* Ⓜ *Nanluoguxiang* ✛ *D2.*

KOREAN

$ ✗ **Siji Minfu** (四季民福烤鸭店 *Sìjì mín fú kǎoyā diàn*). Here's a rare thing: a local restaurant chain that insists on seasonality and says no to MSG. Folks line up out the door for the Peking duck, expertly roasted so that the skin shatters while the flesh remains unctuously tender. Also popular is the *zhajiang mian*, Beijing's austere signature dish of chewy wheat noodles topped with a rich meat sauce and crunchy vegetable accompaniments. A traditional dessert platter includes *wandouhuang*, a dense, sweet cake made from white peas, and *ludagun* (literally "rolling donkey"), a sticky rice cake so named because its dusting of soybean flour resembles a donkey that has rolled on the ground. ⑤ *Average main: Y90* ✉ *Donghua Hotel, 32 Dengshikou Xijie, Wangfujing Dajie, Dongcheng District* ☎ *010/6513–5141* Ⓜ *Dengshikou* ✛ *E4.*

NORTHERN
CHINESE

A BOOKWORM'S FOOD TOUR

Throughout China's history, there has been a love affair between the literati and food. So try the following plates from these famous books:

Qiexiang: a dish of "scented" aubergine strips, as depicted in the classic *Dream of the Red Chamber,* a novel about scholar-gentry life in the 1700s.

Huixiang dou: a bean boiled with star anise, made famous through Lu Xun's short story "Kong Yi Ji," which takes place in a traditional wine house.

Lu Yu zhucha: beef cooked in tea leaves, inspired by Lu Yu, the author of the *Book of Tea.*

3

$$$
SICHUAN

✗ The Source (都江源 *Dōujiāngyuán*). The Source dishes up dainty set menus of Sichuan-inspired favorites (RMB 188 or 288 per person) in a romantic, historic courtyard. Dishes change according to seasonality, but you can expect several hot and cold appetizers, meat and seafood dishes, and a few surprise concoctions from the chef, all tweaked for international palates (the waitresses will ask how spicy you like your food). On a peaceful hutong intersecting busy Nanluogu Xiang, the building was once the backyard of a Qing Dynasty general referred to by the imperial court as "The Great Wall of China" for his military exploits. The grounds have been painstakingly restored; an upper level overlooks a small garden shaded by pomegranate and date trees. $ *Average main: Y188* ✉ *14 Banchang Hutong, Kuanjie, Dongcheng District* ☎ *010/6400–3736* ⚓ *Reservations essential* Ⓜ *Nanluoguxiang* ✛ *D2.*

$
VEGETARIAN

✗ Still Thoughts (静思素食坊 *Jìngsī sùshí fāng*). Though there's no meat on the menu, carnivores can still sate their hunger on mock Peking "duck," "fish" (made of tofu sheets with scales carved into it), and tasty "lamb" skewers that you'd be hard pressed to claim contain no meat at all. In fact, we'd suggest plumping for the straight-up vegetable dishes here, like stir-fried okra with mushrooms, steamed eggplant with sesame paste, or the stone-pot-braised taro, which eschew novelty for sheer deliciousness. The restaurant is a little hard to find: it's inside the alley just east of the large Wahaha Hotel. $ *Average main: Y70* ✉ *Longfu Temple Market, 1 Dongsi Xi Dajie, 1st fl., Building A, Dongcheng District* ☎ *010/6405–2433* ▭ *No credit cards* Ⓜ *Dongsi* ✛ *A2.*

$
VIETNAMESE

✗ Susu (苏苏会 *Sūsū huì*). Tucked away down a dim alley north of the National Art Museum, this hip hutong eatery has quickly gained a following for Beijing's best Vietnamese food. Choose from various light and fresh summer rolls and salads to start, and be sure to order the succulent barbecued La Vong Fish, served on a bed of vermicelli with herbs, peanuts, crispy rice crackers, and shrimp, which goes well with beer from the local Slow Boat Brewery. The lovingly restored courtyard house has a gorgeous patio and rooftop seating for pleasant weather, but the beautifully furnished interiors aren't too shabby either. $ *Average main: Y80* ✉ *10 Qianlang Hutong Xixiang, Dongcheng District* ☎ *010/8400–2699* Ⓜ *National Art Musuem* ✛ *E3.*

Street snacks at Wangfujing, a popular, centrally located shopping area

$$$$ ✕ **Temple Restaurant Beijing.** Worship at the altar of epicureanism and
MODERN   surround yourself with serenity at the city's best international fine-
EUROPEAN   dining restaurant, nestled in the heart of Old Beijing. TRB (as it's also
Fodor's Choice known) serves high-end European cuisine in a spacious, minimalist din-
★   ing room within a fabulously restored Ming Dynasty Buddhist temple
complex. The four-course tasting menu (Y458) includes dishes such as
all-day-braised short rib with burdock chips, and house-cured gravlax
served tableside by Ignace, the most charming restaurateur in town.
The wine list is excellent, with a deep focus on Champagne, Bordeaux,
and Burgundy. Ⓢ *Average main: Y250* ✉ *23 Songzhusi, Shatan Beijie,
Dongcheng District* ☎ *010/8400–2232* ⊕ *www.temple-restaurant.com*
🖥 *Reservations essential* Ⓜ *National Art Musuem* ✛ *D3.*

$ ✕ **Yue Bin** (悦宾饭馆 *Yuèbīn fànguǎn*). Yue Bin was the first private
CHINESE   restaurant to open in Beijing after the Cultural Revolution era, and
its home-style cooking still attracts neighborhood residents, as well
as hungry visitors from the nearby National Art Musuem. The tiny,
no-frills dining room is just big enough for half a dozen tables, where
you'll see families chowing down on specialities such as *suanni zhouzi*,
garlic-marinated braised pork shoulder; *guota doufuhe*, tofu pockets stuffed with minced pork; and *wusitong*, a spring roll filled with
duck and vegetables. Ⓢ *Average main: Y50* ✉ *43 Cuihua Hutong,
Dongcheng District* ☎ *010/6524–5322* ▭ *No credit cards* Ⓜ *National
Art Musuem* ✛ *E3.*

XICHENG DISTRICT 西城区

Mostly contained within the West Second Ring Road, Xicheng extends west of the Forbidden City, and includes Beihai Park and Houhai. Dive into the hutong alleyways here and seek out local snacks and traditional eateries. Head to Houhai for old-style treats at Jiumen Xiaochi, or light Hangzhou style fare at Kong Yi Ji, complete with lake views. To the south, the district of Dashilan is quietly gentrifying, and is a good destination for hipster cafés and hole-in-the-wall eateries.

$ ✕ **Jing Wei Lou** (京味楼 *Jīngwèilóu*). "House of Beijing Flavors" makes
CHINESE up for its rather isolated location by having one of the widest selections of traditional Beijing fare in town. Dishes range from the austere, such as *ma doufu* (mung-bean pulp cooked in lamb fat), and *zha guanchang* (fried starch chips meant to imitate sausage), to more cultivated offerings, including Peking duck or slow-cooked lamb. The Beijing dessert platter is a tasty introduction to the city's long tradition of sweet snacks. The huge, open-plan dining room is bustling and fun, but can get rather smoky. ⓢ *Average main: Y78* ✉ *181 A Di'anmen Xidajie, Xicheng District* ☎ *010/6617–6514* ▭ *No credit cards* Ⓜ *Ping'anli* ✛ *C2.*

$ ✕ **Jinyang Fanzhuang.** Reliable, standard Shaanxi fare is the order of the
NORTHERN day at this slightly out-of-the-way restaurant—dishes might include the
CHINESE region's famous aromatic crispy duck, and "cat-ear" noodles (referring to their ovoid shape), stir-fried with meat and vegetables. End your meal with a "sweet happiness" pastry. Jinyang Fangzhuang is attached to the ancient courtyard home of Ji Xiaolan, a Qing Dynasty scholar, the chief compiler of the *Complete Library of the Four Branches of Literature.* You can visit the old residence without an admission fee and see Ji Xiaolan's study, where he wrote his famous essays. The crab-apple trees and wisteria planted during his lifetime still bloom in the courtyard. ⓢ *Average main: Y90* ✉ *241 Zhushikou Xi Dajie, Xicheng District* ☎ *010/6303–1669* ▭ *No credit cards* ✛ *D5.*

$ ✕ **Jiumen Xiaochi** (九门小吃). A dozen well-known restaurants, some
ECLECTIC dating back more than a century and threatened by the urban renewal of the old Qianmen business district, have found refuge in this large traditional courtyard house in Xiaoyou Hutong. Some of Beijing's oldest and most famous eateries have regrouped here under one roof, and it's become a popular tourist draw. These are our favorites: **Baodu Feng.** This vendor specializes in tripe. The excellent accompanying dipping sauce is a long-guarded family secret. You'll see upon entering that this stall has the longest line. **Chatang Li.** On offer here is miancha, a flour paste with either sweet or salty toppings. Miancha was created by an imperial chef who ground millet, poured boiling water into it, mixed it into a paste, and added brown sugar and syrup. The imperial family loved it, and it soon became a breakfast staple. **Niangao Qian.** This stall makes sticky rice layered with red-bean paste. It's the most popular sticky rice snack made by the Hui, or Chinese Muslims. **Yangtou Ma.** Known for thin-sliced meat from boiled lamb's head, this shop was once located on Ox Street, in the old Muslim quarter. **Doufunao Bai.** These folks sell soft bean curd, recognized for its delicate texture. It's best topped with braised lamb and mushrooms. **En Yuan Ju.** Sample the chaogeda, which are small,

stir-fried noodles with vegetables and meat. **Yue Sheng Zhai**. Line up for excellent jiang niurou (braised beef), shao yangrou (braised lamb), and zasui tang (mutton soup). **Xiaochang Chen**. The main ingredient of this vendor's dish is intestines, complemented with pork, bean curd, and huoshao (unleavened baked bread). The contents are simmered slowly in an aromatic broth. **Dalian Huoshao**. This stall serves pot stickers in the shape of old-fashioned satchels that the Chinese once wore. These pot stickers were the creation of the Yao family of Shunyi, who set up their small restaurant in the old Dong'an Market in 1876. $ *Average main: Y90* ⊠ *1 Xiaoyou Hutong, Gulou Xidajie, just off Houhai lake, Xicheng District* ✛ *C2.*

$$
SHANGHAINESE

✕ **Kong Yi Ji** (孔乙己 *Kǒngyǐjǐ*). Named for the down-and-out protagonist of a short story by Lu Xun (one of China's most famous writers), this elegant restaurant features dishes from Lu's hometown of Shaoxing, near Shanghai. Expect light, delicate offerings such as *longjing xiaren*—plump, peeled shrimp poached in aromatic green tea until ethereally soft. Also served is a wide selection of the region's famed *huangjiu* (sweet rice wine); it comes in heated silver pots and you sip from a shallow ceramic cup. The peaceful lakeside location is a perfect launching point for an after-dinner stroll; private rooms on the second floor have balconies with lovely lake views. $ *Average main: Y110* ⊠ *Southwest shore of Houhai, Deshengmennei Dajie, Xicheng District* ☎ *010/6618–4915* Ⓜ *Shichahai* ✛ *C2.*

$
CHINESE

✕ **Shaguo Ju** (沙锅居 *Shāguō jū*). Established in 1741, this time-honored brand serves a long-standing Manchu favorite—*bairou,* or "white-meat" pork casserole, which consists of thin strips of fatty pork concealing bok choy and glass noodles below. *Shaguo* is the Chinese term for a casserole pot, and there are many others on the menu at this perennially busy restaurant. Historically, Shaguo Ju emerged as a result of ceremonies held by imperial officials and wealthy Manchus in the Qing Dynasty, which included sacrificial offerings of whole pigs. The meat offerings were later given away to the city's night watchmen, who shared the "gifts" with friends and relatives. Such gatherings gradually turned into a small business, and the popularity of "white meat" became more widespread. $ *Average main: Y60* ⊠ *60 Xisi Nan Dajie, Xicheng District* ☎ *010/6602–1126* ▭ *No credit cards* Ⓜ *Xidan* ✛ *C4.*

CHAOYANG DISTRICT 朝阳区

Vast Chaoyang District extends east from Dongcheng, encompassing Beijing's Jianguomen diplomatic neighborhood, the Sanlitun bar area, the Central Business District, and several outdoor markets and upscale shopping malls. The large foreign population living and working here has encouraged many international restaurants to open, making this a fine place to sample dishes from around the world. If you're in Sanlitun, head to the third floor of Taikoo Li Village for the best selection of mid-range and affordable international eats. Home to most of the city's five-star hotels, Chaoyang is also where Beijing's nouveau riche flock for ultra-luxe dining.

Dishing up hotpot

$$ ✗ **Alameda.** Serving contemporary European fare with a Brazilian twist,
BRAZILIAN   Alameda is housed in a funky outdoor mall behind the hubbub of
Sanlitun's bar street. Though most lauded for its good-value weekday
prix-fixe lunch (88 RMB for two courses), which often features filet
mignon or codfish, on weekends the restaurant slow cooks a big batch
of authentic *feijoada*—Brazil's national dish—a hearty black-bean stew
with pork and rice. The glass walls and ceiling make it a bright, pleas-
ant place, but they do magnify the din of the crowded room. $ *Average
main: Y120* ✉ *Nali Mall, Sanlitun Lu, opposite Page One bookstore,
Chaoyang District* ☎ *010/6417–8084* Ⓜ *Tuanjiehu* ✛ *H2.*

$$$$ ✗ **Aria** (阿郦雅 *Ālìyǎ*). Enjoy deluxe hotel dining amid murals and
INTERNATIONAL   paintings of cheerful Italian Renaissance characters at Aria. Choose
from three settings: the posh dining and bar area on the first floor, inti-
mate private rooms upstairs, or alfresco on a terrace, protected from
the din of downtown by neatly manicured bushes and roses. A deca-
dent meal here would include foie gras and seafood bisque, followed
by one of the excellent steaks, with a playful deconstructed cheesecake
for dessert. The best deal at this elegant restaurant is the three-course
weekday business lunch with coffee or tea for Y188. $ *Average main:
Y300* ✉ *China World Hotel, 1 Jianguomenwai Dajie, Chaoyang Dis-
trict* ☎ *010/6505–2266* Ⓜ *Guomao* ✛ *H4.*

$ ✗ **Baoyuan Dumpling** (宝源饺子屋 *Bǎo yuán jiǎozi wū*). The fillings at
NORTHERN   this cheerfully homey joint go far beyond the standard pork and cab-
CHINESE   bage—the photo-filled menu includes dozens of creative filling options,
including beef, lamb, seafood, smoked bean curd, noodles, and just
about every vegetable you can name, many wrapped in bright skins of
purple, green, and orange, thanks to the addition of vegetable juice to

the dough. The minimum order for any kind of dumpling is two *liang* (100 grams, or about ten dumplings). There's a separate menu with a solid selection of family-style Chinese dishes—you'll see the popular *mapo doufu* (spoon-soft tofu with ground pork in a mildly spiced sauce) on many tables. Ⓢ *Average main: Y50* ✉ *North of 6 Maizidian Jie, Chaoyang District* ☎ *010/6586–4967* ▤ *No credit cards* ✛ *H2.*

$$
\begin{array}{ll}
\text{\$\$} & \text{✗ Bellagio (鹿港小镇 } Lùgǎng\ xiǎo \\
\text{TAIWANESE} & zhèn).
\end{array}
$$

$$ ✗ **Bellagio** (鹿港小镇 *Lùgǎng xiǎo*
TAIWANESE *zhèn*). This popular chain of glitzy, see-and-be-seen restaurants dishes up Taiwanese favorites to a largely young and upwardly mobile clientele. A delicious choice is the "three-cup chicken" (*sanbeiji*), served in a sizzling pot fragrant with ginger, garlic, and basil, and the wonderful crispy fried mixed mushrooms with XO sauce. Finish your meal with a Taiwan-style mountain of crushed ice topped with condensed milk and beans, mangoes, strawberries, or peanuts. This branch, beside the Workers' Stadium, is open until 4 am, making it a favorite with Beijing's clubbers. The smartly dressed staff—clad in black and white—sport identical short haircuts. Ⓢ *Average main: Y140* ✉ *6 Gongti Xilu, Chaoyang District* ☎ *010/6551–3533* ✛ *G3.*

$ ✗ **Biteapitta** (吧嗒饼 *Bātà bǐng*). Located upstairs in a dive behind
MIDDLE EASTERN Sanlitun's bar street, this bright and spacious kosher falafel joint is a breath of fresh air. Biteapitta has been filling Beijing tummies for over a decade with quick and tasty Mediterranean fare such as baba ghanoush, roasted chicken, and pita sandwiches brimming with yogurt, tahini, cucumbers, and tomatoes. The cheerful room encourages diners to linger over a lemonade or mint tea, with plenty of power outlets to help them catch up on emails. Ⓢ *Average main: Y80* ✉ *Tongli Studio, Sanlitun Houjie, 2F, Chaoyang District* ☎ *010/6467–2961* ✛ *G3.*

$ ✗ **Comptoirs de France Bakery** (法派 *Fǎpài*). This small chain of con-
FRENCH temporary French-managed patisseries is Beijing's go-to spot for Gallic cakes, pastries, and tarts. A variety of other goodies are on offer, like airy macaroons, flaky croissants, sandwiches in crunchy home-baked baguettes, and savory croquettes and quiches. Beside the standard coffee options, Comptoirs has a choice of unusual hot chocolate flavors. Try the Sichuan pepper–infused variety, which has a mouth-tingling kick. Ⓢ *Average main: Y80* ✉ *China Central Place, Building 15, N 102, 89 Jianguo Lu(just northeast of Xiandai Soho), Chaoyang District* ☎ *010/6530–5480* ⊕ *www.comptoirsdefrance.com* ▤ *No credit cards* Ⓜ *Dawanglu* ✛ *H4.*

3

$$$
NORTHERN
CHINESE

Fodor's Choice
★

✕ **Da Dong Roast Duck** (北京大董烤鸭店 *Běijīng Dàdǒng kǎoyā diàn*). You won't go wrong with the namesake dish at this world-famous eatery. Chef Dadong's version combines crisp, caramel-hued skin over meat less oily than tradition dictates, and is served with crisp sesame pockets in addition to the usual steamed pancakes. But the duck is only half the story. Dadong is an innovative chef and a student of many culinary styles, and his tome-like menu has some of the most original and luxe dishes in the city. Noodles are made from lobster meat, wafer-thin Kobe steaks are blow-torched tableside, and braised thorny sea cucumber is paired with a fresh lemon sorbet. Several locations offer various levels of decor and ambience; this one strikes the best balance between bling and tradition. $ *Average main: Y180* ✉ *1–2 Nanxincang Guoji Dasha, 22 Dongsishitiao, Chaoyang District* ☎ *010/5169–0328* ⚏ *Reservations essential* Ⓜ *Dongsishitiao* ✛ *H3.*

$$
TAIWANESE

Fodor's Choice
★

✕ **Din Tai Fung** (鼎泰丰 *Dǐngtàifēng*). Taipei's best known restaurant, now with several branches in Beijing, specializes in *xiaolong bao*—steamed dumplings filled with piping hot, aromatic soup. Crafted to an exacting standard, there are several beautifully wrapped variations on the standard pork ones, such as crab, chicken, shrimp, or a luxurious pork and black truffle variety. The *dandan* noodles, vegetable dishes, fried rice, and sweet dessert dumplings are also excellent. Service is friendly and efficient, and the dining room strikes an easy balance between refined and casual. $ *Average main: Y150* ✉ *24 Xinyuan Xili Zhongjie, Chaoyang District* ☎ *010/6462–4502* 🌐 *www.dintaifung. com.cn* ✛ *G2.*

$$$$
CHINESE

Fodor's Choice
★

✕ **Duck de Chine** (全鸭季 *Quányājì*). At what is hands-down the city's tastiest destination for Peking duck, the lacquered skin is simply more aromatically flavorful than the competition's. Cantonese father-son chef duo Peter and Wilson Lam spent months formulizing the perfect bird, roasted for exactly 65 minutes over jujube wood. The house-made sauce is a fabulous piece of food theater, and supporting dishes—order the duck liver on toast—are largely faultless. A daily lunchtime dim sum deal is excellent value. The simplicity of the loft-like, industrial space extends to the chefs, who in slate-gray robes wheel out each duck to the sound of a gong. A bottle of Bollinger from the adjoining champagne bar is claimed to be the perfect pairing, but the crisp prosecco, at a fraction of the price, cuts through the rich, oily duck just as well. If it's fully booked, there is a newer, larger location on Jinbao Jie. $ *Average main: Y220* ✉ *1949 The Hidden City, Courtyard 4, Gongti Beilu, Behind Pacific Century Place, Chaoyang District* ☎ *010/6501–8881* Ⓜ *Tuanjiehu* ✛ *H3.*

$
SICHUAN

✕ **Feiteng Yuxiang** (沸腾鱼乡 *Fèiténg yúxiāng*). Be warned: Sichuan spices can be addictive. This restaurant's signature dish is *shuizhuyu*, sliced fish cooked in an oily broth brimming with scarlet chili peppers and piquant peppercorns. The impossibly delicate fish melts in the mouth like butter, while the chilies and peppercorns tingle the lips. It's a sensory experience that heat-seekers will want to repeat over and over. Red-faced diners test the limits of their spice tolerance over *dandan* noodles and *koushuiji* ("mouthwatering") chicken, a salad dish of tender meat tossed with cilantro in spicy oil. The service is unfriendly but efficient. $ *Average main: Y90* ✉ *1 Gongti Beilu(Chunxiu Lu), Chaoyang District* ☎ *010/6417–4988* ✛ *G3.*

$
CHINESE
Fodor's Choice
★

✕ **Haidilao** (海底捞 *Hǎidǐlāo huǒguō*). You can expect to wait for a table at this trendy hotpot haven, but fortunately there's plenty to do while you're in line. Enjoy a complimentary manicure or shoeshine and munch on crunchy snacks to whet your appetite for the main draw: bubbling pots of broth (spices optional), a variety of thinly sliced meat, fresh veggies, greens, mushrooms, and more for dipping, and a DIY sauce bar with loads of choices. Order the "kungfu noodles," then sit back and marvel as a waiter twirls the noodles expertly at your table. More than a dozen locations are around town. $ *Average main: Y90* ✉ *2A Baijiazhuang Lu, Chaoyang District* ☎ *010/6595–2982* ⊕ *www. haidilao.com* ✛ *G3.*

$
NORTHERN
CHINESE

✕ **Hai Wan Ju** (海碗居 *Hǎiwǎnjū*). "Haiwan" means "a bowl as deep as the sea," a fitting name for an eatery that specializes in big bowls of hand-pulled noodles. A *xiao' er* (a "young brother" in a mandarin-collar shirt) greets you with a shout, echoed in thundering chorus by the rest of the staff. The hustle and bustle and rustic decor re-create the atmosphere of an old teahouse. There are two types of noodles: *guoshui,* noodles that have been rinsed and cooled; and *guotiao,* meaning "straight out of the pot," ideal for winter days. Vegetables, including diced celery, radish, green beans, bean sprouts, cucumber, and scallions, are placed on individual small dishes to be mixed in by hand. Hand-pulled noodles are deliciously doughy and chewy, a texture that can only be achieved by strong hands repeatedly stretching the dough. $ *Average main: Y50* ✉ *36 Songyu Nanlu, Chaoyang District* ☎ *010/8731–3518* Ⓜ *Mudanyuan* ✛ *G6.*

$$$
JAPANESE

✕ **Hatsune @ the Village** (隐泉日本料理 *Yǐnquán Rìběn liàolǐ*). Fusion-style California rolls are the name of the game at this hip and trendy Japanese eatery in the heart of Sanlitun. At this Beijing institution, the many unconventional rolls are made with everything from crab and avocado to imported foie gras. Fresh sashimi, crisp tempura, and tender grilled fish go well with the extensive sake menu; ask the manager for pairing recommendations. A cocktail list and range of imported beers make this recently renovated spot popular with a well-heeled, pre-party crowd. The original location is on Guanghua Lu in the CBD. $ *Average main: Y190* ✉ *Sanlitun Village South, 19 Sanlitun Rd., 3rd fl., S8–30, Chaoyang District* ☎ *010/6415–3939* ✎ *Reservations essential* Ⓜ *Tuanjiehu* ✛ *G2.*

$
SOUTHERN

✕ **Home Plate BBQ.** Ground zero for authentic American barbecue in Beijing, this busy joint grills, smokes, and slow-roasts mouthwateringly tender pulled pork, chopped brisket, and sticky ribs alongside wings, fried pickles, cornbread, slaw, chili cheese fries, and a solid cheeseburger. The huge, hipster-friendly Sanlitun location packs in a mixed party crowd, fueled by a wide range of imported American beers and bourbons (they've got A&W Root Beer too). If you've any appetite remaining after your meal, grab a slice of pecan or cherry pie or carrot cake. $ *Average main: Y80* ✉ *Unit 10, Electrical Research Institute, Sanlitun Lu, just past The Bookworm, Chaoyang District* ☎ *400-0967670* Ⓜ *Tuanjiehu* ✛ *H3.*

$
YUNNAN

✕**In and Out** (一坐一忘 *Yīzuò yīwàng*). On a tree-lined street in the heart of Beijing's embassy district, this large Yunnan restaurant, adorned with decorative crafts and paintings from China's southwest, serves as an excellent introduction to the light, fresh, and spicy flavors of the province. Staff in traditional dress dish up crispy potato pancakes, eggs stir-fried with fragrant jasmine flowers, tilapia folded over lemongrass and lightly grilled, and aromatic sticky rice stuffed inside long strips of bamboo. Comfy private rooms are perfect for groups; service can be rather absent at busy periods, so poke your head out of the door and holler. $ *Average main: Y90* ✉ *1 Sanlitun Beixiaojie, Chaoyang District* ☎ *010/8454–0086* ✛ *G2.*

$$$
CHINESE

✕**Jing Yaa Tang** (京雅堂 *Jīng Yātáng*). In the belly of the Opposite House hotel, this high-end Peking duck restaurant gently guides *laowai* (foreigners) through the crowd-pleasing hits of Chinese cuisine. A glassed-in kitchen, raised above the main dining room like a stage, reveals chefs slinging bronzed birds out of a blazing brick oven. The molasses-skinned duck is some of the best in town, and the accompaniments, like molecule-thin pancakes and a rich sauce infused with dates, completes a classy package. Accompanying dishes read like a roll call of Chinese family favorites, from mildly spiced kung pao chicken to Cantonese clay-pot fish, though the Taiwanese-style "three-cup" cod with basil ought to wow even the more seasoned palates. Save room for the delectable *dan ta*—Macau-style mini custard tarts. $ *Average main: Y200* ✉ *The Opposite House, 11 Sanlitun Lu, Chaoyang District* ☎ *010/6410–5230* ✛ *G2.*

$
NORTHERN
CHINESE

✕**Jingzun Roast Duck Restaurant** (京尊烤鸭 *Jīngzūn kǎoyā*). Locals and foreigners alike pack out this pleasant mid-range restaurant for affordable roast duck and tasty, varied Chinese fare with a Beijing slant. The roadside patio, garlanded by twinkling Christmas lights, is a lovely spot for warm-weather dining. Standout dishes include plump shrimp with lemongrass, stir-fried celery with smoked tofu, and the eye-wateringly hot Chinese mustard greens with sesame sauce. A basic wine list and local draft beer are available. To avoid disappointment, order your duck when you reserve a table. $ *Average main: Y90* ✉ *4 Chunxiu Lu, opposite Holiday Inn Express, Chaoyang District* ☎ *010/6417–4075* ✛ *G2.*

$$
HUNAN

✕**Karaiya Spice House** (辣屋 *Làwū*). Hunan cuisine, or *xiang cai*, is famous for its extensive use of colorful chili peppers, resulting in a "dry heat" rather than the more aromatic heat of Sichuan and its famous mouth-numbing peppercorn. This contemporary Hunanese eatery puts an international spin on the region's well-known flavors, like steamed fish with fresh diced chilies, sizzling spice-roasted duck, flame-baked shrimp wrapped in tinfoil, and a giant rack of melt-in-the-mouth, spice-encrusted pork ribs. The dining room is elegant without being showy, and service is friendly and attentive. $ *Average main: Y120* ✉ *Sanlitun Taikoo Li South, 19 Sanlitun Road, S9–30, Chaoyang District* ☎ *010/6415–3535* Ⓜ *Tuanjiehu* ✛ *G3.*

$$
PIZZA

✕**La Pizza** (辣匹萨 *Là bǐsà*). An Italian pizza man can often be seen working the massive brick oven at this glass-enclosed corner joint in Sanlitun, popular with Italian expats for the most authentic Napoli-style

pizzas in Beijing. The classic Margherita is top-notch, with a thin crust, bubbled and charred at the edges, topped with creamy buffalo mozzarella and a perfectly tangy tomato sauce. Or you can say "when in Beijing" and try the Peking duck pizza, one of many available options. A good selection of antipasti, salads, and pastas round out the straightforward menu. ⑤ *Average main: Y110* ✉ *3.3 Mall, 33 Sanlitun Lu, Chaoyang District* ☎ *010/5136–5582* ✛ *G3.*

$$ ✕**Madam Zhu's Kitchen** (汉舍中国菜馆 *Hàn shě zhōngguó càiguǎn*).
CHINESE This sprawling basement venue offers a whirlwind culinary tour of Chinese regional styles in a brightly lit space decked out with sofas, green plants, and stylish photographs of the owner and her friends. Madam Zhu is in fact the founder of the popular Sichuan chain Yuxiang Renjia. Here she's branched out with confident updates of classic Chinese dishes, including delicate "lion's head" meatballs (a Huaiyang dish from Yangzhou) served with crab roe and freshwater bass, crispy duck, tender black-pepper tenderloin, and poached egg whites filled with crabmeat. A great place to discover a contemporary take on Chinese food unconstrained by tradition or convention. ⑤ *Average main: Y130* ✉ *Vantone Center, 6A Chaoyangmenwai Dajie, B1/F, Bldg. D, Chaoyang District* ☎ *010/5907–1625* Ⓜ *Dongdaqiao* ✛ *G4.*

$$ ✕**Makye Ame** (玛吉阿米 *Mǎjíāmǐ*). Fluttering prayer flags lead up to the
TIBETAN second-floor entrance of this Tibetan restaurant, where a pile of *mani* (prayer) stones and a large prayer wheel greet you. Elegant Tibetan Buddhist trumpets, lanterns, and handicrafts adorn the walls, and the kitchen serves a range of hearty dishes that run well beyond the region's staples of *tsampa* (roasted barley flour) and yak-butter tea. Try the vegetable *pakoda* (a deep-fried dough pocket filled with vegetables), curry potatoes, grilled mushrooms, and cumin-roasted lamb ribs. There are live Tibetan performances most nights. ⑤ *Average main: Y110* ✉ *11 Xiushui Nanjie, 2nd fl., Chaoyang District* ☎ *010/6506–9616* Ⓜ *Jianguomen* ✛ *G4.*

$$ ✕**Middle 8th** (中八楼 *Zhōngbālóu*). In the heart of Sanlitun's shopping
YUNNAN and dining district, this trendy Yunnan restaurant, known as a celebrity haunt, is a great place to wrap up a day's exploring. Deep earth tones, soaring ceilings, and traditional handicrafts are a relaxing setting in which to enjoy sticky-sweet pineapple rice, sizzling platters of Yunnan beef with fried potatoes, "crossing the bridge" rice noodles, and the restaurant's signature *paijiu* mushrooms. Don't miss the delicious staple of sweet-potato rice with mushrooms and chives. The libation of choice here is a tall bamboo pitcher of *mijiu*, a cloudy, low-alcohol rice wine with a sweet, fragrant taste. ⑤ *Average main: Y110* ✉ *Taikoo Li, Sanlitun Lu, 4th fl., Chaoyang District* ☎ *010/6415–8858* Ⓜ *Tuanjiehu* ✛ *G3.*

$$$$ ✕**Mio.** Playful creativity is the hallmark of this upscale Italian restau-
ITALIAN rant in the Four Seasons. Tokyo-based Spin Design Studio has taken colored crystal and chrome to gaudy heights in an interior scheme that is a contrast to Head Chef Marco Calenzo's earthy pasta dishes (try the *pici*, a hand-rolled noodle slightly fatter than spaghetti). A pair of brick ovens turns out gourmet pizzas—Calenzo's "white pizza" is made of wood-fired focaccia dough topped with organic egg and shavings of

imported white truffle. The desserts are divine, and the wine list is extensive. $ *Average main: Y280* ⊠ *Four Seasons Hotel, 48 Liangmaqiao Lu, 2nd fl., Chaoyang District* ☎ *010/5695–8858* Ⓜ *Liangmaqiao* ⊹ *H1.*

$$$
INTERNATIONAL

✕ **Mosto.** A hit with the cosmopolitan crowd, this casual fine-dining restaurant rarely fails to impress. The open kitchen turns out innovative, good-value international fare with a Latino twist, such as a braised oxtail and black bean napoleon, grilled tuna steak with *mojo* (a spicy sauce), and a famous chocolate soufflé with Sichuan-pepper ice cream. A solid wine list (there's also wine-paired set menu) and well-mixed cocktails keep the upwardly mobile diners here in high spirits. In warm weather, try to reserve one of the few balcony tables. $ *Average main: Y180* ⊠ *Nali Patio, 81 Sanlitun Beilu, 3rd fl., Chaoyang District* ☎ *010/5208–6030* ⊕ *www.mostobj.com* ⊹ *G2.*

$$$
ASIAN

✕ **My Humble House** (寒舍 *Hánshè*). After a year or so in the restaurant wilderness, this much-heralded contemporary Asian eatery is now in Parkview Green, one of the city's most original and appealing shopping malls. From the decor to the dinnerware, there's nothing really humble here. Designed by a Japanese architect, the skylit dining room is laid out around a pool and flanked with live bamboo. Delicately prepared Southeast Asian dishes, such as Malaysian *laksa* are joined by Chinese fare, including crisp-skinned Peking duck. $ *Average main: Y180* ⊠ *Parkview Green, 9 Dong Da Qiao Lu, L2-12, Chaoyang District* ☎ *010/8518–8811* Ⓜ *Dongdaqiao* ⊹ *G4.*

$
NORTHERN CHINESE
Fodor's Choice
★

✕ **Najia Xiaoguan** (那家小馆 *Nàjiā xiǎoguǎn*). The Manchu ruled all of China during the Qing Dynasty, but it is their roots as a semi-pastoral people living north of the Great Wall that are celebrated at this excellent restaurant. Dishes like pot-braised venison reflect the Manchus' love of hunting, and the hearty, tender ox ribs here would have been ideal fortification for the far northeast's freezing winters. Huge wooden tables, a decent wine list, and excellent service make the affordable fare here even more enjoyable; expect to wait for a table at peak times. $ *Average main: Y90* ⊠ *10 Yonganli, South of LG Twin Towers, Chaoyang District* ☎ *010/6567–3663* ✍ *Reservations essential* Ⓜ *Yong'Anli* ⊹ *G4.*

$$
AMERICAN

✕ **Nola.** This is the only place in Beijing—perhaps all of China—to get genuine New Orleans grits, jambalaya (peppered with dark sausage), traditional gumbo, and other Cajun and Creole fare. For a quick snack, grab a po'boy served in a crusty roll with a side of fries; the pork tenderloin with bacon-wrapped plums will do for bigger appetites. A lovely rooftop terrace makes for romantic alfresco dining overlooking leafy embassy gardens and nearby Ritan Park. Finish with warm apple cobbler and a melting scoop of nutmeg ice cream. $ *Average main: Y110* ⊠ *11A Xiushui Street South, Chaoyang District* ☎ *010/8563–6215* Ⓜ *Yong'Anli* ⊹ *G4.*

$
CANTONESE

✕ **Noodle Bar** (面吧 *Miàn bā*). With a dozen seats surrounding an open kitchen, this petite dining room next to Duck de Chine lives large when it comes to flavor. The brief menu lists little more than beef brisket, tendon, and tripe, which are stewed to tender perfection and added to delicious noodles, hand-pulled while you wait. $ *Average main: Y80*

⊠ *1949 The Hidden City, Gongti Beilu, behind Pacific Century Place, Chaoyang District* ☎ *010/6501–1949* Ⓜ *Tuanjiehu* ✛ *G3.*

$ ✕ **Noodle Loft** (面酷 *Miànkù*). Watch the dough masters work in a flurry while you slurp your noodles at this bright and ritzy restaurant. A seat at the bar lets you observe chefs snipping, shaving, and pulling dough into various styles of noodles amid clouds of steam. The black-and-white decor plays backdrop to a trendy crowd; do as they do and order Shaanxi-style "cat's ears" (*mao' er duo*), so named for the way the nips of dough are curled around the chef's thumb into an ear shape. They are then stir-fried with pork, eggs, cabbage, and wood-ear mushrooms. Ⓢ *Average main: Y60* ⊠ *Fumu Dasha, 33 Guangshun Beidajie, 2nd fl., Chaoyang District* ☎ *010/8472–4700* ✛ *H5.*

NORTHERN CHINESE

$$$$ ✕ **Okra.** This upscale sushi bar, restaurant and cocktail joint is the work of Max Levy, a New Orleans native who became the only non-Japanese sushi chef at New York's famous Sushi Yasuda. Daily *kaiseki* (traditional set menus) star pearlescent sushi and sashimi, dainty hot dishes like slow-cooked octopus, and countless other classy snacks, like the signature *yakitoro*—charcoal-roasted fatty tuna with leeks, garlic, and grill sauce—or the roasted eel and avocado, artfully wrapped in a thin slice of cucumber. The sparse, simple decor doesn't quite match the sophistication of the food; if you like to watch the chefs slicing and dicing up close, book a spot at the seven-seat sushi bar. Ⓢ *Average main: Y450* ⊠ *Courtyard 4, Gongti Beilu, 1949-The Hidden City, Chaoyang District* ☎ *010/6593–5087* ⏱ *Closed Mon.* Ⓜ *Tuanjiehu* ✛ *H3.*

SUSHI

$$$$ ✕ **One East** (东方路一号 *Dōngfāng lù yīhào*). Contemporary fine dining with a major North American influence brings business travelers to the Hilton's flagship restaurant. In addition to succulent steaks, the kitchen serves lighter fare like sea bass with a sweet garlic puree. Or go large with one of Beijing's fanciest burgers, made with Wagyu beef and served with foie gras and black truffle. You'll find a very good wine list here, enjoyed by a crowd that's a mix of loyal Beijing residents and hotel guests drifting down from their rooms. Ⓢ *Average main: Y220* ⊠ *Beijing Hilton Hotel, 1 Dongfang Lu, 2/F, Chaoyang District* ☎ *010/5865–5030* Ⓜ *Liangmaqiao* ✛ *H1.*

AMERICAN

$ ✕ **One Pot.** Chef-owner Andrew Ahn has toned down the glamour at this excellent Korean restaurant, formerly known as Ssam, to focus on reinventing street snacks. Think *kimbap* (Korean-style sushi rolls), rich miso crab stew, and the unpronounceable *tteokbokki*—a popular street food of rice cakes and fish cakes in sweet chili sauce. The twist here is that the rice is stuffed with cheese and stewed tableside in a range of inventive sauces, such as pumpkin gravy. The tiramisu, made with a reduction of the Korean spirit *soju*, is one of the few Ssam survivors. After your meal, order a fabulous cup of coffee (the imported beans are ground table-side) to set you up for a drink or three in one of the many Sanlitun bars nearby. Ⓢ *Average main: Y100* ⊠ *Sanlitun SOHO, Gongti Beilu, Tower 2, B1–238, Chaoyang District* ☎ *010/5395–9475* Ⓜ *Tuanjiehu* ✛ *H3.*

KOREAN

$$$$
ITALIAN
Fodor's Choice
★

✕ **Opera Bombana.** Italian chef Umberto Bombana won three Michelin stars for his acclaimed Hong Kong restaurant. This Beijing franchise could be seen as a bit of a cash-in, though under the stewardship of former Sureno chef Marino D'Antonio it still makes a strong case for being Beijing's best Italian, with delectable signatures like langoustine carpaccio, and Wagyu beef ravioli with pungent Gorgonzola sauce. It's a gorgeous dining environment, too, especially considering its location inside a high-end shopping mall. Opera Bombana is also serious about baking; grab a bag of *bomboloni* to go from the bakery counter—these sugary donuts filled with a rich lemony custard are sinfully good. $ *Average main: Y260 ⊠ Parkview Green, 9 Dongdaqiao Lu, LG2-21, Chaoyang District ☎ 010/5690–7177 Ⓜ Dongdaqiao ⊕ G4.*

$$
NORTHERN
CHINESE

✕ **Peking Duck, Private Kitchen** (私房烤鸭 *Guǒguǒ sīfáng kǎoyā*). Doing away with the banquet-style scene that accompanies the more traditional roast duckeries in Beijing, diners here lounge on comfortable sofas in a moderately sized, warmly lit dining room where the signature dish is made to exacting standards. The set menus, which all include succulent Peking duck, are good value and include other popular dishes such as kung pao shrimp and green beans in sesame sauce. $ *Average main: Y120 ⊠ Vantone Center, 6A Chaowai Dajie, FS2015, Chaoyang District ☎ 010/5907–1920 ☺ No lunch. Ⓜ Dongdaqiao ⊕ G4.*

$$$$
VEGETARIAN

✕ **Pure Lotus** (净心莲 *Jìngxīnliányu*). You'd never guess, but this glamorous vegetarian haven is owned and operated by Buddhist monks. The warm jewel tones and traditional artwork will calm and restore frazzled nerves, and dishes served on mother-of-pearl amid wafting dry ice will delight the senses. The exhaustive, expensive menu artfully transcends the typical tofu and salad offerings by including mock meat dishes, such as Sichuan-style "fish" or Beijing-style "duck" (it's all made from wheat gluten and soy protein.) Alcohol is off the menu, but a wide range of teas and fruit drinks are available. $ *Average main: Y260 ⊠ Tongguang Building, 12 Nongzhanguan Nanlu, Chaoyang District ☎ 010/6592-3627 Ⓜ Tuanjiehu ⊕ H3.*

$$
MIDDLE EASTERN

✕ **Rumi Persian Grill** (入迷 *Rùmí*). Soaring ceilings and enormous mirrors decorated with Arabic script create a casually exotic atmosphere at this all-white Persian favorite. Portions are family-sized, and a mixed appetizer of three choices from the menu is more than enough for a summertime supper. Standouts include Persian flat bread with thick hummus, grilled chicken in a tangy pomegranate sauce, tender marinated lamb chops, or a platter of generously sized meat and seafood kebabs. For dessert, take your rosewater and pistachio ice cream out to the patio to enjoy the breeze. The Baha'i owner doesn't offer alcohol, but you're welcome to bring your own. $ *Average main: Y130 ⊠ 1–1A Gongti Beilu, Chaoyang District ☎ 010/8454–3838 ⊕ www.rumigrill.com ⊟ No credit cards Ⓜ Tuanjiehu ⊕ H3.*

$$
JAPANESE
Fodor's Choice
★

✕ **Sake Manzo.** As Beijing's best all-round Japanese *izakaya*-style restaurant, this is the place for frothy mugs of Asahi draft and perfectly executed dishes like beer-marinated fried chicken with vinegar, a crisp pork cutlet under a mound of diced greens, sublime soba noodles, and some of the best sushi and sashimi in the city for the price. A white-walled, bustling dining area gets the atmosphere just right; larger groups will be ushered to comfy private rooms with sunken seating. The slow-cooked pork belly in miso broth with a poached egg gets rave reviews. Ask the helpful waitstaff for sake recommendations. $ *Average main: Y140* ✉ *8A Tuanjiehu Beisitiao, Chaoyang District* ☎ 010/6436–1608 ✚ *H3.*

$$$$
MEDITERRANEAN

✗ **Sureño.** Housed in the city's hippest hotel, this chic, sceney eatery with an open kitchen is a great spot for people-watching over a glass of wine and excellent tapas. A wood-fired oven takes center stage, baking exquisite thin-crust pizzas and grilled meats, including Wagyu steaks, tuna, and tender baby chicken. The Florentine steak (for two or more) is a hefty showstopper. A basement garden is a pleasant haven for brunch before kicking off a weekend shopping trip at the luxury boutiques of Taikoo Li Sanlitun North. $ *Average main: Y300* ✉ *The Opposite House, 11 Sanlitun Lu, Chaoyang District* ☎ 010/6417–6688 ⊕ *www.surenorestaurant.com* ⌂ *Reservations essential* ✚ *G2.*

$$
INDIAN

✗ **Taj Pavilion** (泰姬楼 *Tàijī lóu*). Since 1998, Beijing's best Indian restaurant has been serving up the classics, like chicken tikka masala, *palak paneer* (creamy spinach with cheese), *rogan josh* (tender lamb in curry sauce), and a range of grilled meats and fish from the tandoor oven. Wash it all down with a cup of masala tea flavored with cardamom, cloves, and ginger. Consistently good service and an informal atmosphere make this a well-loved neighborhood haunt. Newer branches have opened in Lido and Shunyi. $ *Average main: Y130* ✉ *China Overseas Plaza North Tower, No 8 Guanghua Dong Li, Jianguomenwai Ave., 2nd fl., F2-03, Chaoyang District* ☎ 010/6505–5866 ⊕ *www.thetajpavilion.com* Ⓜ *Guomao* ✚ *H4.*

$$$
MEDITERRANEAN

✗ **Taverna+** (塔瓦娜 *Tǎwǎnà*). Refined Mediterranean dishes are a marked contrast to the industrial-chic interior of this former factory. The young, well-heeled crowd fuels up on tasty tapas and wine before heading out into the nightclubs of Sanlitun. Perch yourself on the luxe leather seats against exposed brick walls and sip on a selection from the modern wine list. Or dig in for a heftier meal of authentic paella (served in wide cast-iron pans), roast suckling pig, baby-back ribs, and generous salads. $ *Average main: Y180* ✉ *1949—The Hidden City, Courtyard 4, Gongti Beilu, Chaoyang District* ☎ 010/6501–8882 ⊙ *No lunch.* Ⓜ *Tuanjiehu* ✚ *H3.*

$
CHINESE

✗ **Three Guizhou Men** (三个贵州人 *Sānge Guìzhōurén*). The widespread popularity of Guizhou cuisine and its trademark spicy-sour flavors prompted three Guizhou artist friends to set up shop in Beijing (their paintings and sculptures decorate the dining area). There are many dishes here to recommend, but among the best are "beef on fire" (pieces of beef placed on a bed of chives over burning charcoal) accompanied by ground chilies; pork ribs; spicy lamb with mint leaves; the region's signature *suantangyu* (fish in a spicy-sour soup), and *mi doufu*, a rice-flour cake in spicy sauce. $ *Average main: Y90* ✉ *Jianwai SOHO, Bldg. 7, 39 Dong Sanhuan Zhonglu, Chaoyang District* ☎ 010/5869–0598 Ⓜ *Guomao* ✚ *G5.*

$$$
SICHUAN
Fodor's Choice
★

✗ **Transit** (渡金湖 *Dùjīnhú*). This is one of Beijing's hottest contemporary Chinese restaurants, and we're not just talking about the chilies. Located in the upscale Sanlitun Village North, this glam Sichuan establishment marries the region's famous spicy dishes with slick service and a designer interior entirely at home amid the surrounding luxury boutiques. The region's fiery classics are elegantly prepared; the *koushuiji* (cold chicken appetizer dressed in chili oil), the mouth-numbing *dandan* noodles, and the crisp stir-fried eel with chili have garnered rave reviews. Unlike most Chinese restaurants, Transit serves fabulous cocktails and has an extensive, if pricey, wine list. $ *Average main: Y160* ✉ *Sanlitun Village North, N4–36, Chaoyang District* ☎ *010/6417–9090* 🍴 *Reservations essential* ⊗ *No lunch* ✛ *G2.*

$$ ✕ **Xiao Wangfu** (小王府 *Xiǎowángfǔ*). A foreigner-friendly introduction to Chinese homestyle cooking, this restaurant is popular with the city's expat community. Thanks to rampant reconstruction, it's moved from location to location as neighborhoods have been torn down, but fans can now happily find the newest site inside Ritan Park, located in a small, two-story building with an attractive rooftop area overlooking the park's greenery. The Peking duck is solid, and the *laziji* (deep-fried chicken smothered in dried red chilies) is just spicy enough. The second-floor dining area overlooks the main floor, with plenty of natural sunlight pouring through the surrounding windows. $ *Average main: Y110* ✉ *Ritan Park North Gate, Chaoyang District* ☎ *010/8561–5985* Ⓜ *Jianguomen* ✛ *G4.*

CHINESE

$$$ ✕ **Yotsuba** (四叶 *Sìyè*). This tiny, unassuming restaurant serves arguably the best sushi in the city. The interior comprises a sushi counter manned by a Japanese master working continuously and silently, and two small sunken tatami-style dining areas that evoke an old-time Tokyo restaurant. The seafood is flown in from Tokyo's Tsukiji fish market; the daily chef's selection (about Y280) is a wooden board of sushi made from the best catches of the day. Reservations are a must for this dinner-only Chaoyang gem. There are three locations around town. $ *Average main: Y200* ✉ *2 Xinyuan Xili Zhongjie, Building 2, Chaoyang District* ☎ *010/6464–2365* 🍴 *Reservations essential* ⊗ *No lunch* ✛ *G2.*

JAPANESE
Fodor's Choice
★

$ ✕ **Yuxiang Renjia** (渝乡人家 *Yúxiāngrénjiā*). Of the thousands of Sichuan restaurants in Beijing, the Yuxiang Renjia chain is often the choice of Sichuan natives living in the capital. Huge earthen vats filled with pickled vegetables, hanging bunches of dried peppers and garlic, and servers in traditional garb evoke the Sichuan countryside. The restaurant does an excellent job with classics like *gongbao jiding* (diced chicken stir-fried with peanuts and dried peppers) and *ganbian sijidou* (green beans stir-fried with olive leaves and minced pork). Thirty different Sichuan snacks are served for lunch on weekends, all at very reasonable prices. There are more than a dozen locations around the city. $ *Average main: Y70* ✉ *Lianhe Dasha, 101 Chaowai Dajie, 5th fl., Chaoyang District* ☎ *010/6588–3841* ⊕ *www.yuxiangrenjia.com* Ⓜ *Chaoyangmen* ✛ *G4.*

SICHUAN

HAIDIAN DISTRICT 海淀区

Whether you're visiting the Summer Palace, Beijing's university area, or the electronics mecca of Zhongguancun, you certainly won't go hungry. And if you're hankering for the familiar, wander around the university campuses and pick one of the many Western-style restaurants or cafés catering to the local and international student population.

3

$$$$
CHINESE

✕ **Baijia Dayuan** (白家大宅门 *Báijiā dà zháimén*). Staff dressed in richly hued, Qing-dynasty attire welcome you at this grand courtyard house, the Bai family mansion. Bowing slightly, they'll say *"Nin jixiang"* ("May you have good fortune"). The mansion's spectacular setting was once the garden of Prince Li, son of the first Qing emperor. Cao Xueqin, the author of the Chinese classic *Dream of the Red Chamber,* is said to have lived here as a boy. Featured delicacies (ordered via an iPad) include bird's-nest soup, braised sea cucumber, abalone, and authentic imperial snacks. On weekends, diners are treated to short, live performances of Beijing opera. After dinner, explore the beautiful garden. ⑤ *Average main: Y250* ⊠ *15 Suzhou St., Haidian District* ☎ *010/6265–4186* ⌂ *Reservations essential* Ⓜ *Suzhoujie* ✛ *C1.*

$$
NORTHERN CHINESE

✕ **Ding Ding Xiang** (鼎鼎香 *Dǐngdǐngxiāng*). Hotpot restaurants are plentiful in northern China, but few do it better than Ding Ding Xiang, a self-proclaimed "hotpot paradise." Diners order a variety of meats, sliced paper thin, as well as seafood, mushrooms, tofu, and vegetables to be cooked at the table in a wide selection of broths (the wild mushroom broth is a must for mycophiles), or, better yet, order a partitioned pot to accommodate multiple soup varieties. The dipping sauces, used in the final stage of eating, are thick and delicious. Despite the surly service and gaudy decor, this place is perennially crowded. ⑤ *Average main: Y120* ⊠ *Bldg 7, Guoxing Jiayuan, Shouti Nanlu, Haidian District* ☎ *010/8835–7775* ▭ *No credit cards* Ⓜ *Baishiqiao South* ✛ *C1* ⑤ *Average main: Y120* ⊠ *40 Dongzhong Jie, Dongzhimenwai, Dongcheng District* ☎ *010/6417–9289* ✛ *C1.*

$$$$
JAPANESE FUSION

✕ **Naoki** (直树怀石料理餐厅 *Zhíshùhuáishí liàolǐcāntīng*). Few restaurants in the capital are able to approach the level of refinement found at this Japanese haven, set in the restored imperial grounds of the Aman Resort at the Summer Palace. The set menus introduces diners to chef Naoki Okumura's multi-course meals (*kaiseki*), which marry French cooking techniques to Japanese traditions, such as seared foie gras served on steamed egg custard. If the weather is fine, sit outside by the reflecting pool for a calming, romantic experience. ⑤ *Average main: Y600* ⊠ *Aman at Summer Palace, 1 Gongmenqian Jie, Summer Palace, Haidian District* ☎ *010/5987–9999* ⌂ *Reservations essential* ⊙ *No lunch.* Ⓜ *Xiyuan* ✛ *C1.*

$$
TAIWANESE

✕ **Shin Yeh** (欣叶 *Xīnyè*). The focus at this smartly appointed eatery is on authentic, fresh Taiwanese flavors. Try *caipudan,* a scrumptious turnip omelet, or the poetically named *fotiaoqiang* ("Buddha jumping over the wall"), a delicate soup full of seafood and medicinal herbs. For something a little less austere, the crisp barbecued pigeon is a lip-smacking delight; the accompanying tot of lemon juice is meant to counteract all that oil. Last but definitely not least, try the *mashu,* a glutinous rice cake rolled in ground peanuts. ⑤ *Average main: Y110* ⊠ *Xin Zhongguancun Shopping Center, 19 Zhongguancun Dajie, 4th fl., Haidian District* ☎ *010/8248–6288* Ⓜ *Zhongguancun* ✛ *C1.*

WHERE TO STAY

Updated by
Tom O'Malley

The first real wave of tourists to visit China in the early 1980s had little need for guidebooks—foreigners were only allowed to stay in ugly, state-run, Stalinist-style blocks. But times have changed. Now Beijing has it all: a glorious glut of the world's best hotel brands; cheap and breezy places to make your base; intimate boutique beauties; and historical courtyard conversions.

The main hubs for hotels are around Wangfujing (Beijing's famous shopping strip), in the vicinity of the northeast Third Ring Road, and along Chang'an/Jianguomen, one of the city's main thoroughfares that connect the Central Business District (CBD) to Tiananmen Square. This is where you'll find the city's most recognizable and reputable hotels, all of which offer luxurious rooms, international-standard facilities, and attentive service. Don't despair if you're on a budget: there are plenty of decent dwellings next to the tourist trail at a fraction of the cost.

"Location, location, location" should be your mantra when booking a Beijing hotel, especially if you're only in town for a few days. It's a big city: there's no point schlepping halfway across it for one particular hotel when a similar option is available in a more convenient area. Consider where you'll be going (Summer Palace? Forbidden City? Great Wall?), then pick your bed. Busy execs should choose wisely in order to avoid getting snarled up in Beijing's horrific traffic, which most likely means staying a little farther west near Financial Street or in the other commercial hub of Guomao (the CBD) in the east. Those in search of nightlife will want to be by Sanlitun, home to the capital's best bars and restaurants. If you're after a one-of-a-kind Beijing experience, check out the city's courtyard hotels. These distinctive lodgings are often converted *siheyuan*—traditional homes built as residential quadrangles among the hutongs.

BEST BETS FOR BEIJING LODGING

Fodor's offers a selective listing of quality lodging experiences in every price range, from the city's best budget beds to its most sophisticated luxury hotels. Here we've compiled our top recommendations by price and experience. The very best properties—in other words, those that provide a particularly remarkable experience in their price range—are designated in the listings with the Fodor's Choice logo.

Fodor's Choice ★

3+1 Bedrooms, p. 135

Aman at Summer Palace, p. 150

EAST, Beijing, p. 146

Four Seasons Hotel Beijing, p. 146

Grace Beijing, p. 146

Grand Hyatt Beijing, p. 139

Hilton Beijing Wangfujing, p. 147

Holiday Inn Express Beijing Dongzhimen, p. 140

Langham Place, Beijing Capital Airport, p. 152

Lüsongyuan, p. 141

The Opposite House, p. 149

The Orchid, p. 141

Park Hyatt Beijing, p. 149

Peninsula Beijing, p. 141

Raffles Beijing Hotel, p. 142

The Regent, p. 142

Shan Li Retreats, p. 152

St. Regis, p. 149

Temple Hotel Beijing, p. 143

Waldorf Astoria Beijing, p. 143

Best by Price

$

Day's Inn Forbidden City Beijing, p. 138

Double Happiness Courtyard, p. 139

Holiday Inn Express Beijing Dongzhimen, p. 140

Hotel Kapok, p. 140

Kempinski Hotel Beijing Lufthansa Center, p. 148

The Orchid, p. 141

Park Plaza Beijing, p. 141

Sofitel Wanda, p. 149

$$

Crowne Plaza Beijing Chaoyang U-Town, p. 145

Grace Beijing, p. 146

Red Capital Residence, p. 142

Shangri-La Hotel, Beijing, p. 151

$$$

Hilton Beijing Wangfujing, p. 147

The Opposite House, p. 149

Peninsula Beijing, p. 141

St. Regis, p. 149

$$$$

Aman at Summer Palace, p. 150

Four Seasons Hotel Beijing, p. 146

JW Marriott Hotel Beijing, p. 147

Park Hyatt Beijing, p. 149

Waldorf Astoria Beijing, p. 143

Best by Experience

BEST CONCIERGE

Four Seasons Hotel Beijing, p. 146

Raffles Bejing Hotel, p. 142

BEST SPA

Aman at Summer Palace, p. 150

Fairmont Beijing, p. 146

Peninsula Beijing, p. 141

MOST KID-FRIENDLY

Grand Hyatt Beijing, p. 139

Grandma's Place (Schoolhouse Hotels), p. 151

Kerry Centre Hotel, p. 148

BEST FOR BUSINESS

China World Hotel, p. 144

EAST, Beijing, p. 146

Ritz-Carlton Beijing, Financial Street, p. 144

BEST INTERIOR DESIGN

3+1 Bedrooms, p. 135

Du Ge, p. 139

Grace Beijing, p. 146

The Opposite House, p. 149

Waldorf Astoria Beijing, p. 143

4

PLANNING

MONEY-SAVING TIPS

Beijing's busiest seasons are spring and fall, with summer following closely behind. Special rates can be had during the low season, so make sure to ask about deals involving weekends or longer stays. If you are staying more than one night, you can often get some free perks—ask about free laundry service or free airport transfers. Children 16 and under can normally share a room with their parents at no extra charge—although there may be a modest fee for adding an extra bed. Ask about this when making your reservation.

HOTEL RATINGS

The local rating system doesn't correspond to those of any other country. What is called a five-star hotel here might only warrant three or four elsewhere. This is especially true of the state-run hotels, which often seem to be rated higher than they deserve.

TIPPING

Tipping isn't the norm in China—a remnant from the country's Communist past. This may perhaps partly explain why service, in general, isn't as smooth or smiling as you would normally expect, even in the more established hotels.

LANGUAGE

English isn't widely spoken in Beijing, so it's best to print out the address (in Chinese) and telephone number of your hotel before departure. This will save you a lot of trouble upon arrival—taxi drivers, in particular, will be thankful for your forethought. If you're absolutely set on staying somewhere with English-speaking staff, look to the international chains, but call ahead, if you can, to check up on their language proficiency.

HOTEL REVIEWS

Listed alphabetically within neighborhoods.

Use the coordinate (✛ A1) at the end of each listing to locate a site on the corresponding map.

WHAT IT COSTS IN YUAN			
$	$$	$$$	$$$$
FOR TWO PEOPLE under Y1,100	Y1,101–Y1,400	Y1,401–Y1,800	over Y1,800

Prices are for two people in a standard double room in high season, excluding 10% to 15% service charge.

DONGCHENG DISTRICT 东城区

Dongcheng District covers the eastern half of Beijing's inner core, stretching from the Forbidden City in the center out to the Second Ring Road, which marks the boundary of the old city walls. This area incorporates some of the city's most important historic sites. The hotels off Dongchang'an Jie and Wangfujing Dajie are within walking distance of Tiananmen Square.

$$
HOTEL

Fodor's Choice
★

3+1 Bedrooms. Modern, minimalist design—pure white interiors, freestanding bathtubs, individual courtyards—meets old Beijing at this intimate four-bedroom boutique hotel within the quaint alleyways (*hutongs*) near the historic Drum and Bell towers. **Pros:** spacious rooms; free in-room Wi-Fi and minibar; private terraces. **Cons:** no health club; no restaurants; occasionally absent service. $ *Rooms from: Y1,200* ⊠ *17 Zhangwang Hutong, Jiu Gulou Dajie, Drum Tower, Dongcheng District* ☎ *010/6404–7030* ⊕ *www.3plus1bedrooms.com* ⌇*3 rooms, 1 suite* ⦿*Breakfast* Ⓜ *Gulou Dajie* ✛ *C2.*

$$$
HOTEL

Beijing Hotel (北京饭店 *Běijīng fàndiàn*). Occupying a third of the original Grand Hotel de Pekin complex (with Raffles and the Grand Hotel the other tenants), this venerable hotel retains a modicum of old-world charm, its impressive lobby and enviable location next to the Forbidden City and Tiananmen Square making up for the rather outmoded decor. **Pros:** short walk from the Forbidden City; close to shopping; a sense of history. **Cons:** mediocre restaurants; old-fashioned; a lack of local nightlife. $ *Rooms from: Y1,500* ⊠ *33 Dongchang'an Jie, off Wangfujing Dajie, Dongcheng District* ☎ *010/6513–7766* 🖷 *010/6523–2395* ⊕ *www.chinabeijinghotel.com.cn* ⌇*733 rooms, 51 suites* ⦿*No meals* Ⓜ *Wangfujing* ✛ *D5.*

$$
HOTEL

Beijing International (北京国际饭店 *Běijīng Guójì fàndiàn*). Located on the city's main east–west central axis and close to Beijing railway station, this white monolith—curved like Miami's Fontainebleau hotel—symbolized the rebirth of China's tourism industry in 1987; these days, reliable service and decent facilities continue to draw tour groups and business travelers. **Pros:** close to key transport links; near popular sites; good health facilities. **Cons:** expensive restaurants; can lack character; outdated in places. $ *Rooms from: Y1,250* ⊠ *9 Jianguomennei Dajie, off Wangfujing Dajie, Dongcheng District* ☎ *010/6512–6688* ⊕ *www.bih.com.cn* ⌇*909 rooms, 60 suites* ⦿*No meals* Ⓜ *Dongdan* ✛ *F5.*

$$
HOTEL

Beijing Marriott Hotel City Wall (北京万豪酒店 *Běijīng Wànháo jiǔdiàn*). At the edge of the only remaining scrap of Beijing's once-mighty city walls—there are great views from the lobby coffee shop—this hotel is in a good location, relatively near key tourist sites and the Beijing railway station. **Pros:** close to tourist sites; near the old city wall; spacious rooms. **Cons:** some rooms have odd shapes; lacks intimacy; extra charge for in-room Internet. $ *Rooms from: Y1,300* ⊠ *7 Jianguomen Nanlu, Dongcheng District* ☎ *010/5811–8888* ⊕ *www.marriott.com* ⌇*649 rooms, 30 suites* ⦿*No meals* Ⓜ *Jianguomen* ✛ *F6.*

$
HOTEL

Beijing Sihe Courtyard Hotel (北京四合宾馆 *Běijīng Sìhé bīnguǎn*). Small, quiet, and cute, this appealing courtyard hotel—inside one of the city's hutong and featuring a centuries-old date tree, red lanterns, and other such traditional Chinese decorations—may once have been the home of Mei Lanfang, the legendary male Peking opera star known for playing female roles. **Pros:** lots of privacy; homey atmosphere; authentic experience. **Cons:** not all rooms have courtyard views; no restaurant; bad plumbing. $ *Rooms from: Y795* ⊠ *5 Dengcao Hutong, Dongcheng*

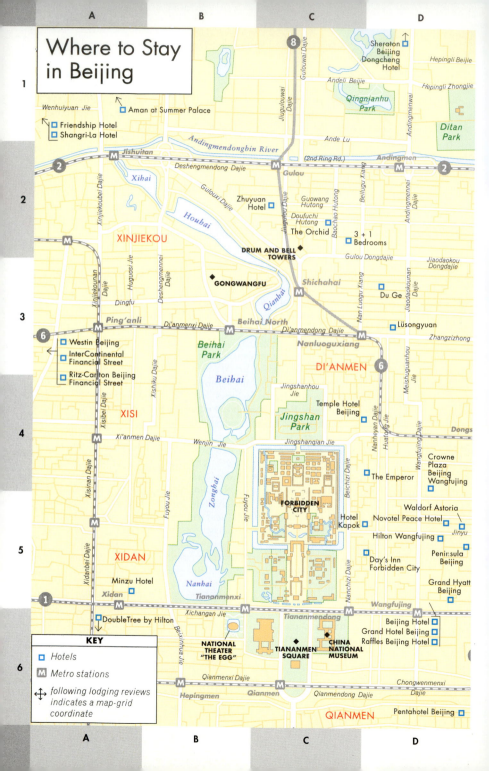

Where to Stay in Beijing

Wenhuiyuan Jie

☐ Aman at Summer Palace

☐ Friendship Hotel
☐ Shangri-La Hotel

Jishuitan

Deshengmendong Dajie

Andingmendongbin River

(2nd Ring Rd.)

Gulou

Andingmen

Sheraton Beijing Dongcheng Hotel

Hepingli Beijie

Andeli Beijie

Hepingli Zhongjie

Qingnianhu Park

Ande Lu

Andingmennei Dajie

Andingmenwai

Ditan Park

Xihai

Xinjiekoubei Dajie

Xinjiekouan Dajie

Gulouxi Dajie

Houhai

XINJIEKOU

Huguosi Jie

Dingfu

Deshengmennei Dajie

Zhuyuan Hotel

Jugulou Dajie

Guowang Hutong

Doufuchi Hutong

The Orchid

Baochao Hutong

Beilugu Xiang

3 + 1 ☐ Bedrooms

Jiaodaokou Dongdajie

Gulou Dongdajie

Nan Luogu Xiang

Jiaodaokounan

Jiaodaokou Dongdajie

☐ Du Ge

Zhangzizhong

◆ **DRUM AND BELL TOWERS**

◆ **GONGWANGFU**

Qianhai

Shichahai

Shichahai

☐ Lüsongyuan

Ping'anli

Di'anmenxi Dajie

Beihai North

Di'anmendong Dajie

Nanluoguxiang

Meishuguanhou Jie

☐ Westin Beijing

☐ InterContinental Financial Street

☐ Ritz-Carlton Beijing Financial Street

Xishiku Dajie

Xisibei Dajie

Beihai Park

Beihai

DI'ANMEN

XISI

Xi'anmen Dajie

Zhongbai

Fuyou Jie

Wenjin Jie

Jingshanhou Jie

Temple Hotel Beijing

Nanheyan Dajie

Huatong Jie

Wangfujing Dajie

Dongs

Jingshanqian Jie

Jingshan Park

Beichizi Dajie

Crowne Plaza Beijing Wangfujing ☐

☐ The Emperor

Xidanbei Dajie

Xidanan Dajie

Zhongnanhai

Fuyou Jie

Beichizi Dajie

FORBIDDEN CITY

Waldorf Astoria ☐

Novotel Peace Hotel ☐

Jinyu

☐ Hilton Wangfujing ☐

Hotel Kapok ☐

Peninsula Beijing

XIDAN

Nanhai

Day's Inn ☐ Forbidden City

Grand Hyatt Beijing

☐ Minzu Hotel

Nanchizi Dajie

Xidan

Tiananmenxi

Wangfujing

☐ DoubleTree by Hilton

Xichang'an Jie

Tiananmendang

Beijing Hotel ☐

Grand Hotel Beijing ☐

Raffles Beijing Hotel ☐

Beixinhua Jie

NATIONAL THEATER "THE EGG"

TIANANMEN SQUARE ◆

◆ **CHINA NATIONAL MUSEUM**

Qianmenxi Dajie

Hepingmen

Qianmen

Qianmendong Dajie

Chongwenmenxi Dajie

QIANMEN

☐ Pentahotel Beijing

CLOSE UP

Apartment and house rentals

There's an abundance of furnished short- and long-term rental properties in Beijing. Prices vary wildly. The priciest are luxury apartments and villas, usually far from the city center and best accessible by (chauffeur-driven) car. Usually described as "serviced apartments," these often include gyms and pools; rents can be over $2,000 a month. There are a lot of well-located mid-range properties in the city. They're usually clean, with new furnishings; rents start at $500 a month. Finally, for longer, budget-friendly stays, there are normal local apartments. These are firmly off the tourist circuit and often cost only a third of the price of the mid-range properties. Expect mismatched furniture, fewer amenities, and—we won't lie—varying insect populations.

Property sites like Wuwoo, Move and Stay, Sublet, and Pacific Properties have hundreds of apartments all over town. For a bit of local flavor, check out the rental options on AirBnB.

Com. These apartments are rented out by the owner and verified by the Web-based service. Centrally located and reasonably priced, they are a worthy alternative to hotel living. The online classifieds pages in local English-language magazines such as *The Beijinger* or *City Weekend* are good places to start.

HOMESTAYS

Single travelers can arrange homestays (often in combination with language courses) through China Homestay Club. Generally these are in upper-middle-class homes that are about as expensive as a cheap hotel—prices range from $150 to $180 a week. Nine times out of 10, the family has a small child in need of daily English conversation classes. China-Homestay.org is a different organization that charges a single placement fee of $300 for a stay of three months or less.

District ☎ *010/5169–3555* ⊕ *www.sihehotel.com* ➟ *12 rooms, 6 suites* ⏹ *Breakfast* Ⓜ *Dongsi (Exit C)* ✛ *E4.*

$ **HOTEL** 🏨 **Crowne Plaza Beijing Wangfujing** (北京国际艺苑皇冠假日酒店 *Běijīng guójì yìyuàn huángguān jiàrì jiǔdiàn*). The best thing about this mid-range choice is its central location on Wangfujing, Beijing's most famous shopping street, where there's a mix of traditional stores, international chains, and a touristy "food" market—scorpions on a stick, anyone? **Pros:** near the main sights; close to shopping; reputable brand. **Cons:** chain-hotel feel; service can be hit and miss; boring design. ⑤ *Rooms from: Y650* ⊠ *48 Wangfujing Dajie, Dongcheng District* ☎ *010/5911–9999* ⊕ *www.crownplaza.com/beijingchn* ➟ *360 rooms, 27 suites* ⏹ *Breakfast* Ⓜ *Wangfujing* ✛ *D4.*

$ **HOTEL** 🏨 **Day's Inn Forbidden City Beijing** (北京香江戴斯酒店 *Běijīng Xiāngjiāng dàisī jiǔdiàn*). Functional rather than fancy, the Day's Inn is about as close as it's possible to get to the Forbidden City without staying in the palace itself, and though guest rooms are tiny, they are definitely inexpensive and relatively comfortable. **Pros:** fantastic price for the location; close to tourist sites; free Internet. **Cons:** restaurant is average at best; bad basement rooms; onset of mold in some shower rooms. $ *Rooms from: Y500* ✉ *99 Nanheyan Dajie, Dongcheng District* ☎ *010/6512–7788* ⊕ *www.daysinn.cn* ➵ *164 rooms* ⦿ *No meals* Ⓜ *Tiananmen East* ✛ *D5.*

$ 🏨 **Double Happiness Courtyard** (北京阅微庄四合院酒店 *Běijīng yuè wēi zhuāng sìhéyuàn jiǔdiàn*). The rooms in this atmospheric warren of wooden corridors, courtyards, and rickety staircases are fairly spacious, with Chinese-style beds, wooden furniture, and small bathrooms, but it's the friendly, English-speaking service, central location, and good rates that make it so popular. **Pros:** traditional architecture; hutong location; good for families. **Cons:** dingy entrance; old-fashioned facilities; can be chilly in winter. $ *Rooms from: Y780* ✉ *37 Dongsi Sitiao, Dongcheng District* ☎ *010/6400–7762* ⊕ *www.hotel37.com/en/index. asp* ➵ *32 rooms; 2 suites* ⦿ *No meals* Ⓜ *Dongsi, Line 5* ✛ *E4.*

$$$ 🏨 **Du Ge** (杜革 *Dù gé*). One step beyond the striking Moon Gate doorway of this 18th-century hutong home—once owned by the Minister of the Imperial Household to Emperor Xianfeng (1860)—and you're transported, thanks to swaying bamboos, flickering lanterns, blazing red walls, and a chic lobby, to a nobleman's courtyard house. **Pros:** gorgeous decor; great location; free soft drinks at the bar all day; outstanding breakfast. **Cons:** small rooms; some service quibbles; Nanluoguxiang alley not as appealing as it once was. $ *Rooms from: Y1,500* ✉ *26 Qian Yuan En Si Hutong, Dongcheng District* ☎ *010/6406–0686* ⊕ *www. dugecourtyard.com* ➵ *6 rooms* ⦿ *No meals* Ⓜ *Gulou Dajie* ✛ *D3.*

$ 🏨 **The Emperor** (皇家驿栈 *Huángjiā yìzhàn*). Lauded for its lovely rooftop bar with views over the Forbidden City, the Emperor has a traditional exterior that belies guest rooms seemingly inspired by the film *2001: A Space Odyssey*: minimalist white decor, sunken beds with tube pillows, lozenge-like sofas, and minibars that rise up from concealed cabinets. **Pros:** best rooftop terrace in the city; unbeatable views of the Forbidden City. **Cons:** no elevator; limited gym facilities; far from the subway. $ *Rooms from: Y1,000* ✉ *33 Qihelou Jie, Dongcheng District* ⊕ *www.theemperor.com.cn* ➵ *46 rooms, 9 suites* ⦿ *No meals* ✛ *D4.*

$$ 🏨 **Grand Hotel Beijing** (北京贵宾楼饭店 *Běijīng Guìbīnlóu fàndiàn*). On the north side of Chang'an Avenue, and adjoining the ritzier Raffles, the Grand offers a decent blend of luxury and comfort without the international brand price tag. **Pros:** good location; classic decor; great rooftop views. **Cons:** some rooms in need of renovation; confusing layout; little atmosphere. $ *Rooms from: Y1,200* ✉ *35 Dongchang'an Jie, Dongcheng District* ☎ *010/6513–7788* 🖷 *010/6513–0048* ⊕ *www. grandhotelbeijing.com* ➵ *214 rooms, 50 suites* ⦿ *No meals* Ⓜ *Wangfujing* ✛ *D5.*

$$$$ 🏨 **Grand Hyatt Beijing** (北京东方君悦酒店 *Běijīng Dōngfāngjūnyuè* FAMILY *jiǔdiàn*). The wow factor at the this top-notch hotel—close to Tiananmen Square and the Forbidden City—comes from its huge glass facade and extraordinary lagoon-like swimming area: entwined around lush vegetation, waterfalls, and statues, it has a "virtual sky" ceiling that imitates different weather patterns. **Pros:** great dining; plenty of shopping; very impressive pool and gym. **Cons:** dull rooms; overpriced bar; Internet is extra. $ *Rooms from: Y2,200* ✉ *1 Dongchang'an Jie, corner of Wangfujing, Dongcheng District* ☎ *010/8518–1234* ⊕ *www.beijing.*

Fodor's Choice ★

4

grand.hyatt.com ⇗ *825 rooms, 155 suites* |○| *No meals* Ⓜ *Wangfujing* ✛ *D5.*

$

HOTEL

FAMILY

Fodor's Choice

★

🏨 **Holiday Inn Express Beijing Dongzhimen** (北京东直门智选 *Běijīng dōngzhīmēn zhìxuǎn jiàrì jiǔdiàn*). Cheap and cheerful does it at this value chain close to Sanlitun (Beijing's lively nightlife center)—yes, it lacks a pool and gym, and the guest rooms are somewhat small, but everything here works, from the gleaming lobby to the surprisingly comfortable beds, while touches such as free-to-use Apple Macs next to the front desk and a games console area add a little something extra. **Pros:** cheap yet extremely modern and clean; tour operator next door; close to some great nightlife and dining. **Cons:** breakfast can be crowded (and no lunch or dinner options); small rooms; subway is a long walk away. $ *Rooms from: Y558* ✉ *1 Chunxiu Road, Dongcheng District* ☎ *010/6416–9999* ⊕ *www.holidayinnexpress.com* ⇗ *350 rooms* |○| *Breakfast* ✛ *G3.*

$$

HOTEL

🏨 **Hotel Cote Cour** (北京演乐70号 *Běijīng yǎn lè 70 hào*). This boutique courtyard hideaway claims to have once served as a rehearsal space for imperial musicians during the Ming Dynasty; renovated rooms wrap around an attractive old courtyard and feature antique pieces, comfy beds with feather duvets, and the usual Western comforts. **Pros:** central location; boutique atmosphere; English spoken. **Cons:** standard rooms a little small; expensive. $ *Rooms from: Y1,300* ✉ *70 Yanyue Hutong, Dongcheng District* ☎ *010/6523–9598* ⊕ *www.hotelcotecourbj.com/indexe.asp* ⇗ *12 rooms, 2 suites* |○| *No meals* ✛ *E4.*

$

HOTEL

🏨 **Hotel Kapok** (木棉花酒店 *Mùmiánhuā jiǔdiàn*). Designed by Studio Pei Zhu (who also worked on the Olympics), this minimalist-style offering helped kick-start the boutique hotel movement in Beijing—it has large, design-conscious guest rooms, internal courtyards enclosed in glass, and bamboo and pebble gardens, as well as a quirky exterior lattice wrapped around the entire building. **Pros:** comfortable rooms; near top sites; friendly staff. **Cons:** no pool; not everyone will like the glass-walled bathrooms; refurbishment needed. $ *Rooms from: Y800* ✉ *16 Donghuamen, Dongcheng District* ☎ *010/6525–9988* ⊕ *www.kapokhotelbeijing.com* ⇗ *89 rooms* |○| *Breakfast* Ⓜ *Tiananmen East* ✛ *D5.*

$$$$

HOTEL

🏨 **Legendale** (励骏酒店 *Lìjùn jiǔdiàn*). The faux European spectacle that is the Legendale screams nouveau riche, but this château-like hotel, with its sparkling chandeliers, gilded staircase, and Parisian fireplace in the lobby, is genuinely comfortable and luxurious. **Pros:** plenty of pampering; in a great neighborhood; luxurious rooms. **Cons:** high prices; vast size can make it feel empty; no traditional Chinese elements. $ *Rooms from: Y2,100* ✉ *90–92 Jinbao Street, Dongcheng District* ☎ *010/8511–3388* ⊕ *www.legendalehotel.com* ⇗ *390 rooms, 81 suites* |○| *Breakfast* Ⓜ *Dengshikou* ✛ *E5.*

$ **Lüsongyuan** (侣松园宾馆 *Lǚsōngyuán bīnguǎn*). The traditional
HOTEL
Fodor's Choice
★
wooden entrance to this delightful courtyard hotel, on the site of an old mandarin's residence, is guarded by two *menshi* (stone lions)—this is a classic Old Beijing experience, turned over to tourism, with no attempts at modern updates or fancy design, but, rather, just a good choice for cheap, traditional living. **Pros:** convenient location; near restaurants; unfussy courtyard conversion. **Cons:** a lack of luxury; can be hard to find; carpets are in need of a clean. $ *Rooms from: Y768* ⊠ *22 Banchang Hutong, Kuanjie, Dongcheng District* ☎ *010/6401–1116* ⤳ *55 rooms* ⓘ⃝*No meals* Ⓜ *Zhangzizhonglu* ⊕ *D3.*

$ **Novotel Peace Hotel** (和平宾馆 *Hépíng bīnguǎn*). This tower of shimmering glass has rooms with floor-to-ceiling windows that afford decent views, but, other than that, there's nothing spectacular here: service is fairly basic and the ambience is decidedly low-key; the big plus is the surrounding area, with plenty of shops and restaurants nearby (as well as Wangfujing and Tiananmen Square), making it a solid base at a good price for the location. **Pros:** convenient location; near plenty of restaurants; close to the sites. **Cons:** mixed room quality; not much ambience; lackluster service. $ *Rooms from: Y550* ⊠ *3 Jinyu Hutong, Wangfujing Dajie, Dongcheng District* ☎ *010/6512–8833* ⊕ *www.accorhotels-asia. com* ⤳ *402 rooms, 25 suites* ⓘ⃝*No meals* Ⓜ *Wangfujing* ⊕ *D5.*
HOTEL
FAMILY

$ **The Orchid.** A firm favorite among travelers looking for somewhere hip but still down-to-earth, the Orchid is a serene spot in the heart of Beijing's most vibrant hutong district, with two tiers of flower-strewn terraces, ludicrously comfy beds, a complimentary à la carte breakfast menu, and friendly staff who have an infectious love for their gentrifying neighborhood. **Pros:** great hutong location; cool interiors; some rooms with gardens. **Cons:** reservations a must; can be hard to find. $ *Rooms from: Y800* ⊠ *65 Baochao Hutong, Gulou Dongdajie, Gulou, Dongcheng District* ☎ *010/8404–4818* ⊕ *www.theorchidbeijing.com* ⤳ *10 rooms* ⓘ⃝*Breakfast* Ⓜ *Guloudajie* ⊕ *C2.*
HOTEL
Fodor's Choice
★

$ **Park Plaza Beijing** (北京丽亭酒店 *Běijīng Lìtíng jiǔdiàn*). Hidden behind the swankier Regent on Beijing's glitziest avenue, this popular mid-range option, especially good for first-time visitors to the city, has clean and compact rooms with decent-sized bathrooms, English TV channels, a pleasant tree-shaded garden, and a fantastic location close to the Forbidden City and Wangfujing. **Pros:** close to the Forbidden City; free Wi-Fi. **Cons:** lobby is small and uninspiring; staff can seem a little harassed. $ *Rooms from: Y700* ⊠ *97 Jinbao St., Dongcheng District* ☎ *010/8522–1999* ⊕ *www.parkplaza.com/beijingcn* ⤳ *216 rooms, 16 suites* ⓘ⃝*No meals* Ⓜ *Dengshikou* ⊕ *E5.*
HOTEL

$$$ **Peninsula Beijing** (王府半岛酒店 *Wángfǔ Bàndǎo jiǔdiàn*). Guests at the Peninsula Beijing enjoy an impressive combination of modern facilities and traditional luxury—the guest rooms are a little small for this sort of hotel, but are superlatively well-appointed, with teak and rosewood flooring, colorful rugs, and high-tech touches like custom bedside control panels that let you adjust lighting, temperature, and the flat-screen TVs; the service is excellent, as is the spa. **Pros:** close to sightseeing, restaurants, and shopping; rooms are impeccable; near the Forbidden City. **Cons:** lobby is squeezed by the surrounding luxury
HOTEL
Fodor's Choice
★

4

shopping mall; hectic; rooms could be bigger. $ *Rooms from: Y1,600* ✉ *8 Jinyu Hutong, Wangfujing, Dongcheng District* ☎ *010/8516–2888* ⊕ *www.peninsula.com* ⇨ *525 rooms, 59 suites* ⚋| *No meals* Ⓜ *Dengshikou* ✛ *D5.*

$ **🏛 Pentahotel Beijing** (北京万怡酒店 *Běi'ertè jiǔdiàn*). This comfort-
HOTEL   able, good-looking mid-range hotel offers modern facilities wrapped up in a slick, business-friendly package; it's close to the Temple of Heaven and Pearl Market, and surrounded by shopping malls. **Pros:** business-friendly; good meeting rooms; next to the subway. **Cons:** in a traffic-clogged area; not much around for tourists. $ *Rooms from: Y750* ✉ *3 Chongwenmenwai Dajie, Dongcheng District* ☎ *010/6708–1188* ⊕ *www.pentahotels.com* ⇨ *307 rooms, 15 suites* ⚋| *Breakfast* Ⓜ *Chongwenmen* ✛ *D6.*

$$$$ **🏛 Raffles Beijing Hotel** (北京饭店莱佛士 *Běijīng fàndiàn Láifóshì*). Raf-
HOTEL   fles is an iconic brand in Asia, and this property doesn't disappoint; in
Fodor's Choice   2006, Singaporean designer Grace Soh restored half of what was the
★   Beijing Hotel into its former glory (crystal chandeliers in the lobby; a broad white staircase enveloped in a royal-blue carpet) while retain-ing its history—service is excellent, and the location, for tourism pur-poses, is flawless. **Pros:** within easy walking distance of the Forbidden City; nifty location for sightseeing; switched-on staff; spacious rooms. **Cons:** pricey restaurants; not in the right part of town for business travelers; occasional problems with the pool. $ *Rooms from: Y2,500* ✉ *33 Dongchang'an Jie, off Wangfujing Dajie, Dongcheng District* ☎ *010/6526–3388* ⊕ *www.raffles.com/beijing* ⇨ *171 rooms, 24 suites* ⚋| *No meals* Ⓜ *Wangfujing* ✛ *D5.*

$$ **🏛 Red Capital Residence** (新红资客栈 *Xīnhóngzī kèzhàn*). Each of the
HOTEL   four rooms at this boutique courtyard hotel—located in a carefully restored home in Dongsi Hutong—are decorated with antiques and according to different themes, such as the Chairman's Suite, in playful homage to Mao, and the two Author's Suites (one inspired by Edgar Snow, a 1930s U.S. journalist who lived in Beijing, and the other by Han Suyin, the Japanese novelist who wrote *Love is a Many-Splendored Thing,* among other best sellers). **Pros:** Fodorites rave about the friendly service, unique atmosphere, and intimate feel. **Cons:** small rooms; limited facilities; quaint more than comfortable; dysfunctional web-site. $ *Rooms from: Y1,200* ✉ *9 Dongsi Liutiao, Dongcheng District* ☎ *010/6402–7150* ⊕ *www.redcapitalclub.com.cn* ⇨ *4 rooms* ⚋| *Break-fast* Ⓜ *Zhangzizhonglu* ✛ *E4.*

$$$$ **🏛 The Regent** (北京丽晶酒店 *Běijīng Lìjīng jiǔdiàn*). Luxurious (if busi-
HOTEL   nesslike) rooms, a prestigious location on the corner of ritzy Jinbao Jie
Fodor's Choice   to Wangfujing, and a spectacularly soaring glass-walled lobby are
★   reasons why the Regent is a top choice for high rollers. **Pros:** conve-nient location; close to the subway; spacious rooms. **Cons:** unimpres-sive breakfast; occasional blemishes in some rooms; check-in can be slow. $ *Rooms from: Y2,250* ✉ *99 Jinbao Street, Dongcheng District* ☎ *010/8522–1888* ⊕ *www.regenthotels.com* ⇨ *500 rooms, 25 suites* ⚋| *No meals* Ⓜ *Dengshikou* ✛ *E5.*

$$ **🏛 Sheraton Beijing Dongcheng Hotel** (北京金隅喜来登 *Běijīng Jīnyú*
HOTEL   *Xǐláidēng*). Though it can feel a little in the middle of nowhere, near

the 2008 Olympic area, the Sheraton Dongcheng, with its cubic glass facade, great-value lunch deals, and spacious, clean, and up-to-date rooms, is a decent high-end choice. **Pros:** lots of dining opportunities; close to the Bird's Nest and Water Cube; plenty of taxis and easy subway access. **Cons:** out of the way; not much to do nearby. $ *Rooms from: Y1,400* ⊠ *36 North Third Ring Rd. East, Dongcheng District* ☎ *010/5798–8888* ⊕ *sheraton.com/beijingdongcheng* ⇘ *441 rooms, 70 suites* ❄❄ *No meals* Ⓜ *Hepingxiqiao* ✛ *D1.*

$$$$
HOTEL
Fodor's Choice
★

🏛 **Temple Hotel Beijing** (东景缘 *Dōng jǐng yuán*). Five hundred years in the making, this beguiling combination of boutique luxury and heritage architecture is one of Beijing's most romantic hotel experiences. **Pros:** historic buildings in hutong location; great for art lovers; exceptional. **Cons:** no gym, pool, or spa; expensive. $ *Rooms from: Y2,400* ⊠ *23 Shatan Beilu, Dongcheng District* ☎ *010/8401–5680* ⊕ *www. thetemplehotel.com* ⇘ *8 rooms* ❄❄ *No meals* ✛ *D4.*

$$$$
HOTEL
Fodor's Choice
★

🏛 **Waldorf Astoria Beijing** (北京华尔道夫酒店 *Běijīng huá'ěr dàofū jiǔdiàn*). No expense has been spared on this stunning, boutique-inspired hotel in central Wangfujing; the public areas have walls of Suzhou silk, staircases of gold-flecked Italian marble, and countless pieces of art, while guest rooms strike a delightful balance of contemporary style and high-tech luxury, with Apple TVs, Bose sound systems, Nespresso machines, Japanese toilets, heated bathroom floors, and a Samsung tablet beside the bed to control the lights, TV, and curtains, and also order various services. **Pros:** Beijing's most beautiful hotel; brand-new; central location. **Cons:** expensive; not much nightlife in the immediate area. $ *Rooms from: Y2,500* ⊠ *5-15 Jinyu Hutong, Dongcheng District* ☎ *010/8520–8989* ⊕ *waldorfastoria3.hilton.com/ en/hotels/china/waldorf-astoria-beijing-bjswawa/index.html* ⇘ *176 rooms* ❄❄ *No meals* Ⓜ *Dengshikou* ✛ *D5.*

$
HOTEL
FAMILY

🏛 **Zhuyuan Hotel** (竹园宾馆 *Zhúyuán bīnguǎn*). The charming "Bamboo Garden" was actually once the residence of Kang Sheng, a sinister character responsible for "public security" during the Cultural Revolution, who nevertheless had fine taste in Chinese art and antiques (some which are still on display). **Pros:** traditional feel; interesting hutong neighborhood; free Wi-Fi. **Cons:** room quality is variable; pricey for what you get; not that close to the big-name sights. $ *Rooms from: Y880* ⊠ *24 Xiaoshiqiao Hutong, Jiugulou Dajie, Dongcheng District* ☎ *010/5852–0088* ⊕ *www.bbgh.com.cn* ⇘ *40 rooms, 4 suites* ❄❄ *No meals* Ⓜ *Gulou Dajie* ✛ *C2.*

XICHENG DISTRICT 西城区

Xicheng District lies to the west of Dongcheng. It makes up the other half of Beijing's inner core, with the Forbidden City's western edge as its starting point. This area is home to many of Beijing's old hutong alleyways and is a great place to stroll around the neighborhood's famous lake.

$
HOTEL
FAMILY

🏛 **DoubleTree by Hilton Beijing** (北京希尔顿逸林酒店 *Běijīng Xī'ěrdùn yìlín jiǔdiàn*). Soaring 22 stories into the air, the DoubleTree is a solid hotel with perks that compensate for its out-of-the-way location, from the warm chocolate-chip cookies in the lobby to the alluring oasis of the terraced outdoor swimming pool. **Pros:** gorgeous pool area; decent value. **Cons:** a little too remote; lack of good dining options. ⑤ *Rooms from: Y880* ✉ *168 Guang'anmenwai Dajie, Xicheng District* ☎ *010/6338–1888* ⊕ *www.beijing.doubletreebyhilton.com* ⤴ *543 rooms, 118 suites* ⑩ *No meals* Ⓜ *Caishikou* ✛ *A6.*

$$$ 🏨 **InterContinental Financial Street Beijing** (金融洲际酒店 *Běijīng*
HOTEL   *Jīnróngjiē zhōujì jiǔdiàn*). The spacious rooms at this well-appointed business hotel show hints of traditional Chinese art. **Pros:** convenient location within Beijing's financial hub; great for business travelers; excellent facilities. **Cons:** no appealing quirks; lack of culture nearby; business vibe may put off families. ⑤ *Rooms from: Y1,500* ✉ *11 Financial St., Xicheng District* ☎ *010/5852–5888* ⊕ *www.ichotelsgroup.com* ⤴ *318 rooms, 10 suites* ⑩ *No meals* Ⓜ *Fuchengmen (Exit C)* ✛ *A3.*

$$$$ 🏨 **Ritz-Carlton Beijing, Financial Street** (北京金融街丽思卡尔顿酒店
HOTEL   *Běijīng Lìsīkǎ'ěrdùn jiǔdiàn*). With ample amounts of glass and chrome, the Ritz-Carlton could be mistaken for one of the many sleek office buildings that crowd this very business-oriented area; the interior is equally swish and contemporary, with smart East-meets-West decor that's up to the Ritz standard—its location, excellent amenities, and eager-to-please staff make it popular with tour groups as well as businesspeople. **Pros:** impeccable service; luxurious atmosphere; incredible Italian dining. **Cons:** far from the city's attractions; expensive; lobby lacks pizzazz. ⑤ *Rooms from: Y2,000* ✉ *18 Financial St., Xicheng District* ☎ *010/6601–6666* ⊕ *www.ritzcarlton.com* ⤴ *253 rooms, 33 suites* ⑩ *No meals* Ⓜ *Fuchengmen* ✛ *A3.*

$$ 🏨 **Westin Beijing Financial Street** (威斯汀酒店 *Wēisītīng jiǔdiàn*). It's busi-
HOTEL   ness as usual at this worthwhile spot: comfortable rooms with plush beds, neutral tones, and marble bathrooms; a plethora of amenities, including dining spots both formal and fun; and not forgetting the perhaps-to-be-expected, well-staffed executive lounge. **Pros:** sumptuous beds; high-tech gadgets; business location. **Cons:** glass between bathroom and bedroom not for the timid; gym could be bigger; not in a good spot for tourists. ⑤ *Rooms from: Y1,400* ✉ *9B Financial Street, Xicheng District* ☎ *010/6606–8866* ⊕ *www.westin.com/beijingfinancial* ⤴ *486 rooms, 25 suites* ⑩ *No meals* Ⓜ *Fuchengmen* ✛ *A3.*

CHAOYANG DISTRICT 朝阳区

Chaoyang District is outside the old city walls and extends east of Dongcheng, so there's little of historical interest here. This is, however, home to Beijing's more modern, urban center, including the Central Business District. You'll also find some of the city's best restaurants, bars, and shopping malls here. The nightlife hub of Sanlitun is of particular note.

$$$ 🏨 **China World Hotel** (中国大饭店 *Zhōngguó dàfàndiàn*). Once placing
HOTEL   high on lists of top Beijing hotels, this place now does opulence in a rather unsubtle way—gold highlights in the lobby; marble tubs in the luxe rooms; high-priced fine dining—but it still just about lives up to its look: the service is slick, the restaurants are very good (Aria, serving contemporary European cuisine, is particularly special), and the

attached mall/cinema is a welcome escape. **Pros:** convenient location for business travelers; very good dining; close to both the subway and shopping. **Cons:** the bustle here can be overwhelming; big and impersonal; rooms are small for the price. $ *Rooms from: Y1,500 ⊠ 1 Jianguomenwai Dajie, Chaoyang District* ☎ 010/6505–2266 ⊕ *www.shangri-la.com* ⤴ *716 rooms, 26 suites* ⦿*No meals* Ⓜ *Guomao* ⊕ *H5.*

4

$$$ 🏨 **China World Summit Wing** (北京国贸大酒店 *Běijīng Guómào dànjiǔdiàn*). Occupying the upper floors of Beijing's tallest building, the business-chic Summit Wing offers knee-trembling views from its luxurious guest rooms—if you need a drink to steady your nerves, the excellent 80th-floor cocktail bar makes a perfect Old Fashioned. **Pros:** jaw-dropping views; close to the CBD; Grill 79 does a great steak. **Cons:** traffic in the area can be hellish; dining gets very expensive; lack of culture nearby. $ *Rooms from: Y1,800 ⊠ 1 Jianguomenwai Avenue, Chaoyang District* ☎ 010/6505–2299 ⊕ *www.shangri-la.com* ⤴ *278 rooms, 17 suites* ⦿*No meals* Ⓜ *Guomao* ⊕ *H5.*

$$$$ 🏨 **Conrad Beijing.** One of the capital's newest luxury hotels is in a distinctively curved, tapering tower on the east Second Ring Road; its standout personality extends to touches like Vivid, a rooftop nightclub and lounge, and the skyline views from the guest rooms, enlivened through lozenge-shaped windows. **Pros:** sparklingly new; original design; fun rooftop bar. **Cons:** not that near to most of the sights; restaurants still a work in progress. $ *Rooms from: Y2,100 ⊠ 29 Bei Dong San Huan, Chaoyang District* ☎ 010/6584–6000 ⊕ *conradhotels.hilton.com* ⤴ *272 rooms, 17 suites* ⦿*No meals* Ⓜ *Hujialou* ⊕ *H4.*

$ 🏨 **Courtyard by Marriott Beijing Northeast** (北京人济万怡酒店 *Běijīng Rénjì wànyí jiǔdiàn*). More an option for business travelers than casual tourists—meaning it's not too far from the airport and a number of work hubs—this hotel near Wangjing High Tech Park understands that a functional location doesn't have to mean a completely utilitarian aesthetic. **Pros:** good value; well located for doing business in Beijing's northeast; reliable. **Cons:** extremely far from the tourist hot spots or downtown; little to do nearby; more for work than pleasure. $ *Rooms from: Y800 ⊠ 101 Jingmi Lu, Chaoyang District* ☎ 010/5907–6666 ⊕ *courtyardbeijingnortheast.com* ⤴ *258 rooms, 43 suites* ⦿*No meals* Ⓜ *Sanyuanqiao* ⊕ *H1.*

$$ 🏨 **Crowne Plaza Beijing Chaoyang U-Town** (北京国际朝阳皇冠假日酒店 *Běijīng Cháoyáng yōutáng huángguàn jiàrì jiǔdiàn*). Expect modern, good-sized guest rooms, a great pool and gym, a sparkling marble lobby, and many convenient dining and shopping options in the integrated U-Town shopping mall (even a German-themed bar that brews its own beer). **Pros:** conveniently attached to a buzzing mall; nicely functional. **Cons:** not close to tourism; lacks character. $ *Rooms from:*

Y1,200 ✉ *3 Sanfeng North Area, Chaoyangmen Wai Dajie, Chaoyang District* ☎ *010/5909–6688* ⊕ *www.crowneplaza.com* ↩ *360 rooms, 13 suites* ⦿*No meals* Ⓜ *Chaoyangmen* ✚ *F4.*

$$
HOTEL
Fodor's Choice
★

⛨ **EAST, Beijing** (北京东隅 *Běijīng Dōngyú*). From the folks behind the Opposite House, EAST is a business hotel with pizzazz, from the contemporary, light-filled guest rooms done out with oak floors and huge windows (the corner rooms have the best views), to Xian, a hip bar, lounge, and music venue with delicious wood-fired pizza and a connoisseur's selection of single malts. **Pros:** a business hotel with style; impeccable service; great in-house dining and drinking. **Cons:** far from the main tourist sights (other than 798); nearby subway yet to open. Ⓢ *Rooms from: Y1,250* ✉ *22 Jiuxianqiao Lu, Jiangtai, Chaoyang District* ☎ *010/8426–0888* ⊕ *www.east-beijing.com* ↩ *346 rooms, 23 suites* ⦿*No meals* ✚ *H1.*

$$$$
HOTEL

⛨ **Fairmont Beijing** (北京华彬费尔蒙酒店 *Běijīng Huábīn fèi'ěrméng jiǔdiàn*). Glowing inside and out in rich shades of bronze and gold, the Fairmont Beijing, close to the Silk Market and the diplomatic district surrounding Ritan Park, stays just on the right side of tasteful, with guest rooms that mix marble floors and deep carpets, Japanese tech toilets, bathtub TVs, iPod players, and a pillow menu. **Pros:** handy for business and shopping; great executive lounge; excellent spa facilities. **Cons:** traffic can be grueling; breakfast is mediocre; surrounded by offices. Ⓢ *Rooms from: Y2,000* ✉ *8 Yong An Dong Li, Chaoyang District* ☎ *010/8511–7777* ⊕ *www.fairmont.com* ↩ *222 rooms* ⦿*Breakfast* Ⓜ *Yong An Li* ✚ *G6.*

$$$$
HOTEL
Fodor's Choice
★

⛨ **Four Seasons Hotel Beijing** (北京四季酒店 *Běijīng Sìjì jiǔdiàn*). Even the most modest "deluxe" rooms at the Four Seasons Beijing come with state-of-the-art tech, bathtubs with city views, and clever architecture that seems to amplify the already generous 46 square meters (500 square feet) of living space. **Pros:** some of the best service in the city; elegant rooms; impeccable attention to detail. **Cons:** very expensive; not particularly close to key tourist hubs; lobby feels a little cramped. Ⓢ *Rooms from: Y3,200* ✉ *48 Liangmaqiao Rd., Chaoyang District* ☎ *010/5695–8888* ⊕ *www.fourseasons.com/beijing* ↩ *247 rooms, 66 suites* ⦿*No meals* Ⓜ *Liangmaqiao* ✚ *H2.*

$$
HOTEL
Fodor's Choice
★

⛨ **Grace Beijing** (一驿 *GēǐruiĀsī Běijīng*). Housed in a redbrick Bauhaus factory building in Beijing's 798 Art District, this stylish boutique hotel mixes French-colonial and art-deco touches, with contemporary artworks dotted throughout the stylish guest rooms, which range from boxy singles to spacious suites with freestandng tubs. **Pros:** unique art-themed hotel; on-site restaurant is excellent; perfect for visiting 798. **Cons:** far from everything else; no subway; no pool. Ⓢ *Rooms from: Y1,100* ✉ *D-Park, Jiuxianqiao Lu 2 Hao Yuan, 798 Art District, Chaoyang District* ☎ *010/6436–1818* ⊕ *www.gracehotels.com* ↩ *30 rooms* ⦿*Breakfast* ✚ *H1.*

$
HOTEL

⛨ **Grand Millennium Beijing Hotel** (北京千禧大酒店 *Běijīng Qiānxǐ dàjiǔdiàn*). Deep in the heart of the Central Business District, this glass tower is a well-appointed business hotel with smart, unassuming guest rooms and a top-notch pool and gym. **Pros:** centrally located; near subway; close to the Silk Market. **Cons:** food outlets are expensive; difficult to get a taxi; some rooms need sprucing up. ⑤ *Rooms from: Y1,000* ✉ *7 Dongsanhuan Zhonglu, Chaoyang District* ☎ *010/8587–6888* ⊕ *www. millenniumhotels.com* ➽ *521 rooms, 118 suites* ⑩ *No meals* Ⓜ *Jintai Xizhao* ✛ *H5.*

$$$
HOTEL
🏨 **Hilton Beijing** (北京稀尔顿酒店 *Běijīng Xī'ěrdùn jiǔdiàn*). At one of the elder statesmen of the city's hospitality scene, good deals can be had. **Pros:** One East restaurant does a great roast; good fitness center. **Cons:** far from the tourist sights; neighborhood lacks charm. ⑤ *Rooms from: Y1,690* ✉ *1 Dongfang Lu, Dongsanhuan Beilu, Chaoyang District* ☎ *010/5865–5000* ⊕ *www.beijing.hilton.com* ➽ *502 rooms, 52 suites* ⑩ *No meals* Ⓜ *Liangmaqiao* ✛ *H1.*

$$$
HOTEL
Fodor's Choice
★
🏨 **Hilton Beijing Wangfujing** (北京王府井稀尔顿酒店 *Běijīng Wángfǔjǐng Xī'ěrdùn jiǔdiàn*). Even the smallest rooms at this big-brand boutique-style hotel come with walk-in wardrobes, freestanding tubs, and six-head showers, and if you can stand the very bachelor-pad brown and slate interiors, you'll reap the benefits of being just a stroll from the Forbidden City and Tiananmen Square. **Pros:** central location; quiet; huge guest rooms. **Cons:** not easy to get cabs; service can get a little strained. ⑤ *Rooms from: Y1,800* ✉ *8 Wangfujing Dong Jie, Dongcheng District* ☎ *010/5812–8888* ⊕ *www3.hilton.com* ➽ *197 rooms, 58 suites* ⑩ *No meals* ✛ *D5.*

$$$$
HOTEL
🏨 **Hotel Eclat** (北京怡亨酒店 *Běijīng yí hēng jiǔdiàn*). Attached to Parkview Green, Beijing's artsiest and most upscale shopping mall, this playfully ultra-luxe option has "lagoon" suites with their own private swimming pools, and a fabulous art collection that includes original works by Salvador Dalí and Andy Warhol. **Pros:** excellent service; free minibar and other welcome treats; attached to shopping mall. **Cons:** expensive; not that close to sights; immediate area lacks local color. ⑤ *Rooms from: Y2,300* ✉ *9 Dongdaqiao Lu, Chaoyang District* ☎ *010/8561–2888* ⊕ *www.eclathotels.com/beijing/default-en.html* ➽ *74 guest rooms; 26 suites* ⑩ *No meals* Ⓜ *Dongdaqiao, Line 6* ✛ *G5.*

$
HOTEL
🏨 **Hotel Kunlun** (北京昆仑饭店 *Běijīng Kūnlún fàndiàn*). A bewildering array of restaurants, bars, and lounges coupled with spacious, well appointed guest rooms means this popular Chinese business hotel deserves even wider recognition. **Pros:** gorgeous decors throughout; well-finished, restful rooms; a good choice of dining. **Cons:** staff can be a little slow; not a top choice for sightseeing; quite business-oriented. ⑤ *Rooms from: Y980* ✉ *2 Xinyuan Nanlu, Sanlitun, Chaoyang District* ☎ *010/6590–3388* ⊕ *www.hotelkunlun.com* ➽ *600 rooms, 50 suites* ⑩ *Breakfast* Ⓜ *Liangmaqiao* ✛ *H2.*

$
HOTEL
🏨 **Jianguo Hotel Beijing** (建国饭店 *Jiànguó fàndiàn*). One of Beijing's first modern hotels, Jianguo was built in 1982 as an exact replica of the Palo Alto Holiday Inn, with direct dialing from rooms and other innovations (for the time). **Pros:** central location; fairly reasonable rates for the area; welcoming. **Cons:** limited amenities; rooms are small; can be a little noisy. ⑤ *Rooms from: Y750* ✉ *5 Jianguomenwai Dajie, Chaoyang District* ☎ *010/6500–2233* ⊕ *www.hoteljianguo.com* ➽ *459 rooms* ⑩ *No meals* Ⓜ *Yonganli* ✛ *G5.*

$$$$
HOTEL
🏨 **JW Marriott Hotel Beijing** (北京万豪酒店 *Běijīng JW Wànháo jiǔdiàn*). As you might expect at one of Beijing's older luxury hotels, the guest

rooms and bathrooms are pokier than current top-end expectations, but the JW makes up for it in the details: immaculate service, elegant public areas, fabulous dining (including a branch of the world-famous sushi destination Nobu), and some of the city's best high-end shopping in nearby Shin Kong Place. **Pros:** sleek style; spectacular service; attention to detail. **Cons:** rooms and bathrooms a little small; traffic-clogged area; not particulary close to sights. $\boxed{S}$ *Rooms from: Y2,000* ✉ *83 Jianguo Road, Chaoyang District* ☎ *010/5908–6688* ⊕ *jwmarriottbeijing.com* ➷ *586 rooms, 100 suites* |◎| *No meals* Ⓜ *Dawanglu* ✛ *H6.*

$ **⛨ Kempinski Hotel Beijing Lufthansa Center** (凯宾斯基饭店 *Kǎibīnsījī*
HOTEL *fàndiàn*). One of the capital's older luxury hotels, the Kempinski could stand to give its guest rooms a refresh, but the facilities remain first-rate thanks to a well-equipped gym, easy access to shopping in the attached Lufthansa Center, and plenty of dining opportunities. **Pros:** excellent service; a good bar; easy access to the airport. **Cons:** some areas are in need of renovation; far from the big tourist spots. $\boxed{S}$ *Rooms from: Y1,100* ✉ *50 Liangmaqiao Lu, Chaoyang District* ☎ *010/6465–3388* ⊕ *www.kempinski.com* ➷ *526 rooms, 114 suites* |◎| *No meals* Ⓜ *Liang-maqiao* ✛ *H2.*

$$ **⛨ Kerry Centre Hotel** (北京嘉里中心饭店 *Běijīng Jiālǐ zhōngxīn*
HOTEL *fàndiàn*). Recently renovated, this Shangri-La owned stalwart is now
FAMILY more appealing than ever, with the stylish Centro Bar joined by the excellent all-day Kerry's Kitchen, and a brand new top-of-the-range health club that has a play area just for kids. **Pros:** reasonably priced luxury; great for kids; nearby shopping. **Cons:** smallish rooms; congested area; expensive bar. $\boxed{S}$ *Rooms from: Y1,250* ✉ *1 Guang Hua Lu, Chaoyang District* ☎ *010/6561–8833* ⊕ *www.shangri-la.com/beijing/kerry* ➷ *487 rooms, 23 suites* |◎| *No meals* Ⓜ *Guomao* ✛ *H5.*

$ **⛨ Metropark Lido Hotel** (丽都假日饭店 *Běijīng Lìdū wěijíng jiǔdiàn*).
HOTEL In a leafy northeastern suburb of Beijing lies Lido Place, an enormous
FAMILY commercial and residential complex in which you'll find the Metropark Lido as well as a British-style pub, a Tex-Mex joint, and a buffet restaurant that makes this feel like Anywheresville. **Pros:** plenty of restaurants nearby; quiet streets; convenient for 798 Art District and airport. **Cons:** slightly sterile neighborhood; far from the sights; part of an expat enclave. $\boxed{S}$ *Rooms from: Y731* ✉ *6 Jiangtai Lu, Chaoyang District* ☎ *010/6437–6688* ⊕ *www.hkctshotels.com/lidohotel* ➷ *433 rooms, 89 suites* |◎| *No meals* Ⓜ *Sanyuanqiao* ✛ *H1.*

$ **⛨ New Otani Changfugong** (北京长富宫饭店 *Běijīng Chángfúgōng*
HOTEL *fàndiàn*). This Japanese-run hotel deserves praise for its crisp service and a great downtown location that makes it a reliable middle-ground for businessmen and (largely Japanese) tour groups alike; rooms are modern and crisp, plus the hotel overlooks a delightful garden where guests can participate in morning exercises. **Pros:** close to the sights; efficient staff. **Cons:** pricey food; worn-out carpets. $\boxed{S}$ *Rooms from: Y800* ✉ *26 Jianguomenwai Dajie, Chaoyang District* ☎ *010/6512–5555* ⊕ *www.cfgbj.com* ➷ *460 rooms, 18 suites* |◎| *No meals* Ⓜ *Jianguomen* ✛ *F6.*

$$$
HOTEL

Fodor's Choice
★

The Opposite House (瑜舍 *Yúshě*). In the heart of the Sanlitun nightlife district and designed by the famed architect Kengo Kuma, this exemplar of 21st-century China has a huge atrium and contemporary art in the stunning lobby, plus spacious and warm guest rooms kitted out with natural wood and Scandi-Asian minimalist chic. **Pros:** a design addict's dream; fantastic food and drink options (both within and around); unique experience. **Cons:** too trendy for some; not close to the tourist trail; awful traffic. $ *Rooms from: Y1,725* ⊠ *11 Sanlitun Lu, Chaoyang District* ☎ *010/6417–6688* ⊕ *www.theoppositehouse.com* ⤳ *98 studios, 1 penthouse* ⦿*No meals* ✛ *H3.*

$$$$
HOTEL

Fodor's Choice
★

Park Hyatt Beijing (北京柏悦酒店 *Běijīng Bòyuè jiǔdiàn*). An easy-to-like (if costly) slice of luxury, this 63-story tower hotel offers plenty of pampering (just imagine your own spa-inspired bathroom with over-sized rain shower, deep-soak tub, and heated floors), with large guest rooms that are a tad businesslike but packed with the obligatory modern amenities. **Pros:** spectacular views of the city; the hotel's buzzing Xue bar has a fab rooftop terrace; good location for business. **Cons:** pricey; lacks intimacy; hard area for walking around. $ *Rooms from: Y2,000* ⊠ *2 Jianguomenwai Dajie., Chaoyang District* ☎ *010/8567–1234* ⊕ *beijing.park.hyatt.com* ⤳ *237 rooms, 18 suites.* ⦿*No meals* Ⓜ *Guomao* ✛ *H6.*

$$$$
HOTEL

The Ritz-Carlton, Beijing (北京丽思卡尔顿酒店 *Běijīng Lìsīkǎ'ěrdùn jiǔdiàn*). In an area where Ferragamo, Chanel, and other couture practically spills out onto the street, this Ritz-Carlton feels rather at home; the dinky marble lobby, mahogany-decorated rooms, excellent Italian restaurant (Barolo), and Davidoff-sponsored cigar bar feel like something from another age, which is no bad thing if you can afford it. **Pros:** superior service; great location; impressive restaurants. **Cons:** dark public areas; expensive food; small lobby. $ *Rooms from: Y2,040* ⊠ *83A Jianguo Lu, Chaoyang District* ☎ *010/5908–8888* ⊕ *www.ritzcarlton.com* ⤳ *305 rooms* ⦿*No meals* Ⓜ *Dawanglu* ✛ *H6.*

$
HOTEL

Sofitel Wanda (北京万达索菲特大饭店 *Běijīng Wàndásuǒfèitè dà jiǔdiàn*). Tang Dynasty style mixes with contemporary French flair at this plush hotel, where swanky rooms and suites are enlivened with subtle Asian motifs; a well-equipped fitness center boasts a 25m-long pool and state-of-the-art gym; the hotel restaurant Héritage serves high-end French. **Pros:** good design; plenty of tech touches; near subway. **Cons:** traffic-clogged area; the view could be better; tourists may want to be closer to the sights. $ *Rooms from: Y1,100* ⊠ *97 Jianguo Road, Tower C (Wanda Plaza), Chaoyang District* ☎ *010/8599–6666* ⊕ *www.sofitel-wanda-beijing.com* ⤳ *417 rooms, 43 suites* ⦿*No meals* Ⓜ *Dawanglu* ✛ *H6.*

$$$
HOTEL

Fodor's Choice
★

St. Regis (北京国际俱乐部饭店 *Běijīng guójì jùlèbù fàndiàn*). At this favorite of business travelers and dignitaries, the luxurious interiors combine classic Chinese elegance with modern furnishings, but it's the facilities that really stand out: the health club is equipped with a Jacuzzi that gets its water directly from a natural hot spring, the glass-atrium swimming pool offers a sun-drenched backstroke, and the smart, wood-paneled Press Club Bar has the air of a private club. **Pros:** grand lobby; fantastic facilities; good Asian and European restaurants. **Cons:** the little extras really add up; local area a bit tired; not many good places to eat nearby. $ *Rooms from: Y1,742* ✉ *21 Jianguomenwai Dajie, Chaoyang District* ☎ *010/6460–6688* ⊕ *www.stregis.com/beijing* ⤳ *156 rooms, 102 suites* Ⓜ *Jianguomen* ✚ *F6.*

$
HOTEL
🏨 **Swissôtel Beijing** (港澳中心瑞士酒店 *gǎngao zhōngxīn Ruìshì jiǔdiàn*). With easy access to the Second Ring Road and Line 2 of the subway, this mid-range hotel is a decent enough hub for sightseers: the marble lobby is impressive, the health club includes an open-air tennis court, and rooms are a decent value. **Pros:** regular jazz performances in the lobby bar; good amenities; easy access to the city. **Cons:** can be noisy; generally mediocre food; a little on the old side. $ *Rooms from: Y750* ✉ *2 Chaoyangmennei Dajie, Dongsishiqiao Flyover Junction (Second Ring Rd.), Chaoyang District* ☎ *010/6553–2288* 🖷 *010/6501–2501* ⊕ *www.swissotel-beijing.com* ⤳ *430 rooms, 50 suites* ⓘ⃝ *No meals* Ⓜ *Dongsishitiao* ✚ *F3.*

$$
HOTEL
🏨 **W Beijing Chang'an** (北京長安街W 酒店 *Běijīng cháng'ān jiē W jiǔdiàn*). The sassy Starwood brand W has finally landed in China's capital, bringing tech-laden guestrooms, comfy beds, pillow menus, and free snacks. **Pros:** Brand new; hip design. **Cons:** A little farther out than the Wangfujing hotels. $ *Rooms from: Y1288* ✉ *2 Jianguomen Nan Dajie, Chaoyang District, Beijing, China* ☎ *010/6515-8855* ⤳ *349* ✚ *H6.*

$$
HOTEL
🏨 **Westin Beijing Chaoyang** (金茂北京威斯汀大饭店 *Jīnmào Běijīng Wēisīdtīng dàjiǔdiàn*). With 34 floors of guest rooms, the Westin Beijing Chaoyang isn't exactly a small affair, but what the hotel lacks in intimacy, it more than makes up for in luxury: highlights include the trademark "Heavenly" beds and thunderous rain-forest showers, waking up to the best and most abundant breakfast buffet in the city, and service that is relaxed, charming, and attentive. **Pros:** convenient location near the airport expressway; beautiful atrium-style swimming pool; great breakfast buffet. **Cons:** in northeast of the city, far from tourist sites; not as shiny as it used to be; check-in can sometimes be slow. $ *Rooms from: Y1,400* ✉ *1 Xinyuan Nanlu, Chaoyang District* ☎ *010/5922–8888* ⊕ *www.westin.com/chaoyang* ⤳ *550 rooms* ⓘ⃝ *No meals* Ⓜ *Liangmaqiao* ✚ *H2.*

HAIDIAN DISTRICT 海淀区

The Haidian District, in the far northwestern corner of Beijing, is where you'll find the university district, the city zoo, and numerous parks. The main attractions here for visitors are the Summer Palace and Old Summer Palace.

$$$$
HOTEL
Fodor's Choice
★
🏨 **Aman at Summer Palace** (北京颐和安缦 *Běijīng yíhé ānmàn*). The epitome of blissful indulgence, this luxury hotel (part of the famed Aman chain) is spread out across a series of carefully renovated ancient Qing Dynasty courtyards—it even has its own private entrance to the Summer Palace—with guest rooms decorated in restful earth tones (lovely traditional wooden screens and bamboo blinds) and grounds that are positively stunning. **Pros:** right next to the Summer Palace; restaurant Naoki serves fine *kaiseki* (Japanese) cuisine; beautiful setting. **Cons:** very pricey; extremely far from downtown; too isolated

for some. $ *Rooms from: Y4,100* ⊠ *1 Gongmen Qian Street, Summer Palace, Haidian District* ☎ *010/5987–9999* ⊕ *www.amanresorts.com* ⌫ *51 rooms, 33 suites* ⑩ *Breakfast* Ⓜ *Yiheyuan* ✛ *A1.*

$ 🏨 **Friendship Hotel** (友谊宾馆 *Yǒuyì bīnguǎn*). One of the largest garden-
HOTEL style hotels in Asia, the Friendship Hotel was built in 1954 to house foreigners (mostly Soviets) who had come to help rebuild the nation; these days, it relies more on tour groups and those who need to be close to the university area. **Pros:** a bit of history; inexpensive; gardens are attractive. **Cons:** far from the city center; needs updating; not much to do nearby (unless you're a student in search of cheap drinks). $ *Rooms from: Y538* ⊠ *1 Zhongguancun Nan Dajie, Haidian District* ☎ *010/6849–8888* ⊕ *www.bjfriendshiphotel.com* ⌫ *1,700 rooms, 200 suites* ⑩ *No meals* Ⓜ *Renmin University* ✛ *A1.*

$$ 🏨 **Shangri-La Hotel, Beijing** (北京香格里拉饭店 *Běijīng Xiānggélǐlā*
HOTEL *fàndiàn*). With its landscaped gardens, luxury mall, and the addition of a more modern wing, the Shangri-La is a slice of charm for business travelers and those who don't mind being far from the city center; the service is spot-on throughout, from the pristine rooms to the efficient check-in, while the dining options are excellent (the pick of the bunch being the superb and expensive S.T.A.Y, a French restaurant from the brain of Michelin-loved, three-starred chef Yannick Alléno). **Pros:** nice gardens; excellent amenities; great restaurants. **Cons:** far from the city center; no subway; older wing not as good as the newer one. $ *Rooms from: Y1,180* ⊠ *29 Zizhuyuan Lu, Haidian District* ☎ *010/6841–2211* ⊕ *www.shangri-la.com* ⌫ *670 rooms, 32 suites* ⑩ *Breakfast* ✛ *A1.*

OUTSIDE THE CITY CENTER

$$$ 🏨 **Commune by the Great Wall** (长城脚下公社 *Chánghéng jiǎoxià*
RENTAL *gōngshè*). An hour from Beijing, Commune is a design-led cluster of
FAMILY villas in wildly contrasting architectural styles set amid the hills and scrubland of the Great Wall; there's plenty of space, so it's an ideal spot for families and small groups (and includes private access to the Wall); Bamboo House and Suitcase House are the best of the villas, but overall the service and upkeep is spotty following changes in ownership. **Pros:** rustic environment; comfortable accommodation; near the Great Wall. **Cons:** you will likely share the villa with other guests; sketchy service; not in the city. $ *Rooms from: Y1,600* ⊠ *Exit 20 at Shuiguan, Badaling Highway, Yanqing County* ☎ *010/8118–1888* ⊕ *www.communebythegreatwall.com* ⌫ *40 houses* ⑩ *Breakfast.*

$$$$ 🏨 **Grandma's Place (Schoolhouse Hotels)** (奶奶家 *Nǎinaijiā*). This two-
RENTAL bedroom rental cottage is part of a project that offers gorgeous self-
FAMILY catering stays in remote villages around the Great Wall; Grandma's Place is the pick of the bunch, created using stones salvaged from Ming and Qing Dynasty structures, as well as massive beams from an old village house, with a cozy, traditional *kang*—a brick bed heated from beneath—and a very private fruit garden and terrace that provides jaw-dropping views of the Great Wall. **Pros:** a wonderfully rustic getaway with modern comforts; views of the Great Wall; The Schoolhouse restaurant is nearby. **Cons:** guests need a car to get here; no hotel

services; outside of Beijing. $ *Rooms from: Y2,600* ✉ *The Schoolhouse, 12 Mutianyu Village, Huairou District* ☎ *010/6162–6282* ⊕ *www. grandmasplaceatmutianyu.com* ⇥ *2 rooms (8 homes available)* ▭ *No credit cards* ⑩ *Breakfast.*

$$ **Hilton Beijing Capital Airport** (北京首都机场稀尔顿酒店 *Běijīng*
HOTEL *Shŏudūjīchăng Xī'ĕrdùn jiŭdiàn*). The number of worthwhile hotels next to Beijing's airport has flourished in recent years, and the Hilton doesn't disappoint, with surprisingly good restaurants considering the lack of passing trade, and plush, soundproofed rooms decked out in cozy deep-red wood accents. **Pros:** less than 1 km (0.6 mile) from airport terminal; good choice of restaurants; slick rooms. **Cons:** not suitable as a base for the sights; a pain to get a taxi from. $ *Rooms from: Y1,200* ✉ *1 San Jing Road, Beijing Capital International Airport (Terminal 3)* ☎ *010/6458–8888* ⊕ *beijingairport.hilton.com* ⇥ *265 rooms, 57 suites* ⑩ *No meals* Ⓜ *Airport Express* ✛ *H1.*

$$$ **Langham Place, Beijing Capital Airport** (北京首都机场朗豪酒店
HOTEL *Běijīng Shŏudūjīchăng Lănghăo jiŭdiàn*). Airport hotels have a repu-
Fodor's Choice tation for dullness—not so with Langham Place, a fun and funky spot
★ next to Terminal 3 that screams style with high-tech guest rooms, luxu-
rious marble bathrooms, and soundproofed floor-to-ceiling windows; the in-house contemporary art gallery and stylish dining options point to this hotel's playful sense of creativity. **Pros:** airport hotels are rarely this stylish; fantastic service; good facilities. **Cons:** far from the city center; overly long corridors; can feel too quiet at times. $ *Rooms from: Y1,608* ✉ *1 Er Jing Road, Beijing Capital International Airport (Terminal 3)* ☎ *010/6457–5555* ⊕ *beijingairport.langhamplacehotels. com* ⇥ *372 rooms, 67 suites* ⑩ *No meals* Ⓜ *Airport Express* ✛ *H1.*

$$$ **Shan Li Retreats** (山里逸居 *Shānlĭ yìjū*). These five village houses
RENTAL have been renovated into gloriously beautiful rental properties, with
FAMILY old wooden beams and traditional-style beds mixed with subtle mod-
Fodor's Choice ern touches, all nestled among the mountains and valleys of Huang-
★ yankou village (120 km from the city), next to crumbling Great
Wall watchtowers on the hill above. **Pros:** a bucolic escape from the city; good hikes nearby; beautifully restored village homes. **Cons:** a car is required to get there; guests need to take their own food. $ *Rooms from: Y1,500* ✉ *Huangyankou Cun, Beizhuang, Miyun County* ☎ *138/1171–6326* ⊕ *www.shanliretreats.com* ⇥ *Five houses* ☾ *Closed Nov.–Mar.* ⑩ *No meals.*

SHOPPING

Updated by
Yuan Ren

Shopping is an integral part of any trip to Beijing. Between the hutongs, the markets, the malls, and the shopping streets, it sometimes seems like you can buy anything here.

Large markets and malls are the lifeblood of Beijing, and they're generally open from 9 am to 9 pm, though hours vary from shop to shop. If a stall looks closed (perhaps the lights are out or the owner is resting), don't give up. Many merchants conserve electricity or take catnaps when business is slack. Just knock or offer the greeting "*ni hao*" and, more often than not, the lights will flip on and you'll be invited to come in. Shops in malls have more regular hours and will only be closed on a few occasions throughout the year, such as Chunjie (Chinese New Year) and October's National Day Golden Week.

Major credit cards are accepted in pricier venues but cash is the driving force here. ATMs abound, however it's worth noting that before accepting any Mao-faced ¥100 notes, most vendors will hold them up to the light, tug at the corners, and rub their fingers along the surface. Counterfeiting is becoming increasingly sophisticated in China, and banks are reluctant to accept responsibility for ATMs that dispense fake notes.

The official currency unit of China is the yuan or *renminbi* (literally, "the people's currency"). Informally, though, the main unit of currency is called *kuai* (using "kuai" is the equivalent of saying a "buck" in the United States). On price tags, renminbi is usually written in its abbreviated form, RMB, and yuan is abbreviated as ¥. 1 RMB = 1 Renminbi = 1 Yuan = 1 Kuai = 10 Jiao = 10 Mao = 100 Fen

If you're looking to bargain, head to the markets; Western-style shops generally go by the price tags. Stalls frequented by foreigners often have at least one employee with some degree of fluency in English. In many situations—whether or not there's a common tongue—the shop assistant will whip out a calculator, look at you to see what they think you'll cough up, then type in a starting price. You're then expected to punch in your offer (start at one third of their valuation). The clerk will usually come down a surprisingly large amount, and so on and so on. A good tip to note is that there's a common superstition in Chinese markets that if you don't make a sale with your first customer of the

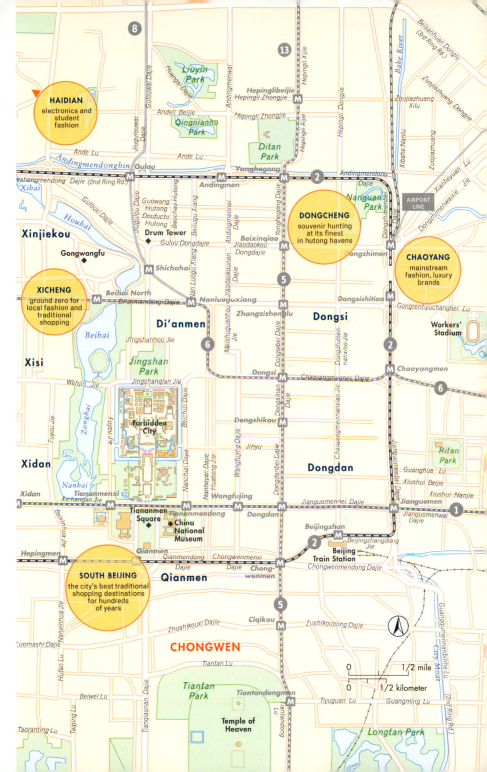

day, the rest of the day will go badly—so set out early, and if you know you're the first customer of the day, bargain relentlessly.

DONGCHENG DISTRICT 东城区

Strolling the old *hutongs* (alleyways) of Dongcheng is one of the simplest pleasures to be found in Beijing. This area is rife with them and, despite a local council that's itching to modernize, many remain relatively unscathed—and filled with households that have lived there for generations. Efforts to reinvigorate some of the hutongs have resulted in a thriving boutique culture, with Nanluoguxiang the first to receive the attentions of tourist dollars. Its bohemian mix of hipster-chic stores, silk shops, and Old China wares attracts huge interest. Next to bask in the limelight was the quieter, but no less hip, Wudaoying Hutong, opposite Lama Temple. Today both command high rents and almost as much attention as nearby Houhai. For some truly unusual finds, try exploring some of the lesser-trod tributaries off Gulou Dongdajie, such as Baochao, Fangjia, and Beiluoguxiang instead.

ART AND ANTIQUES

Beijing Postcards (北京卡片 *Běijīng Kǎpiàn*). Run by historians, this small gallery near bustling Nanluoguxiang showcases a small collection of hundred-year-old Beijing maps and photos of the Drum and Bell towers. As well as selling postcards, reprints, and calenders, the company also runs town walks and historical talks—some of the best you'll find in the city. Check the website for upcoming events as well as a list of other stores selling its products. To visit the gallery, email or phone for an appointment. ⊠ *Chaodou hutong, Dongcheng District* ☎ *156/1145–3992* ⊕ *www.bjpostcards.com* Ⓜ *Zhangzizhonglu.*

Lost & Found (失物招领 *Shīwù zhāolǐng*). Stylish and sensitive to Beijing's past, American designer Paul Gelinas and Chinese partner Xiao Miao salvage objects—whether they're chipped enamel street signs from a long-demolished hutong, a barbershop chair, or a 1950s Shanghai fan—and lovingly remove the dirt before offering them on sale in their treasure trove of a store. This branch is tucked down a tree-lined hutong where imperial exams once took place, and there's another a few doors down. ⊠ *42 Guozijian, Dongcheng District* ☎ *010/6401–1855* ⏰ *Mon.–Thurs. 10:30–8; Fri.–Sun. 10:30–8:30* Ⓜ *Yonghegong* ⊠ *57 Guozijian, Dongcheng District* ☎ *010/6400–1174* ⏰ *Mon.–Thurs. 10:30–8; Fri.–Sat. 10:30–8:30* Ⓜ *Yonghegong.*

Zi'an Print & Graphics (子安版画 *Zí ān Bānhuà*). Exquisite Chinese and European prints (from Y50) decorate the shelves of this adorable little store on Fangjia Hutong. Owner Zi'an is an avid collector of graphic art, engravings, and *ex libris* (aka bookplates—the small prints sometimes pasted into the front of books). Many of the works on display here date from the 19th century onwards, and nearly all have links to China's past, depicting everything from life during the Three Kingdoms period to the Opium Wars. ⊠ *30 Fangjia Hutong, Dongcheng District* ☎ *131/4649–3917* ⏰ *Tues.–Sun. noon–6* Ⓜ *Beixinqiao.*

⚠ **Deception is the only real "art" practiced by the charming "art students" who will approach you at tourist destinations and invite you**

One of the many tea shops in Beijing

to their college's art show. The artworks are, in fact, usually mass-produced copies. If you want to support Beijing's burgeoning art scene, explore the galleries of Dashanzi (798 Art District), Caochangdi, or drop by one of the galleries listed in Chapter 6.

CLOTHING

Mega Mega Vintage. In Gulou, the only real currency is "vintage." Fresh-from-the-factory retro T-shirts have their place, but nothing can replace leafing through the racks at Mega Mega Vintage in search of gold. Distressed denim, classic tees, leather bags, and old-style dresses crown a collection that rises high above the "frumpery" peddled by countless copycat boutiques. ✉ *241 Gulou Dong Dajie, Dongcheng District* ☎ *010/8404–5637* ⊕ *www.douban.com/group/mmvintage* ⊙ *Daily 1:30–9:30* Ⓜ *Beixinqiao.*

Plastered T-Shirts. Now over 15 years old, this store is a must-visit for anyone in search of that rarest of all things: a souvenir you'll actually use when home. Stop here for T-shirt designs that capture the nostalgic days of Old Peking, as well as retro posters, notebooks, and even thermoses from the '80s. It's fun and kitschy, and everything costs around Y100. ✉ *61 Nanluoguxiang Hutong, Dongcheng District* ☎ *136/8339–4452* ⊕ *www.plasteredtshirts.com* ⊙ *Daily 9:30 am–11 pm* Ⓜ *Nanluoguxiang.*

Woo (妩 *Wǔ*). The gorgeous scarves displayed in the windows here lure in passersby with their bright colors and luxurious fabrics. In contrast to those of the vendors in the markets, the cashmere, silk, and bamboo used here are 100% natural. The design and construction are comparable to top Italian designers, while the prices are much more affordable. ⊠ *110/1 Nan-luoguxiang, Dongcheng District* ☎ *010/6400–5395* ⊘ *Daily 9:30 am–10 pm* Ⓜ *Nanluoguxiang.*

MALLS AND DEPARTMENT STORES

Malls at Oriental Plaza (东方广场购物中心 *Dōngfāng guǎngchǎng gòuwù zhōngxīn*). This enormous shopping complex originates at the southern end of Wangfujing, where it meets Chang'an Jie, and stretches a city block east to Dongdan Dajie. It's a true city within a city and certainly geared toward higher budgets. Some of the more upscale shops include Kenzo and Armani Exchange; ladies should check out the boutique from iconic Chinese-American designer Anna Sui for clothes, accessories, and makeup. ⊠ *1 Dongchang'an Jie, Dongcheng District* ☎ *010/8518–6363* ⊘ *Daily 10–10* Ⓜ *Wangfujing.*

MARKETS

FAMILY **Hongqiao Market** (红桥市场 *Hóngqiaó shìchǎng*). Hongqiao, or Pearl Market, is full of tourist goods, knockoff handbags, and cheap watches, but it's best known for its three stories of pearls. Freshwater, seawater, black, pink, white: the quantity is overwhelming, and quality varies by stall. Prices also range wildly, though the cheapest items are often fakes. Fanghua Pearls (No. 4318), on the fourth floor, displays quality necklaces and earrings, with photos of Hillary Clinton and Margaret Thatcher shopping there to prove it. Fanghua has a second store devoted to fine jade and precious stones. Stallholders in the market can be pushy, but try to accept their haggling in the gamelike spirit it's intended. Or wear headphones and drown them out. ⊠ *9 Tiantan Lu, east of the northern entrance to Temple of Heaven, Dongcheng District* ☎ *010/6711–7630* ⊘ *Daily 9:30–7* Ⓜ *Tiantan Dongmen.*

SHOES

Pi'erman Maoyi (皮尔曼贸易公司 *Pí'ěrmàn màoyì gōngsī*). If you've always wanted to have shoes made just for you, this traditional cobbler is highly rated by Beijing expats. If you're in the city at least two weeks—you can have a pair of shoes or boots made for very reasonable prices. Bring in a photo or a pair that you wish to copy, as the cobbler doesn't speak much English. ⊠ *37 Gulou Dong Dajie, Dongcheng District* ☎ *010/6404–1406* ⊘ *Daily 9:30–9* Ⓜ *Beixinqiao.*

⚠ **Fakes abound—and that includes jade, antiques, cashmere, pashminas, silk, and leather as well as handbags and Calvin Klein underwear. Many foreign tourists and local people buy fakes, but keep in mind that the low price generally reflects poor quality, often in ways that aren't**

CLOSE UP

The Ultimate Shopping Tour

Day 1 (weekend): Can't sleep from jet lag? No worries. Rise before dawn and join the hordes at the **Panjia-yuan** antiques market for Beijing Shopping 101. Spend some time on a reconnaissance tour of its vast collection of stores before making any purchases. Bags in tow, head directly across the street to furniture market **Zhaojia Chaowai** and hit the fourth floor for ceramics and more Old China trinkets. Next, direct a pedicab driver to **Beijing Curio City** for all manner of kitsch and souvenirs. From here, take a cab to haggle hard for knock-offs and cheap silk garments at **Silk Alley.** Have lunch, then make the trek to **Qianmen and Dashilan** for a walk down old streets newly renovated for modern shoppers. Travel their length on foot (or take the Qianmen tram); by this time of day its shops will begin to close and it's time to head back to your hotel.

Day 2: Kick off the day by sampling tea from the seemingly infinite number of vendors peddling their wares on **Maliandao Tea Street.** Buy clay or porcelain service sets and loose tea leaves galore. Then take a cab to Qing Dynasty–style shopping street **Liulichang** for calligraphy, scrolls, paintings, and more. Linger here a while before returning to modernity and heading to **Wangfu-jing.** Then, if its mix of malls, snack shops, and souvenir stalls doesn't wipe you out, take a cab to **Hongqiao Market** for a pearl-shopping spree.

Day 3: Start the day in the heart of Beijing's lake district on the pictur-esque **Yandai Xiejie**, beside Houhai. Ethnic garments and Communist relics litter its stores. Afterwards, stretch your legs along the nearby, boutique-packed Gulou Dongdajie until you reach **Nanluoguxiang**, the popular shopping hutong. Affordable local designs, cute and ironic T-shirts, and gorgeous scarves abound. After one lap, continue east until you reach Yonghegong Dajie; here you'll find the quieter **Guozijian** and **Wudaoy-ing** hutong, and plenty more stores to sate your lust for trinkets. From here, grab a taxi and hit Sanlitun for a visit to **Yashow Market** and, next door, **Sanlitun Village.** Designer boutiques and chic malls scatter what used to be just a bar district. Shop, shop, shop, and then drop—wherever you land, a waiter will appear to offer you an ice-cold *jianyi kele* (Diet Coke) or Tsingtao beer.

5

immediately apparent. **Never buy fake beauty products or perfumes, as these can cause serious skin irritation, and reserve your big purchases for accredited shops or merchants who can prove the quality of their product. Some countries limit the number of knockoffs you can bring back through customs, so don't go overboard on the handbags or DVDs. If you're buying authentic antiques, just ask the vender for a receipt (or *fapiao* 发票), embossed with an official red seal.**

SILK AND FABRICS

Daxin Textiles Co. (大新纺织 *Dàxīn fǎngzhī*). For a wide selection of all types of fabrics, from worsted wools to sensuous silks, head to this shop. It's best to buy the material here and find a tailor elsewhere, as sewing standards can be shoddy. ⊠ *Northeast corner of Dongsi, Dongcheng District* ☎ *010/6403–2378* Ⓜ *Dongsi.*

XICHENG DISTRICT 西城区

Xicheng is best known as the home of the Forbidden City, but it also has a few choice shopping areas. Located to the south of Tiananmen Square, **Qianmen** might not rank high on the authenticity scale, thanks to a pre-Olympics renovation, but it still offers plenty of color (as well as brand names)—a ride on the tram down what is one of the city's oldest shopping streets is a must. To the east lies the similarly spruced-up **Dashilar** area, a series of shiny hutongs (alleyways) that are a bit too clean to be real but house old-school Chinese medicine stores, silk shops, and "ancient" souvenirs aplenty.

TO BUY A BIKE OR NOT

Riding a bike is the best way to see Beijing. If you're here for a while, a cheap way of getting around rental prices is to just buy a secondhand bike at **Jindian Xinqiao Xintuo** (金点新桥信托) at 43 Dongsi Beidajie. Prices start at around Y150, and you can always sell it back to them afterwards. Note: the men standing outside are selling stolen bikes that are cheaper and better quality, but that way lies the Dark Side!

Head northwest of the Forbidden City and you'll find Beijing's lake district of Shichahai, comprising Qianhai, Xihai, and Houhai. The latter is surrounded by a morass of hutongs that include Yandai Xiejie, a side street packed with stores and hawkers pushing jewelry, clothes, Mao-shape oddities, and plenty of stuff you don't need but simply can't resist. Meanwhile, farther west of here lies **Xidan**, a giant consumer playground swarming with high-rise malls and bustling underground markets stuffed with cheap clothing and accessories—it's the go-to place for Beijing's young and fashionable. At 13 stories, **Joy City** is the largest mall, while **Mingzhu** and **77th Street** are best for market browsing. And for those who are especially flush with cash, **Galeries Lafayette** is luxury-brand heaven, with the likes of Alexander McQueen, Jimmy Choo, and Gucci.

CHINESE MEDICINE

Tongrentang (同仁堂 *Tóngréntáng*). A first-time consultation with a Chinese doctor can feel a bit like a reading with a fortune-teller. With one test of the pulse, many traditional Chinese doctors can describe the patient's medical history and diagnose current maladies. Serving as official medicine dispenser to the imperial court until its collapse, Tongrentang now has branches all over the city. At its 300-year-old store in Dashilan you can browse the glass displays of deer antlers and pickled snakes, dried seahorses and frogs, and delicate tangles of roots with precious price tags of Y48,000. If you don't speak Chinese and wish to have a consultation with a doctor, consider bringing along a translator. ✉ *24 Dashilan, Qianmen, Exit C, Xicheng District* ☎ *010/6701–5895* ⏱ *Daily 8:30–5* Ⓜ *Qianmen.*

⚠ **Chinese medicine can be effective, but that's unlikely to be the case when it's practiced by lab-coated "doctors" sitting behind a card table on the street corner. If you're seeking Chinese medical treatment, visit a** local hospital, Tongrentang medicine shop, or ask your hotel concierge for a legitimate recommendation.

MALLS AND DEPARTMENT STORES

Seasons Place (金融街购物中心 *Jīnróngjiē gòuwùzhōngxīn*). If you're staying at one of the business hotels in Beijing's Financial Street area, this ritzy mall can fulfill any international luxury-brand needs you may have. Louis Vuitton, Gucci, and Versace are here, as is the Beijing branch of Hong Kong's fab department store, Lane Crawford. ✉ *2 Jinrong Jie, Xicheng District* ☎ *010/6622–0581* ⊕ *www.seasonsplace. com* ⊙ *Daily 10–9* Ⓜ *Fuxingmen*.

MARKETS

Baoguosi Temple Antiques Market (报国寺收藏品市场 *Bàoguósì shōucángpǐn shìchǎng*). This little-known market, atmospherically set in the grounds of Baoguosi Temple, is a smaller, more manageable version of Panjiayuan. It sees very few foreigners, and no one will speak English, but armed with a calculator, stallholders will get their point across. As well as memorabilia from the Cultural Revolution, look out for stalls that sell original photos, ranging from early-20th-century snaps to people posing with their first TVs in the 1970s. ✉ *Guanganmennei Dajie, Xicheng District* ☎ *8223–4583* ⊙ *Daily 9:30–4:30* Ⓜ *Caishikou*.

SILK AND FABRICS

Beijing Silk Shop (北京谦祥益丝绸商店 *Běijīng qiānxiángyì sīchóu shāngdiàn*). Since 1830, the Beijing Silk Shop has been supplying the city with bolts of quality silks and other fabrics. There are tailors on-site to whip up something special, and the second floor has ready-to-wear clothing. To reach the shop, walk all the way down Dashilan then head directly onto Dashilan West Street. ✉ *50 Dashilan Xi Jie, Xicheng District* ☎ *010/6301–4732* ⊙ *Daily 9–8:30* Ⓜ *Qianmen*.

SPECIALTY SHOPS

Tea Street (马连道茶叶批发市场 *Mǎliándào cháyè pīfā shìchǎng*). Literally a thousand tea shops perfume the air of this prime tea-shopping district, west of the city center. Midway down this near-mile-long strip looms the **Teajoy Market**, the Silk Alley of teas. Unless you're an absolute fanatic, it's best to visit a handful of individual shops, crashing tea parties wherever you go. Vendors will invite you to sit down in heavy wooden chairs to nibble on pumpkin seeds and sample their large selections of black, white, oolong, jasmine, and chrysanthemum teas. Prices range from a few kuai for a decorative container of loose green tea to thousands of yuan for an elaborate gift set. Tea Street is also the place to stock up on clay and porcelain teapots and service sets. Green and flower teas are sold loose; black teas are sold pressed into disks and wrapped in natural-colored paper. Despite the huge selection of drinking vessels available, you'll find that most locals drink their tea from a recycled glass jar. ✉ *Maliandao Lu, Xicheng District* ✛ *South end of Maliandao Lu near Guang'anmen Waidajie* Ⓜ *Xuanwumen*.

TOYS

Three Stones Kite Store (三石斋风筝店 *Sānshízhāi fēngzhēng diàn*). For something more traditional, go fly a kite. Here, for three generations, the same family has hand-painted butterflies and birds onto bamboo

Crowded souvenir stalls on the Dashilan Shopping Street

frames to delight adults and children alike. They're a far cry from the run-of-the-mill types you can find elsewhere. ✉ *25 Di'anmen Xidajie, Xicheng District* ☎ *010/8404–4505* ⊕ *www.cnkites.com* ⊙ *Daily 10–9* Ⓜ *Shichahai.*

CHAOYANG DISTRICT 朝阳区

The vast Chaoyang District is *the* area to shop in Beijing, although given that it's the size of many cities, that is somewhat understating things. It stretches all the way from downtown to the airport, encompassing 798 Art District, Sanlitun, and the Central Business District areas. Its consumerist joys lie mainly in its collection of labyrinthine markets and ever more futuristic malls, with a smattering of boutiques in between. Parkview Green and Indigo are just some of the more impressive examples of shopping malls to dot this part of new-look China. Elsewhere, shopping highlights include Panjiayuan Antique Market, Silk Road Market, the indie stores of 798, and the local capitalist's mecca that is Sanlitun Village.

BOOKS

The Bookworm (书虫 *Shūchóng*). Thousands of English-language books fill the shelves at this pleasant café in the heart of Sanlitun. Read for free over a coffee or a simple bistro meal, or join the lending library for a fee. The Bookworm is also a good spot to buy new international magazines and best sellers. This is a popular venue for guest speakers, poetry readings, film screenings, and live-music performances. The kitchen offers a three-course set lunch and dinner. For a quick bite, sandwiches, salads, and a cheese platter are also available. ✉ *4 Sanlitun Nan Lu, set*

CLOSE UP

You Can Judge a Pearl by Its Luster

All the baubles of Beijing could be strung together and wrapped around the Earth 10 times over—or so it seems with Beijing's abundance of pearl vendors. It's mind-boggling to imagine how many oysters it would take to produce all those natural (and cultured) pearls. But, of course, not all are real: some are fake.

The attentive clerks in most shops are eager to prove their products' quality. Be wary of salespeople who don't demonstrate, with an eager and detailed pitch, why one strand is superior to another. Keep in mind the following tips as you judge whether that gorgeous strand is destined to be mere costume jewelry or the next family heirloom.

Color: Natural pearls have an even hue; dyed pearls vary in coloration.

Good Luster: Pick only the shiniest apples in the bunch. Pearls should have a healthy glow.

Shape: The strand should be able to roll smoothly across a flat surface without wobbling.

Blemishes: We hate them on our faces and we hate them on our pearls.

Size: Smaller pearls are obviously less expensive than larger ones, but don't get trapped into paying more for larger poor-quality pearls just because they're heftier.

The cost of pearls varies widely. A quality strand will generally run around US$50 to $200, but it's possible to buy good-looking but lower-quality pearls much more cheaply. As with any purchase, choose those pearls you adore most, and only pay as much as you think they warrant. After all, most women could always use an extra strand of good-looking fakes. Also, if you plan on making multiple purchases and you have time to return to the same shop, go ahead and establish a "friendship" with one key clerk. Each time you return, perhaps bringing someone else along, the price will miraculously drop.

back slightly in an alley 50 meters south of the Gongti Beilu junction, Chaoyang District ☎ *010/6586–9507* ⊕ *www.beijingbookworm.com* ⊗ *Daily 9 am–midnight* Ⓜ *Tuanjiehu.*

Page One. Spread over two floors, this newest addition to the popular Page One chain is *huge*, and when it opened, was open 24 hours a day. Soon, however, the realities of such an epic endeavor hit home (it's located on Bar Street), and normal business hours now apply. As the most comprehensive English language bookstore in the city, there's a little bit of everything here. The second floor has a large area dedicated to arty stationery, gadgets, and funky knickknacks, along with a large selection of children's titles and magazines in English. What isn't here? Many places to sit, so take your seat on a step on the wide staircase, along with the rest of the booklovers. ✉ *Sanlitun Village South, No.19 Sanlitun Rd., Chaoyang* ☎ *010/6417–6626* ⊕ *www.pageonegroup. com/1/china.html* ⊗ *Mon.–Thurs. 10–10, Fri.–Sun. 10–midnight* Ⓜ *Tuanjiehu.*

CLOTHING

Best New China. Showcasing an eclectic collection from more than 100 homegrown designers, Best New China makes a bold statement about China's emerging fashion. Many of the clothes, shoes, and accessories here are created by subtly tinkering with tradition—they have been given a twist of modern chic while remaining distinctly "period." The store's celebrity founder, Hong Huang, has been a driving force behind the concept, and also helped create its celebrity following. From high-fashion to simple linen and even gargoyle art, there's something for just about everyone. Prices start from under 100 yuan for accessories to a few thousand for clothing. ⊠ *Floor B1, Sanlitun Village North, Chaoyang District* ☎ *010/6416–9045* ⊕ *www.brandnewchina.cn* Ⓜ *Tuanjiehu.*

Candy & Caviar. Chinese-American fashion designer Candy Lin owns and operates this gem. From her peaceful and professional store, she designs for both men and women—her label has attracted a celebrity following, including Will.i.am from the Black Eyed Peas and Taiwanese superstar Jay Chou. Expect lots of sharp tailoring, stark colors, and relatively high prices. ⊠ *921, Bldg. 16, China Central Place, 89 Jianguo Lu, Chaoyang District* ☎ *010/5203 6581* ⊕ *www.candyandcaviar.com* ⊙ *Mon.–Fri. 9–5:30* Ⓜ *Guomao.*

Dong Liang Studio (栋梁工作室 *Dòngliáng Gōngzuòshì*). Prices begin at steep and climb to positively perpendicular at this boutique. A visit here is key for anyone wanting to get under the skin of the local fashion scene. Its stock reads like a who's who of rising Chinese designers, with clothes by Vega Wang, He Yan, Manchit Au, and many more. ⊠ *Shop 102, Bldg. 2, Central Park, 6 Chaoyangmenwai Dajie, Chaoyang District* ☎ *010/8404–7648* ⊙ *Daily 11–9* Ⓜ *Yong'anli.*

Fei Space (飞 *Fēi*). Fei Space more than holds its own against the other galleries in the 798 Art District, with a funky interior design and eclectic selection of clothes and housewares. Some of the fashion brands are unique to the store (including the first foray into China by Topshop and Topman), and all of them are uniformly stylish—and expensive. That includes the collection of jeans by Victoria Beckham. ⊠ *B-01, 798 Art District, 4 Jiuxiangqiao Lu, Chaoyang District* ☎ *010/5978–9580* ⊙ *Daily 10–7.*

Heyan'er (何燕服装店 *Héyán fúzhuāng diàn*). He Yan's design philosophy is stated in her label: "*bu yan bu yu*" ("no talking"). Her linen and cotton tunics and collarless jackets speak for themselves. With their earth tones, aubergine hues, peacock patterns, He Yan's designs echo traditional Tibetan styles. ⊠ *15–2 Gongti Beilu, Chaoyang District* ☎ *010/6415–9442* ⊙ *Daily 9:30–9:30* Ⓜ *Dongsishitiao* ⊠ *Holiday Inn Lido, 6 Fangyuan Xilu* ☎ *010/6437–6854* ⊙ *Daily 9:30–9:30* Ⓜ *Sanyuanqiao.*

The Red Phoenix (红凤凰服装工作室 *Hóng fènghuáng fúzhuāng gōngzuòshì*). In this cramped-but-charming Sanlitun showroom, the fashion diva Gu Lin designs embroidered satin qipaos, cropped jackets, and men's clothing for stylish foreigners and China's *xin xin ren lei* (literally the "new, new human being," referring to the country's latest flock of successful young professionals). ⊠ *30 Sanlitun Bei Jie,*

Chaoyang District ☎ *010/6417–3591* 🖃 *Mon.–Sat. 9–11 and 1–6* Ⓜ *Nongzhanguan.*

UCCA Store (东八时区 *UCCA Shāngdiàn*). The 798 Art District is home to a burgeoning collection of housewares, fashion, and design shops. The most innovative of these is an offshoot of the Ullens Center for Contemporary Art (UCCA), located just one door down from the gallery. Clothes, posters, ingenious knickknacks, and artist Sui Jianguo's iconic (and pricey) "Made in China" plastic dinosaurs make it a must-visit for anyone in the area. 🖂 *798 Art District, 4 Jiuxianqiao Lu, Chaoyang District* ☎ *010/5780–0224* ⊕ *ucca.org.cn/en/uccastore* ⊘ *Daily 10–7.*

COMPUTERS AND ELECTRONICS

Beijing Xinshiweiye CD DVD Shop (北京华实伟业商店 *Běijīng Huáshíwěiyè CD DVD Shāngdiàn*). Easily the most reliable DVD store in the city, this store has plenty of oldies as well as the usual "just released in cinemas" Hollywood blockbusters. Look for the "CD DVD Shop" sign out front—the stall is otherwise unlabeled. Because of the many pirated titles among its merchandise, the shop is occasionally raided by police (this isn't be too arduous for them, as it's only a 10-second walk from the nearest station). If that's happened recently, you'll find largely bare shelves with nothing but the odd black-and-white classic on display. Usually normal service is resumed pretty fast. DVDs start at Y10 each; box sets range from Y60 to Y500. 🖂 *Shop 3, East Yashow Market, 58 Gongti Beilu, Chaoyang District* ☎ *010/6417–8633* ⊘ *Daily 10–9* Ⓜ *Tuanjiehu.*

Buy Now Computer Shopping Mall (百脑会电脑广场 *Bàinaǒhuìdiànnaǒ guǎngchǎng*). Buy Now (or Bainaohui) is home to hundreds of stalls selling laptops, PCs, iPods, speakers, phones, and just about any electonic malarkey you can imagine. Both real and knockoff goods tend to be mixed in with each other, so choose wisely. Some stall owners will bargain, others won't, but it's always worth a try. 🖂 *10 Chaoyangmenwai Dajie, Chaoyang District* ☎ *010/6599–5912* ⊘ *Daily 9–8* Ⓜ *Hujialou.*

Kuntai Shopping Mall (昆泰商城 *Kūntài shāngchéng*). Sitting above Walmart in this mall are cameras, tripods, flash memory, phones, and MP3 players (called MP-San in Chinese). If you forgot the USB cable for your digital recorder or need extra camera batteries, this is the place. Bargain hard and you'll be rewarded. 🖂 *12 Chaoyangmenwai Dajie, Chaoyang District* 🖃 *Daily 9:30-7:30* Ⓜ *Dongdaqiao.*

HOUSEWARES

Spin (旋 *Xuán*). This trendy ceramics shop near the 798 Art District features the work of several talented Shanghainese designer who take traditional plates, vases, and vessels and give them a unique and delightful twist. Prices are surprisingly inexpensive. 🖂 *6 Fangyuan Xilu, Lido, Chaoyang District* ☎ *010/6437–8649* ⊘ *Daily 10–7.*

JEWELRY

Shard Box Store (慎德阁 *Shèndégé*). The signature collection here includes small to midsize jewelry boxes fashioned from the broken shards of antique porcelain. Supposedly the shards were collected during the Cultural Revolution, when scores of antique porcelain pieces were smashed in accordance with the law. Birds, trees, pining lovers, and dragons decorate these affordable ceramic-and-metal containers, which range from Y20 to Y200. ⊠ *4 Ritan Beilu, Chaoyang District* ☎ *010/8561–3712* ⊗ *Daily 9–7* Ⓜ *Yong'anli* ⊠ *2 Jiangtai Lu, near the Holiday Inn Lido* ☎ *010/5135–7638* ⊗ *Daily 9–7* Ⓜ *Sanyuanqiao.*

MALLS AND DEPARTMENT STORES

China World Mall (国贸商城 *Guómào Shāngchéng*). Nothing embodies Beijing's lusty embrace of luxury goods quite like China World Mall, which is home to a giant branch of the Hong Kong designer emporium Joyce. The average spend here must run into millions of yuan. However, for smaller budgets, there are plenty of cafés and affordable restaurants; the cinema is decent, and there's also a good ice rink for kids. The mall is open every day, from 10 am to 9:30 pm. ⊠ *1 Jianguomenwai Dajie, Chaoyang District* ☎ *010/8535–1698* Ⓜ *Guomao.*

Indigo (颐堤港 *Yítígǎng*). Located just on the edge of Dashanzi (798 Art District), this complex is one of the city's many impressive "super malls." Light, airy, and with a few new stores still not open, the mall houses brands that include the GAP, H&M, and Sephora as well as the the Parisian Bread and Butter and homebred earthy fashion house JNBY; there is also a branch of the excellent Page One bookstore. The indoor garden isn't much to write home about, but a gigantic outdoor park area might be when it's finished. ⊠ *18 Jiuxianqiao Lu, Chaoyang District* ☎ *010/8426–0898* ⊕ *www.indigobeijing.com* ⊗ *Daily 10–10.*

Parkview Green, Fangcaodi (芳草地 *Fāngcǎodî*). Scattered in and around this giant, green pyramid-shaped "biodome" is a boutique hotel, a mall that doubles as a walk-through gallery, and one of the largest private collections of Salvador Dalí works on display outside Spain. For shoppers, stores by designers Stella McCartney and Mulberry rub shoulders with the likes of GAP; meanwhile a branch of the world-famous Taiwanese dumpling-slingers Din Tai Fung is always worth a visit. Even if designer knickknacks aren't your thing, stopping by just to gawk at the sheer grandiosity of it all comes highly recommended. ⊠ *9 Dongdaqiao Lu, Chaoyang District* ☎ *010/5690–7000* ⊕ *www.parkviewgreen.com/ eng* ⊗ *Daily 10–10* Ⓜ *Dong Daqiao.*

The Place (世贸天阶 *Shìmào tiān jiē*). Shopping-wise you'll find all the usual suspects here—Zara, JNBY, et al.—even if a lack of good dining spots ensures that you won't linger too long. However, visitors largely flock to The Place to witness its eye-wateringly gigantic LED screen, which bursts into life every hour in the evenings and shows some pretty stunning mini-movies (the meteorites are the best!) before lapsing back into screensavers and commercials. ⊠ *9 Guanghua Lu, Chaoyang District* ☎ *010/6587–1188* ⊕ *www.theplace.cn* ⊗ *Daily 10–10* Ⓜ *Jintaixizhao.*

Sanlitun Village (三里屯 *Sānlìtún Village*). The default destination for all expats, this fashionable complex, split into two zones, gets the nod for its great range of stores at all price points, cool architecture, and fun people-watching. Village South houses the biggest Adidas store in the world, as well as branches of Uniqlo, Steve Madden, I.T, and the

5

Inspecting the goods at the Panjiayuan Antiques Market

busiest Apple store you'll ever see. The newer and more upscale Village North has designer stores such as Alexander Wang and Emporio Armani. There's also a good cinema and some great restaurants and bars. ⊠ *19 Sanlitun Jie, Chaoyang District* ☎ *010/6417–6110* ⊕ *www. sanlitunvillage.com* ⊙ *Daily 10–10* Ⓜ *Tuanjiehu.*

Solana Lifestyle Shopping Park (蓝色港湾 *Lánsè Gǎngwān*). This California-style, outdoor shopping complex has a rather enviable location alongside Chaoyang Park, a huge expanse of green space on the east side of the city. It's certainly something Solana's impressive lakeside strip of wine bars and terraces takes full advantage of. As for the shopping, it pulls in a decent list of names: H&M, Zara, Stradivarius, and Muji— as well as Demeter's always-interesting selection of scents—"wet dirt" fragrance anybody? ⊠ *6 Chaoyang Gongyuan Lu, Chaoyang District* ⚓ *A shuttle service runs from Liangmaqiao station Exit C to Solana every 15 minutes daily from 3 pm* ☎ *010/5905–6663* ⊕ *www.solana. com.cn* ⊙ *Daily 10–10* Ⓜ *Tuanjiehu.*

MARKETS

Beijing Curio City (北京古玩城 *Beijīng gǔwán chéng*). This complex has four stories of kitsch and curio shops and a few furniture stores, some of which may actually be selling authentic antiques. Prices are high (they are driven up by free-spending tour groups), so don't be afraid to lowball your offer. Ignore the overpriced duty-free shop at the entrance. ⊠ *21 Dongsanhuan Nan Lu, Chaoyang District* ☎ *010/6774–7711* ⊙ *Daily 10–6* Ⓜ *Panjiayuan.*

Fodor's Choice
★ **Panjiayuan Antiques Market** (潘家园市场 *Pānjiāyuán shìchǎng*). Every day the sun rises over thousands of pilgrims rummaging in search of

antiques and curios, though the biggest numbers of buyers and sellers are on weekends. With over 3,000 vendors crowding an area of 48,500 square meters, it's a sure bet that not every jade bracelet, oracle bone, porcelain vase, and ancient screen is authentic, but most people are here for the reproductions anyway. Behold the bounty: watercolors, scrolls, calligraphy, Buddhist statues, opera costumes, old Russian SLR cameras, curio cabinets, Tibetan jewelry, tiny satin lotus-flower shoes, rotary telephones, jade dragons, antique mirrors, and infinite displays of "Maomorabilia." If you're buying jade, first observe the Chinese customers, how they hold a flashlight to the milky-green stone to test its authenticity. As with all Chinese markets, bargain with a vengeance, as many vendors inflate their prices astronomically for *waiguoren* ("outside-country people").

A strip of enclosed stores forms a perimeter around the surprisingly orderly rows of open-air stalls. Check out photographer Xuesong Kang and his **Da Kang** store (No. 63-B) for some fascinating black-and-white snaps of Beijing city life, dating from the start of the 20th century up to the present day. Also be sure to stop by the **Bei Zhong Bao Pearl Shop** (甲-007) for medium-quality freshwater pearls cultivated by the Hu family. Also here are a sculpture zoo, a book bazaar, reproduction-furniture shops, and an area stashing propaganda posters and Communist literature. Stalls start packing up around 4:30 pm, so make sure to get there on the early side. ✉ *18 Huaweili, Panjiayuan Lu, Chaoyang District* ☎ *010/6774–1869* ⊘ *Weekdays 8:30–6; weekends 6–6* Ⓜ *Panjiayuan.*

Ritan Office Building Market (日坛商务楼 *Rìtán shāngwù lóu*). Don't let the gray-brick and red-trim exterior fool you: The three stories of offices inside the Ritan Building are strung with racks of brand-name dresses and funky-fab accessories. Unlike the tacky variations made on knockoff labels and sold in less expensive markets, the collections here, for the most part, retain their integrity—perhaps because many of these dresses are actually designer labels. They're also more expensive, and bargaining is discouraged. The **Ruby Cashmere Shop** (No. 1009) sells genuine cashmere sweaters and scarves at reduced prices, while **Fandini** (No. 1011) carries a modern selection of typical "street" clothing for men and women. ✉ *15A Guanghua Lu, east of the south entrance to Ritan Park, opposite the Vietnam Embassy, Chaoyang District* ☎ *010/85619556* ⊘ *Daily 10–8* Ⓜ *Yong'anli.*

Fodor's Choice
★

Silk Alley Market (秀水市场 *Xiùshuǐ shìchǎng*). Once a delightfully chaotic sprawl of hundreds of outdoor stalls, the Silk Alley Market is now corralled inside a huge shopping center. The government has been cracking down on an increasing number of certain copycat items, so if you're after a knockoff Louis Vuitton purse or Chanel jacket, just ask; it might magically appear from a stack of plastic storage bins. You'll face no dearth, however, of fake Pumas and Nikes or Paul Smith polos. Chinese handicrafts and children's clothes are on the top floors. Bargain relentlessly, carefully check the quality of each intended purchase, and guard your wallet against pickpockets. ✉ *8 Xiushui Dong Jie, Chaoyang District* ☎ *010/5169–9003* 🌐 *www.silkstreet.cc* ⊘ *Daily 9:30–9* Ⓜ *Yong'anli.*

Yashow Market (雅秀市场 *Yǎxiù shìchǎng*). Especially popular among younger Western shoppers, Yashow is yet another indoor arena stuffed to the gills with low-quality knockoff clothing and shoes. Prices are slightly cheaper than Silk Alley, but the haggling no less essential—don't pay any more than Y50 for a pair of "Converse" sneakers. Also, don't be alarmed if you see someone sniffing the shoes or suede jackets: they're simply trying to see if the leather is real. On the third floor, **Wendy Ya Shi** (No. 3066) is the best of the many tailors on offer, with a basic suit usually starting out at around Y1,500 (including fabric) after a good haggle. ■ TIP→ The Lily Nails salon on the first floor offers inexpensive manicures and foot rubs if you need a break. ⊠ *58 Gongti Beilu, Chaoyang District* ☎ *010/6416–8699* ⊙ *Daily 9:30–9* Ⓜ *Tuanjiehu.*

HAIDIAN DISTRICT 海淀区

If you're in Haidian, the chances are that you're a student, Korean, or both. An abundance of universities and a large Korean population around **Wudaokou** make this a rather bustling, fun area, although it's not worth the journey for that alone—unless you have a penchant for kimchi, cheap shots, and overcrowded dance floors. But, if you're on your way to the Summer Palace or Beijing Zoo, it's worth stopping by, if only to wind down with a massage at one of the many cheap Korean joints. Inexpensive and cheerful boutiques and restaurants are in abundance, while the usual mainstream chain stroes can be found farther east at the shopping malls in **Zhongguancun**, which is also home to Beijing's largest IT and electronics market.

ART AND ANTIQUES

AIKA International Collection Market (镾爱家红木大楼 *Ài jiā guó jì shōu cáng pǐng jiāo liú shì chǎng*). Collectors can spend hours perusing the quiet halls of this large antiques, jade, art, and calligraphy market that's just under the South Fourth Ring Road, beside the Big Bell Temple Museum. ⊠ *31 Beisanhuanxilu, Haidian District* ☎ *010/82132704* ⊕ *mall.cang.com/ajsc* ⊙ *Daily 9:30–7* Ⓜ *Dazhongsi.*

Zhongguancun Electronics City (中关村电器成 *Zhōngguāncūn diànqì chéng*). There's little in the world of IT and electronics that can't be found in Hailong, Dinghao, and the other multistory malls around the Zhongguancun subway station. Before you buy, make sure you compare prices among a few of the stalls (literally hundreds may be offering the same product or serices). Never accept the initial quote without driving a hard bargain, and don't hesitate to pit sellers' prices against each other—it's the thing to do when the competition is this intense. ⊠ *Zhongguancun Dajie, Haidian District* ☎ *010/8266–3883* ⊙ *Daily 9–7.*

6

NIGHTLIFE AND PERFORMING ARTS

Updated
by Adrian
Sandiford

Beijing has blossomed. China is now a global superpower and the capital has become a major center for nightlife, culture, and the arts. The traditional options still endure: Peking opera, acrobatics, classical music, martial arts, and more, but alongside them are more and more exciting contemporary events venues.

From avant-garde plays and modern music to world-class cocktail bars and international talent performing in the hottest clubs, Beijing has ascended to the world stage. You can take in the best of Old Beijing while sipping a world-class martini or Manhattan, or dance the night away at a happening dance club. There are bars for every taste, from beer gardens to classy lounges to vampire-themed venues and English-style pubs.

The performing arts, led by the programming at the National Centre for the Performing Arts (aka "The Egg") are thriving, with talent from as far as the United States and as close as two blocks away taking over the stage nightly. With concerts by the likes of Elton John and Justin Bieber, the city has become a must-stop destination on many international tours. No matter what your interest, Beijing awaits.

PLANNING

GETTING AROUND

Most bars and clubs are clumped together in districts, so you can amble from pub to wine bar to cocktail lounge on foot. Beijing's public transportation system shuts down for the most part after 11 pm. Your best bet is to rely on taxis to get back to your hotel—make sure you pick up a business card from your hotel to show the driver.

LAST CALL

After hours is where Beijing is still playing catch-up to the rest of the world. There are a handful of 24-hour joints, with the bleary-eyed drinkers who populate them but most partiers wind down around 3 or 4 am and decamp to 24-hour dim sum joints to recover.

HAIDIAN
youthful kicks
in Beijing's
university district

8

13

Liuyin
Park

Huangsi Dajie

Gulouwai Dajie

Andeli Beilie

Qingnianhu
Park

Hepinglibeijie
Hepingli Zhongjie

Hepingli Zhongjie

Hepingli Xijie

Hepingli Dongjie

Hepingli Xilu

Zoujiazhuang
Xilu

Beisanhuan Donglu (3rd Ring Rd.)

Bahe River

Zuojiazhuang Dongjie

Xibahe Nanlu

Xibahe Nanlu

Ande Lu

Ande Lu

Ditan
Park

Yonghegong

2

Andingmendong
Dajie

Nanguan
Park

Xianheyuan Lu

Dongzhimenwaixie

**AIRPORT
LINE**

Jishuitan

Andingmendongbin

Gulou

Deshengmennei Dajie

Xinjiekouwai Dajie

Deshengmenwai Dajie

Deshengmendong Dajie (2nd Ring Rd.)

Xihai

Guowang
Hutong
Doufuchi
Hutong

Baochao Hutong

Andingmennei Dajie

Andingmen

Andingmen

Yonghegong Dajie

Dongzhimennei Dajie

Dongzhimen

Dongzhimen

Xinjiekou

Gulouxi Dajie

Houhai

Gulou Dajie

Andu Xiang

Bailyu Xiang

Drum Tower

Gulou Dongdajie

CHAOYANG
international
eateries for every
pocketbook

DONGCHENG
hutong hideaways,
cozy courtyards,
and world-class
theaters

Gongwangfu

Shichahai

Nan Luogu Xiang

Beixinqiao
Jiaodaokou
Dongdajie

Dongsishitiao

Gongrentiyuchangbei Lu

Xinjiekounan Dajie

Qianhai

Beihai North

Zhangzizhonglu

Zhangzizhong
Lu

Dongsi Tiao

5

Dongsishitiao

**Workers'
Stadium**

D'anmenxi Dajie

6

Nanluoguxiang

Meishuguanhou
Jie

Meishuguanqian
Dajie

Ping'anli

**Beihai
Park**

Di'anmen

Xiaojie

4

Zishiku Dajie

Beihai

Jingshanhou Jie

Dongsi

Chaoyangmennei Dajie

Dongsinandajie

2

Yisibei Dajie

Xisi

Wenjin Jie

Zhonghai

**Jingshan
Park**

Jingshannan Jie

Meishuguanqiannanxiao Jie

Dengshikou

Chaoyangmen

Chaoyangmenwai Dajie

6

Xi'anmen Dajie

Beichizi Dajie

Chaoyangmennanxiaojie

Chaoyangbeixiaojie

Liuyin Jie

**Forbidden
City**

Xidan

Xidaihe Dajie

Fuyou Jie

Nanchang Jie

Nanheyan Dajie

Jinyu

Dongdan

Xiushui Nanjie

Nanhai

Jingshanqian Jie

Wangfujing Dajie

Dongdanbei Dajie

Xidan

Baixinhua Jie

Tiananmenxi

Xichangan Jie

1

Xichangan Jie

Tiananmendong

Wangfujing

Jianguomennei Dajie

Jianguomen

Jianguomenwai
Dajie

1

**Tiananmen
Square**

Tiananmendong

Dongdan

Beijingzhan

**Great
Hall of
the People**

**China
National
Museum**

Beijingzhandong
Jie

**Beijing
Train Station**

2

Xuanwumen

Qianmennei Dajie

Qianmendong

Chongwenmenxi

**Chong-
wenmen**

Chongwenmennei Dajie

Chongwenmendong Dajie

Guangqumennanbinhe Lu

Xuanwumendong Dajie

Hepingmen

Dajie

Qianmen

Dajie

Chongwenmenxi Dajie

Qianmen

Qianmen

Qianmen Dajie

Ciqikou

5

Zushikoudong Dajie

City Moat

Guangqumen (2nd Ring Rd.)

Luomashi Dajie

XICHENG
thrills and spills
at Beijing's
best shows

Zhushikouxi Dajie

Zushikoudong Dajie

CHONGWEN

4

Tiantan Lu

Hufang Lu

Tianqiaonan Dajie

Beiwei Lu

**Tiantan
Park**

Tiantandongmen

Tiyuguan Lu

Guangming Lu

Taiping Lu

**Temple of
Heaven**

Tiantandong Lu

Longtan Park

Taoranting Lu

0   1/2 mile

0   1/2 kilometer

SMOKING

Smoking inside bars and clubs remains common in Beijing. There are a handful of no-smoking bars, such as Mao Mao Chong, off Nanluoguxiang, and nearby Great Leap Brewing, which prohibits smoking inside while allowing smokers to light up in the courtyard, but in general, be prepared for a heavy dose of secondhand smoke at most venues.

WHAT'S ON?

The best way to find out what's on or where to party is to pick up one of the free listing magazines found at many bars and restaurants. The best ones are the monthly *The Beijinger* and *That's Beijing,* as well as the biweekly *City Weekend:* all have frequently updated websites and give bilingual addresses in their listings.

WHAT TO WEAR

A rapidly expanding middle class combined with runaway economic growth means that the local population has developed an insatiable appetite for international luxury brands such as Prada and Louis Vuitton, and it shows in many of the classiest venues in Beijing. That said, there's no strictly enforced dress code and you're just as likely to see the pajamas-and-sweat pants crowd out and about at the same places.

NIGHTLIFE

With intimate bars, world-class cocktail lounges, happening dance halls, sports bars, and even English-style pubs, Beijing has just about every kind of experience you can imagine. Keep in mind, though, that establishments seemingly rise up overnight, and can disappear just as quickly in the breakneck pace of development that is endemic to Beijing.

DONGCHENG

BARS

Fodor's Choice ★ **Amilal** (按一拉尔 *Àn yī lā'ěr*). If you have the patience to find this cozy courtyard bar in a tiny alley, you'll be rewarded with one of the city's hidden gems. Grab a seat at one of the rough wooden tables, listen to the low-key live music that's often playing, and enjoy the laid-back hutong vibe that's so unique to Beijing. For such a small bar, there's an unexpectedly good selection of whiskies on offer, too. ⊠ *48 Shoubi Hutong, off the east end of Gulou Dongdajie, Dongcheng District* ☎ *010/8404–1416.*

Cu Ju (蹴鞠 *Cùjū*). Proprietor Badr Benjelloun is a Moroccan expat who's lived in the city for many years and has myriad interests. This fun bar is the culmination of all his many passions, including rum, Moroccan food, and sporting events. Like many of Beijing's best hutong bars, it can be a bit tricky to find, but is well worth it once you're there. ⊠ *28 Xiguan Hutong, off Dongsi Bei Dajie, Dongcheng District* ☎ *010/6407–9782* ⊕ *www.cujubeijing.com.*

Drum & Bell Bar (鼓钟咖啡馆 *Gǔzhōng kāfēiguǎn*). Situated next to the Drum and Bell towers (hence the name), this busy bar has one of Beijing's nicest views from its roof deck (when the surrounding area is not undergoing renovation, as tends to happen around here from time to time). An all-you-can-drink deal on Sunday only serves to sweeten the deal. ✉ *41 Zhonglouwan Hutong, next to the Drum and Bell towers, Dongcheng District* ☎ *010/8403–3600.*

El Nido (方家小酒馆59号 *Fāngjiāxiǎojiǔguǎnwǔshíjiǔhào*). Little more than a hole in the wall, this hutong gem is stuffed to the gills with imported beers, fine cheeses and charcuterie, and the owner's home-made infused liquors. In the summer it's a little roomier, since overflow crowds spill onto picnic tables set up in the front. El Nido is a great first stop of the night. If you aren't feeling the crowds, grab some bottles to go and sip on the streets with the rest of the Beijing old-timers—and thank your lucky stars for the lack of open container laws. ✉ *59 Fangjia Hutong, Andingmennei Dajie, Dongcheng District* ☎ *010/8402–9495* Ⓜ *Andingmen.*

4Corners (肆角餐吧 *Sìjiǎocānba*). Tucked inside a tiny hutong near the western end of Houhai, 4Corners has a working fireplace in the winter and a breezy patio in the summer. There's inventive, pan-Asian cuisine from its Vietnamese-Canadian chef-owner, delicious cocktails, and refreshing beer such as Vedett White on tap. ✉ *27 Dashibei Hutong, Gulou Xidajie, Dongcheng District* ☎ *010/6401–7797.*

Great Leap Brewing (大跃啤酒 *Dàyuèpíjiǔ*). At Beijing's first proper microbrewery, the beers are made with ingredients such as tea and Sichuan peppercorns. The courtyard operation also hosts weekly movie screenings and the odd special event. Don't miss the bar peanuts—spicy and salty, they'll keep you going back to the bar for just one more brew. This place has been so successful, in fact, that the owners have since opened a much-larger flagship space in downtown Sanlitun (on Xinzhongjie). ✉ *6 Doujiao Hutong, Dongcheng District* ☎ *010/5717–1399* ⊕ *www.greatleapbrewing.com.*

Mao Mao Chong (毛毛虫 *Máomáochóng*). This bar is known for top-quality infused cocktails, including a chili-infused vodka Bloody Mary and a Sichuan peppercorn Moscow Mule. Another standout is the owners' own Bangkok Hilton: Thai tea–infused Scotch, crème de cassis, bitters, syrup made from *pandanus* (screw pine) leaves, and an orange twist. The pizzas and artwork are an added reason to stop in. ✉ *12 Banchang Hutong, Jiaodaokounan, Dongcheng District* ☎ *010/6405–5718* ⊕ *www.maomaochongbeijing.com* ⊙ *Closed Mon.*

Slow Boat Brewery Taproom (慢船啤酒厂 *Màn chuán píjiǔ chǎng*). At this sleek yet cozy taproom inside the hutongs, there are at least a dozen beers on tap at any given moment, including all-weather tipples such as pale ales and IPAs, as well as seasonal specialities (warming stouts in the winter, refreshing citrusy brews come summertime). A luxurious bonus if you're here during the frigid winter season are the heated floors. ✉ *56 Dongsi Batiao, Dongsi Beidajie, Dongcheng District* ☎ *010/6538–5537* ⊕ *www.slowboatbrewery.com* ⊙ *Closed Mon.* Ⓜ *Zhangzizhong Lu (Line 5).*

Yin (饮皇家驿栈屋顶 *Huángjiā Yìzhàn*). The Emperor Hotel's rooftop terrace bar certainly has the "wow" factor when it comes to the view, thanks to a vista that overlooks the Forbidden City, plus there's even a hot tub on hand if you need to relax. Unsurprisingly, drink prices are high, and, more often than not it tends to be too empty for real fun, but it can be a good place to show visitors. Befitting the design focus of the hotel, red lanterns and fashionably outfitted staff add to the classiness of the experience. If only it had a bit more buzz. ⊠ *The Emperor Hotel, 33 Qihelou Dajie, top floor, Dongcheng District* ☎ *010/6526–5566* Ⓜ *Tiananmen East.*

DANCE CLUBS

Dada Bar (达达 *Dá dá*). A chilled-out, unpretentious place where you can dance, Dada is the sort of underground club a cool older cousin might have once sneaked you into. Talented resident and guest DJs from all over the world perform, and you can expect industrial-chic decor and cheap, strong drinks. It's a great final destination on a night out, and beloved by both long-term expats and local scenesters. ⊠ *Rm. 101, Bldg. B, 206 Gulou Dongdajie, Dongcheng District* ☎ *183/1108–0818.*

Tango (糖果 *Tángguǒ*). This warehouse-style space is way more interesting than the competition. Without the usual gaudy decor, Tango is roomy enough to take the crowds, and often plays some very loud, but good music. Beijing's best midsize live-music venue is on the third floor and (unimaginatively) called Tango 3F. ⊠ *79 Hepingli Xijie, Dongcheng District* ☎ *010/6428–2288* Ⓜ *Yonghegong.*

XICHENG DISTRICT

BARS

East Shore Live Jazz Café (东岸咖啡 *Dōng'àn kāfēi*). There's no competition: This place has the most fabulous views of Houhai lake, hands-down, and authentic jazz on stage every night. ⊠ *2nd fl., 2 Qianhai Nanyanlu, west of the Post Office on Di'anmen Waidajie, Xicheng District* ☎ *010/8403–2131.*

CHAOYANG DISTRICT

BARS

Apothecary (药剂员 *Yào jì yuán*). Like an old-fashioned pharmacist doling out carefully concocted medicinals, the bartenders at this low-key venue artfully turn all of your favorite ingredients into cocktails that will soothe the soul. Mixologist-in-chief Leon Lee is something of a local celebrity for good reason. The location (in the trendy Nali Patio complex) and the tasty bar food are bonuses. ⊠ *3/F, Nali Patio, 81 Sanlitun Beilu, Chaoyang District* ☎ *010/5208–6040* Ⓜ *Tuanjiehu.*

China Bar (北京亮酒吧 *Běijīng liàng jiǔbā*). Perched atop the 65-story Park Hyatt, this upmarket cocktail bar offers bird's-eye views of the city, smog and all. Dark and sultry, the modern Asian decor is minimalist and doesn't distract from the views, or the drinks. Cocktails are expertly mixed; Scotch purists can choose from a 20-plus strong list of single malts. ⊠ *Park Hyatt, 2 Jianguomenwai Dajie, 65th fl., Chaoyang District* ☎ *010/8567–1838* Ⓜ *Guomao.*

The Den. This old-school joint's main attractions are the sports showing on its wide-screen TVs and the fact that it never, ever shuts. It's buzzing every night, especially during happy hour, when you can grab half-price drinks and pizza until 10 pm. This is also the social HQ for the city's amateur rugby club, so you'll often find its players in here, drinking rowdily. Yes, it's somewhat of a dive bar, populated by a questionable cast of characters in the small hours, but it's also an always-reliable watering hole, too. ⊠ *4 Gongti Donglu, next to the City Hotel, Chaoyang District* ☎ *010/6592–6290* Ⓜ *Tuanjiehu.*

D.Lounge. Raising the bar for bars in Beijing, this New York–style lounge is swank, spacious, and has an innovative drink list. This is where many of the city's cool kids like to hang, and the doormen occasionally restrict entry to the more dapperly dressed. It's a bit tricky to find: if you are facing Q Mex, then walk down the lane that runs north–south, parallel to the side of that building. ⊠ *Courtyard 4, Gongti Beilu, behind the Bookworm, Chaoyang District* ☎ *010/6593–7710.*

Face (飞色 *Fēi sè*). Stylish without being pretentious, Face has been around longer than most, and remains popular with a mature and usually well-heeled crowd. The complex holds a multitude of restaurants, but the real gem is the bar. Grab a lounge bed surrounded by silky drapes, take advantage of the happy-hour drink specials, and enjoy some premier people-watching. ⊠ *26 Dongcaoyuan, Gongti Nanlu, Chaoyang District* ☎ *010/6551–6788* ⊕ *www.facebars.com* Ⓜ *Dongdaqiao.*

First Floor (壹楼 *Yīlóu*). An unpretentious bar perfect for a night out with friends, First Floor is the sort of place where you stop in for one, and end up drinking through to the early hours. Expect a relaxed but busy crowd, with plenty of friendly folk happy to strike up a conversation while the beer keeps flowing. Happy hour runs from 5 to 9 pm. ⊠ *Tongli Studio, Sanlitun Houjie, 1st Floor, Chaoyang District* ☎ *010/6413–0587.*

Ichikura (一藏 *Yī cāng*). This tiny bar is the place to go if you're a discerning whiskey drinker—there are hundreds of varieties on offer. The dimly lit interior, minimalist decor, and hushed conversation give it an air of exclusivity—it's worthy of James Bond. Drinks are taken very seriously here, and it shows in both the quality of the alcohol and the professionalism with which it's mixed by the Japanese-led bar staff. The entrance is via stairs at the south wall of the Chaoyang Theatre. ⊠ *Chaoyang Theatre, 36 Dongsanhuan Beilu, 2nd fl., Chaoyang District* ☎ *010/6507–1107* Ⓜ *Hujialou.*

Mokihi. Tucked behind an Italian-fusion restaurant on an unassuming strip mall of establishments near Chaoyang Park, Mokihi is a perfect oasis from the hustle and bustle of everyday Beijing. Have the Japanese-trained bartenders mix up one of their signature cocktails and nibble on delightful hors d'oeuvres while engaging in quiet conversation with your drinking companions. ⊠ *C12, Haoyun Jie (Lucky Street), 3rd fl., Chaoyang District* ☎ *010/5867–0244.*

Fodor's Choice ★ **Q Bar.** This tucked-away lounge south of the main Sanlitun drag is an unpretentious option for an evening out. The cocktails here—strong, authentic, and not ridiculously expensive—are a bit of a legend in Beijing, thanks to the involvement of Echo Sun, who has been a real pioneer on the local drinks scene. Don't be put off by the fact that it's on the top floor of a bland, 1980s-style hotel; in the summer the terrace more than makes up for that. ⊠ *Top floor of Eastern Inn Hotel, 6 Baijiazhuang Lu, corner of Sanlitun Nanlu and Gongti Nanlu, Chaoyang District* ☎ *010/6595–9239* ⊕ *www.qbarbeijing.com* Ⓜ *Tuanjie Hu.*

The Tree. For years now, expats have crowded this bar for its Belgian beer, wood-fired pizza, and quiet murmurs of conversation. It does, however, get a bit smoky; if you're sensitive you may want to give this venue a pass. For pasta instead of pizza, there's always Nearby the Tree just 100 yards to the southeast. ⊠ *43 Sanlitun Beijie, Chaoyang District* ☎ *010/6415–1954* ⊕ *www.treebeijing.com.cn* Ⓜ *Tuanjiehu.*

Twilight (暮光 *Mùguāng*). Opened by some of the same people involved with Apothecary in Sanlitun, Twilight is an oasis of cool in the otherwise somewhat dry Central Business District (CBD). Have the bartender make you a perfect Old Fashioned, which you can pair with one of the bar's tasty pizzas. ⊠ *Bldg. 5, Jianwai SOHO, 39 Dongsanhuan Zhonglu, 3rd fl., Chaoyang District* ☎ *010/5900–5376.*

The World of Suzie Wong (苏西黄俱乐部 *Sūxīhuáng jùlèbù*). It's no coincidence that this bar is named after a 1957 novel (and 1960 film) about a Hong Kong prostitute. Come here late at night and, as well as groups of friends on the dance floor, you're also likely to find those on the prowl, and in search of a good time. The vibe is enhanced by the 1930s-opium-den design, with China-chic beds overrun with cushions. Over the years, Suzie Wong's has built a reputation for decent cocktails and good, crowd-pleasing music. It has, however, begun to drop off the local party circuit in recent years. ⊠ *1A Nongzhanguan Lu, Chaoyang West Gate, Chaoyang District* ☎ *010/6500–3377.*

DANCE CLUBS

Cargo Club. Fierce promotions have attracted some top-name international DJs to this spot: in spite of the smallish dance floor, many expats consider Cargo the best mainstream club along Gongti Xilu. Perhaps it's the 1980s kitsch. ⊠ *6 Gongti Xilu, Chaoyang District* ☎ *010/6551–6898.*

GAY NIGHTLIFE

Alfa (餐吧 *Alfa cānba*). Home to nostalgia-fueled theme nights, including 80s and disco, Alfa is a hopping little dance spot that's particularly popular with local gay men. ⊠ *6 Xingfu Yicun, opposite the north gate of the Workers' Stadium, Chaoyang District* ☎ *010/6413–0086.*

Destination (目的地 *Mùdìdì*). The city's best and most popular gay club has a bouncy dance floor, energetic DJs, and a small lounge area. It gets extremely packed on weekends and attracts a varied crowd of almost all male expats and locals. Unlike most places in Beijing, there's a cover here. ⊠ *7 Gongti Xilu, Chaoyang District* ☎ *010/6551–5138* Ⓜ *Dongsi Shitiao.*

DID YOU KNOW?

Chinese acrobatics has existed for more than two thousand years. Like vaudeville in the West, acrobatic performances in old China were considered low-class; they were even banned from theaters. Many of the acts used props such as chairs, tables, and plates. Today you'll see amazing feats like traditional group gymnastics, springboard stunts, and gymnastics on double-fixed poles.

HAIDIAN DISTRICT

BARS

Lush. The go-to hangout in the university district of Wudaokou, Lush is a home-away-from-home for many a homesick exchange student. With weekly pub quizzes, open-mike nights, and large, strong drinks, Lush is an excellent place to start the night for those in this part of town. ⊠ *2nd fl., Bldg. 1, Huaqing Jiayuan, Chengfu Lu, Haidian District* ☎ *010/8286–3566* ⊕ *www.lushbeijing.com* Ⓜ *Wudaokou.*

The Red House (色家 *Hóng jiā*). The simple, no-frills exterior here reflects the bar as a whole—bare walls warmed by a roaring fire, friendly bar staff, and a loyal crowd looking for a home away from home in which to booze in peace. The pizza oven never stops churning out tasty pies, a good accompaniment to the beers on tap. ⊠ *Wudaokou, Wangzhuang Lu, Haidian District* ☎ *010/6291–3350* Ⓜ *Wudaokou.*

PERFORMING ARTS

The performing arts in China took a long time to recover from the Cultural Revolution (1966–76), and political works are still generally banned or avoided. In recent years, names such as Kevin Spacey and the Royal Shakespeare Company have alighted on Beijing, reinforcing the capital's reputation as an arts destination. For culture vultures, there are avant-garde plays, chamber music, traditional Peking opera, acrobatics shows, and lots more.

As most of the stage is inaccessible to non-Chinese speakers, visitors to Beijing are more likely to hunt out the big visual spectacles, such as Beijing opera or kung fu displays. These long-running shows are tailored for travelers: your hotel will be able to recommend performances and venues and will likely be able to help you book tickets.

ACROBATICS AND KUNG FU

Chaoyang Theater (朝阳剧场 *Cháoyáng jùchǎng*). This space is the queen bee of acrobatics venues, especially designed to unleash oohs and ahhs. Spectacular individual and team acrobatic displays involving bicycles, seesaws, catapults, swings, and barrels are performed here nightly. It's touristy but fun. ⊠ *36 Dongsanhuan Beilu, Chaoyang District* ☎ *010/6507–2421* ⊕ *www.chaoyangjuchang.com* Ⓜ *Hujialou.*

Fodor's Choice ★ **The Red Theatre** (红剧场 *Hóng jùchǎng*). If it's Vegas-style stage antics you're after, the *Legend of Kung Fu* show is what you want. Extravagant martial arts—performed by dancers, not martial artists—are complemented by neon, fog, and heavy-handed sound effects. Shows are garish but also sometimes glorious. ⊠ *44 Xingfu Dajie, Dongcheng District* ☎ *010/5165–1914, 135/5252–7373* ⊕ *www.redtheatre.cn* Ⓜ *Tiantan Dong Men.*

Tianqiao Acrobatic Theater (天桥乐茶馆 *Tiānqiáo cháyèguàn*). The Beijing Acrobatics Troupe of China is famous for weird, wonderful shows. Content includes a flashy show of offbeat contortions and tricks, with a lot of high-wire action. There are two shows per night, usually

The National Centre for the Performing Arts

scheduled for 5:30 and 7:15 pm, but it's best to phone ahead and check. ✉ *5 Tianqiao Shichang Lu, east end of Beiwei Lu, Xicheng District* ☎ *010/6303–7449.*

MUSIC

Beijing Concert Hall (北京音乐厅 *Běijīng yīnyuètīng*). One of Beijing's main venues for Chinese and Western classical-music concerts also hosts folk dancing and singing, and many celebratory events throughout the year. The 1,000-seat venue is also the home of the China National Symphony Orchestra. ✉ *1 Bei Xinhua Jie, Xicheng District* ☎ *010/6605–7006* Ⓜ *Tiananmen West.*

Fodor's Choice
★ **Forbidden City Concert Hall** (北京中山音乐堂 *Zhōngshān gōngyuán yīnyuètáng*). One of the nicest venues in Beijing, the 1,400-seat Forbidden City Concert Hall plays host to a variety of classical, chamber, and traditional music performances in plush surroundings and with world-class acoustics. Though the facilities are completely modern, concertgoers are treated to a moonlit walk through Zhongshan Park, a former imperial garden dotted with historical landmarks. ✉ *In Zhongshan Park, Xichang'an Jie, Xicheng District* ☎ *010/6559–8285* ⊕ *www. fcchbj.com* Ⓜ *Tiananmen West.*

MAO Live House. With some of the most committed gig fans in the city, and live music almost every night of the week, MAO Live House is *the* place to experience the vibrant local music scene. ✉ *111 Gulou Dongdajie, Dongcheng District* ☎ *010/6402–5080* ⊕ *www.mao-music.com* Ⓜ *Gulou Dajie.*

Poly Theater (保利剧院 *Bǎolì jùyuàn*). This is a modern shopping-center-like complex on top of Dongsishitiao subway station. One of Beijing's better-known theaters, the Poly hosts Chinese and international concerts, ballets, and musicals. ■TIP→ **If you're seeking a performance in English, this is one of your best bets.** ⊠ *1/F Poly Plaza, 14 Dongzhimen Nandajie, Dongcheng District* ☎ *010/6500–1188* ⊕ *www.polytheatre. com* Ⓜ *Dongsishitiao.*

Yugong Yishan (愚公移山 *Yúgōngyíshān*). Housed in a Republican-era courtyard, Yugong Yishan is the city's other premier destination for live music by both local rock bands and touring foreign acts. If you're in the mood to catch a good show, check the venue website to see who's playing when you're in town. ⊠ *3–2 Zhangzizhong Lu, Dongcheng District* ☎ *010/6404–2711* ⊕ *www.yugongyishan.com* Ⓜ *Zhangzizhonglu.*

CHINESE OPERA

Chang'an Grand Theater (长安大戏院 *Cháng'ān dàxìyuàn*). In this theater specializing in Chinese opera, spectators can choose to sit either in the traditional seats or at cabaret-style tables. Besides Peking-style opera, the theater also puts on performances of other regional styles, such as *yueju* (from Guangdong) and *chuanju* (from Sichuan). ⊠ *7 Jianguomennei Dajie, Dongcheng District* ☎ *010/6510–1309* ⊕ *www. changantheater.com* Ⓜ *Jianguomen.*

Huguang Guild Hall (湖广会馆 *Húguǎng huìguǎn*). Built in 1807, the Huguang Guild Hall was at its height one of Beijing's "Four Great" theaters. In 1925 the Guild Hall hosted Dr. Sun Yat-sen at the founding of the Chinese Nationalist Party (KMT). Today, the Guild Hall has been restored to its former splendor and hosts regular opera performances. The venue also has a small museum of Peking opera artifacts. ⊠ *3 Hufang Lu, Xicheng District* ☎ *010/6351–8284* Ⓜ *Caishikou.*

Lao She Teahouse (老舍茶馆 *Lǎoshě cháguǎn*). Named for famed Beijing author Lao She, this teahouse in the Qianmen area plays host to a variety of traditional performances, including acrobatics, opera, and vaudeville shows. Dinner is served on the premises; reservations are required one day in advance for the nightly shows. ⊠ *Building 3, 3 Qianmenxi Dajie, Xicheng District* ☎ *010/6303–6830.*

Fodor's Choice ★

Liyuan Theater (梨园剧场 *Líyuán jùchǎng*). The unabashedly touristy shows here are still a great time. You can first watch performers put on makeup before the show (come early) and then graze on snacks and sip tea while watching English-subtitled shows. Glossy brochures complement the crooning. ⊠ *1/F, Qianmen Hotel, 175 Yong'an Lu, Xicheng District* ☎ *010/6301–6688* ⊕ *www.qianmenhotel.com/en/liyuan.html.*

THEATER

Beijing Exhibition Theater (北京展览馆剧场 *Běijīng zhǎnlǎnguǎn jùchǎng*). Chinese plays, Western (and Chinese) operas, and ballet performances are staged in this Soviet-style building that's part of the exhibition center complex. Talk about a wide range of shows: the Michael Jackson musical *Thriller* was once staged here, swiftly followed by some

Beijing Opera

For hundreds of years, Beijing opera troupes have delighted audiences with rich costumes, elaborate makeup, jaw-dropping acrobatics, and tales of betrayal and intrigue. Nowadays, operas staged in Beijing's theaters are typically of the Jing Ju style, which emerged during the Qing Dynasty, although there are more than 350 other kinds of Chinese opera, each distinguished by different dialects, music, costumes, and stories.

WHAT YOU'LL SEE AND HEAR

A night at the opera gives a glimpse into China's past—not to mention a fascinating mix of drama, color, movement, and sound. To master the art of Beijing opera's leaping acrobatics, stylized movements, sword dances, and dramatic makeup techniques, actors begin their grueling training as young children.

Opera instrumentation consists of the percussive Wuchang—the gongs, drums, cymbals, and wooden clappers that accompany exaggerated body movements and acrobatics—and the melodic Wenchang, including the Chinese fiddle (*erhu*), the lutelike *pipa*, horns, and flutes. Neophytes may find two hours of the staccato clanging and nasal singing of Beijing opera hard to take (and most young Chinese fed on a diet of Western-style pop agree) but this dramatic, colorful experience can be one of the most memorable of your trip.

BEFORE YOUR TRIP

Watch Chen Kaige's *Farewell My Concubine*, a 1993 film that follows the life, loves, and careers of two male opera performers against a background of political turmoil. It also depicts the brutality of opera schools, where children were forced to practice grueling routines (balancing water jugs, doing headstands).

MEI LANFANG: GAY ICON AND OPERA HERO(INE)

Born in Beijing into a family of stage performers, Mei Lanfang (1894–1961) perfected the art of female impersonation during his five decades on stage. He's credited with popularizing Beijing opera overseas and was so popular in his day that there was even a brand of cigarettes named after him. His gender-bending abilities earned him a special place in the hearts of gay activists across China. *The Worlds of Mei Lanfang* (2000) is an American documentary about him, with footage of his performances.

WHERE TO WATCH

There is opera performance any night of the week in Beijing, but there are more options on weekends. Shorter shows put on at venues such as Liyuan Theater and Huguang Guild Hall are full of acrobatics and fantastic costumes. Shows usually start around 7 pm and cost between Y50 and Y200. The free-listing magazines have information, and staffers at your hotel can recommend performances and help you book tickets. ■TIP→ **You can get a free taste of Chinese opera before you spring for tickets if you have access to a television; China Central Television broadcasts nonstop opera on its CCTV 11 channel.**

6

traditional folk art performances. ✉ *135 Xizhimenwai Dajie, Xicheng District* ☎ *010/6835–4455* Ⓜ *Xizhimen.*

Capital Theater (首都剧场 *Shǒudū jùchǎng*). This is a busy, modern theater near Wangfujing shopping street. It often has performances by the respected Beijing People's Art Theatre and various international acts, such as the British troupe TNT. ✉ *22 Wangfujing Dajie, Dongcheng District* ☎ *010/6525–0996* ⊕ *www.bjry.com* Ⓜ *Wangfujing.*

FAMILY **China National Puppet Theater** (中国木偶剧院 *Zhōngguó guójiā mùǒujùyuà*). The shadow and hand-puppet shows at this theater convey traditional stories—it's lively entertainment for children and adults alike. This venue also attracts foreign performers, including the Moscow Puppet Theater. ✉ *1 Anhuaxili, Chaoyang District* ☎ *010/6425–4847* ⊕ *www.puppetchina.com* Ⓜ *Anhuaqiao.*

Fodor's Choice **National Centre for the Performing Arts** (国家大剧院 *Guójiā dàjùyuàn*). ★ Architecturally, the giant silver dome of this performing arts complex is stunning, and its interior holds a state-of-the-art opera house, a music hall, and a theater. "The Egg," as it's been called, offers a world-class stage for national and international performers. If you don't wish to see a show, you can tour the inside of the building by paying for an entrance ticket. ✉ *2 Xi Chang'an Jie, Xicheng District* ☎ *010/6655–0000* ⊕ *www.chncpa.org* Ⓜ *Tiananmen West.*

Tianqiao Theater (天桥乐茶馆 *Tiānqiáolè cháguǎn*). A traditional theater that hosts everything from contemporary dance performances to ballet, folk music, and cross-talk revues. ✉ *30 Beiwei Lu, Xicheng District* ☎ *010/8315–6300.*

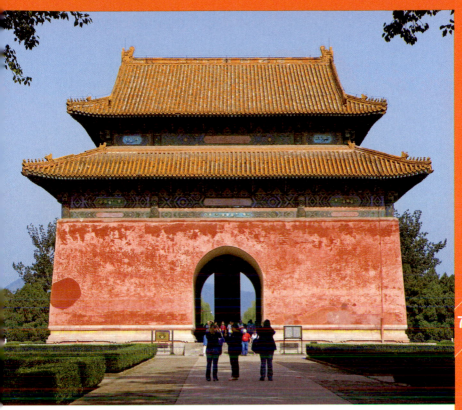

BEST SIDE TRIPS

Including the Great Wall, Chengde,
and Thirteen Ming Tombs

WELCOME TO SIDE TRIPS FROM BEIJING

TOP REASONS TO GO

★ **Walk on the Wall:** Postcard views of large sections of the restored wall rise majestically around you. The sheer scope of this ancient project boggles the mind.

★ **Add Ming to the Mix:** It's easy to arrange a tour or your own transportation to the Great Wall and the Thirteen Ming Tombs—especially if you go to the Badaling section of the wall.

★ **Have an Adventure:** Traveling through rural China, even for a day trip, is always something of an adventure. Endless greenery peppered with ramshackle villages and roadside fruit stalls ensure that short stops along the way are a must rather than an inconvenience.

★ **Meet the Locals:** People in rural China can be extremely kind, inviting you to their homes for tea, a meal. If you accept an invite, a small gift is always appreciated.

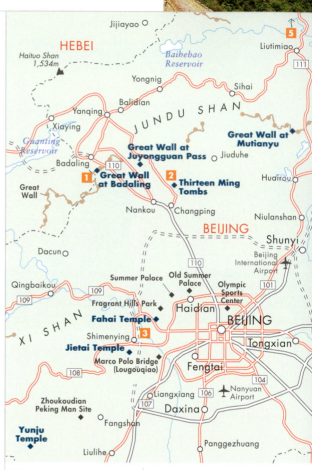

1 **The Great Wall.** The longest man-made structure on Earth is one of the country's most accessible and cosmopolitan attractions. On any given day you'll find hikers, hawkers, and sightseers at various points along this UNESCO World Heritage Site.

2 **Thirteen Ming Tombs.** The grandeur of the final resting place for 13 Ming Dynasty emperors gives you an idea of the importance of ancestor worship in ancient China.

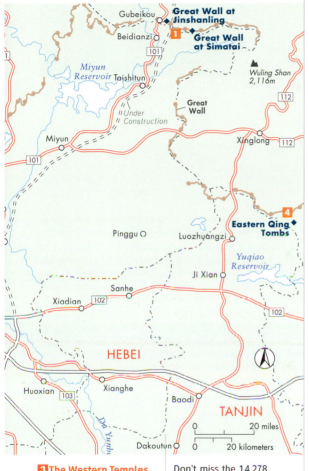

GETTING ORIENTED

With the exception of Chengde, the best side trips from Beijing, including the Great Wall, can be visited on a day trip. It's easy to get out of Beijing by taxi, even to sites as far away as farther-flung sections of the Great Wall and the Qing Tombs in Zunhua (126 km [78 miles] northeast). Train travel is an option for some side trips; organized bus tours are especially convenient as they take care of the details. Chengde, a 4-hour train ride from Beijing, needs more than a day.

7

3 The Western Temples. Li Tong, a favorite eunuch in Emperor Zhengtong's court, built Fahai; its frescos are considered some of the finest examples of Buddhist mural art from the Ming Dynasty. Jietai, China's most ancient Buddhist site, is located just west of Beijing.

Don't miss the 14,278 delicately carved Buddhist tablets at Yunju.

4 The Eastern Qing Tombs. This mausoleum complex was modeled after the Thirteen Ming Tombs in Changping, but the tombs are even more extravagant and much less touristy.

5 Chengde. Originally an imperial summer retreat, this town's magnificent temples, palaces, and deer-filled parks now attract weekenders hunting for culture.

Updated by
Yuan Ren

The wonders of Beijing aren't confined to the city center. Venturing into the outskirts and beyond, you'll discover a wealth of sights that provide a further look at imperial might, offer natural delights and some refreshing relief from city crowds, and even deliver a whiff of adventure.

Of course, the Great Wall is a good starting point for any exploration, and while it isn't (as the old propagandist myth goes) visible to the naked eye from space, it's nonetheless an awesome sight. It might have failed to prevent the Manchus from invading, but few more soaring testimonies to human endeavor are more visually rewarding. You needn't stop there, though. Imperial tombs and Buddhist temples also surround the capital, with remarkable mausoleum complexes to the east near Changping and the west at Zunhua and a satisfying swath of temples in the western suburbs. A bit farther afield, a half day's travel by train brings you to Chengde, where emperors left behind lavish summer pavilions, pagodas, and gardens. Beijing might be one of the most intriguing cities on earth, and you'll soon discover the fascination extends well beyond the city limits.

PLANNING

GETTING THERE

TAXI TRAVEL

Taxis, which in Beijing are both plentiful and reasonably priced, are a good way to get to sights outside the city. Set a price beforehand; the metered fare can add up quickly (generally, rides start at Y13 for the first 3 km (2 miles), with an additional Y2.3 for each additional km and another Y2 per every five minutes of waiting time during rush-hour (Y1 otherwise). Also make sure that this covers the return journey, or face the prospect of haggling with illegal cab drivers on the way back—and they will fleece you! At the time of writing, a Y1 fuel surcharge is added for all trips. A small surcharge is also added between 11 pm and 5 am. Private-car services are available, and even if they aren't always cheap, they're in most cases worth the investment for the comfort, reliability, and ease of dealing with English-speaking operators and drivers.

Beijing Limo. A variety of cars and buses, complete with English-speaking drivers, are available. Prices range from Y900 for four hours of rental within the city to Y1,500 for trips farther out into the countryside. ☎ *010/6546–1588* ⊕ *www.beijinglimo.com/english* ☯ *Mon.–Sun. 9–8.*

TRAIN TRAVEL

Some day-trip-worthy sites, such as Yesanpo, Tianjin, Beidaihe, and Shanhaiguan, are accessible by train. Plan to get to the station at least 30 minutes before your train leaves, as stations are huge and often confusing for visitors (as well as being crowded). It's easy to buy train tickets once there, but these sell out fast on peak dates, so if you're on a tight schedule and can't afford a delay, buy a ticket beforehand.

If you decided to take the train to Chengde, most hotels will help you buy tickets up to four days in advance for a fee (typically Y5 to Y15 per ticket). There are also small train-ticket windows scattered around the city: look for the China Railways logo and make sure to bring your passport.

TIMING

It'll take you several days to see all the sights outside of Beijing, and visits to the various sites require separate, often day-long excursions. If you only have time to see one site, you'll want to go to the **Great Wall**; if you go the section at Badaling, you can also work the nearby 13 Ming Tombs into one outing. If you want to treat yourself to seeing several sites in one outing, and get an eye full of temples, head west, where you can make stops at the **Fahai Temple,** about an hour's drive from the center, as well as the tomb of Tian Yu, and the **Jietai** and then the **Tanzhe Temples,** all in one day if you're touring by car. Another rewarding day's outing takes you east to Zunhua, and the elaborate **Qing Tombs** complex. Wear walking shoes and bring a lunch to enjoy the surrounding countryside.

If you have time and inclination to go farther afield, consider a four-hour train trip and an overnight in **Chengde**, where in the 18th century Qing Dynasty Emperor Kangxi established a summer retreat of temples, gardens, and monasteries. If you're looking for a little summertime relaxation, take a day and a night (or, for real relaxation, two days) at **Beidaihe,** to bask on the beach, chow down on seafood, or see where the Great Wall meets the sea at Shanghaiguan.

WHAT TO WEAR

The weather in Beijing and neighboring areas is notoriously fickle, so make sure you dress appropriately. In the summer it's hot; travel with sunglasses, sunscreen, and a wide-brimmed hat. It gets terribly cold in the winter, so dress in layers and pack gloves, a hat, and a scarf. And if you plan to do any hiking, make sure to bring sturdy, comfortable shoes.

Also, checking the weather forecast before an excursion is always a good idea for last-minute wardrobe changes. ■TIP➔ **Don't carry too much cash or expensive jewelry**. Other things to bring along? A camera, a change of clothes if you're staying overnight, and your common sense.

7

THE GREAT WALL

60–120 km (37–74 miles) north and west of Beijing.

Any visitor to Beijing should aside at least a day to visit one of the incredible sections of the Great Wall, just outside the city. Badaling is the closest to Beijing, just about an hour from the city center. The farther you get from Beijing, the more rugged the terrain, so you'll add the excitement of seeing the wall tumbling across the countryside.

See the highlighted feature in this chapter for more about the Great Wall.

GETTING HERE AND AROUND

The easiest and most comfortable way to visit the wall is by private car. Though taxis are occasionally willing to make the trip to more accessible sections like Badaling and Mutianyu, most hotels can arrange a four-passenger car and an English-speaking driver for eight hours at around Y500–Y700. Settle details in advance, and remember that it's polite to invite your driver to eat meals with you. To ensure your driver doesn't return to Beijing without you, pay after the trip is over.

TOURS

In addition to the tour buses that gather around Tiananmen Square, most hotels and tour companies offer trips (in comfortable, air-conditioned buses or vans) to Badaling, Mutianyu, Juyongguan, and Jinshanling. Smaller, private tours are generally more rewarding than large bus trips. Trips will run between Y400 and Y1,500 per person, but costs vary depending on the group size, and can sometimes be negotiated. Wherever you're headed, book in advance.

For further help in planning your trip to the wall, while adding a bit of adventure to the mix, consider the following.

Albatros Adventure Great Wall Marathon. Not for the faint of heart, the Great Wall Marathon (and half marathon) takes place each May and covers approximately 6.5 km (4 miles) of the Great Wall, with the rest of the course running through lovely valleys in rural Tianjin. Visitors must book through Albatros, a Danish tour company that arranges weeklong packages, or a local operator. ✉ *Albatros, Tøndergade 16, Copenhagen, Denmark* ☎ *45/3698–9838* ⊕ *great-wall-marathon.com.*

Beijing Hikers. Arrange weekly day-treks to the wilder parts of the Great Wall throughout the year, as well as personalized tours. ☎ *010/6432 2786* ⊕ *www.beijinghikers.com.*

Beijing Service. Private guided tours by car include stops at Badaling, Mutianyu, Jinshanling, and Juyongguan for small groups of up to four people. ✉ *9-6 West Block of Chang'an Block, Miyun* ☎ *010/5166–7026* ⊕ *www.beijingservice.com.*

Bespoke Beijing. This firm designs private tours with English-speaking guides to suit your interests. ✉ *107 Dongsi Bei, Dongcheng District* ☎ *010/6400–0133* ⊕ *www.bespoke-beijing.com.*

CITS (China International Tour Service). The company runs bus tours to Badaling and private tours to Badaling, Mutianyu, and Jinshanling. ✉ *1 Dongdan Bei, Dongcheng District* ☎ *010/6522–2991* ⊕ *www.cits.net.*

Cycle China. This company runs good guided hiking tours of the unrestored wall at Jiankou. ⊠ *12 Jingshan East St., opposite of the east gate of Jingshan Park, Dongcheng District* ☎ *10/6402–5653* ⊕ *www.cyclechina.com.*

EXPLORING

Great Wall at Badaling. Only one hour by car from downtown Beijing and located not far from the Ming Tombs, the Great Wall at Badaling is where visiting dignitaries go for a quick photo op. Postcard views abound here, with large sections of the restored Ming Dynasty brick wall rising majestically to either side of the fort while, in the distance, portions of early-16th-century Great Wall disintegrate into more romantic but inaccessible ruins.

The downside is that Badaling suffers from its popularity, with tour groups flocking here en masse. This has led to its reputation as "one to be avoided" by those allergic to shoulder-bumping and being gouged by hawkers. Nevertheless, with popularity come tourist-friendly facilities, and those with disabilities find access to the wall here to be far better than at other sections. Either take the cable car to the top or walk up the gently sloping steps, relying on handrails if necessary. On a clear day, you can see for miles across leafy, undulating terrain from atop the battlements. The admission price also includes access to the China Great Wall Museum and the Great Wall Circle Vision Theater.

A car for four people from central Beijing to Badaling should run no more than Y600 for five hours, and you can sometimes make arrangements to include a stop at the Thirteen Ming Tombs. By public transportation, trains leave Beijing North Station for Badaling Station (Y6) almost every hour from 6:12 am and take 1 hour 20 minutes. From there, it's just a 20-minute walk to the entrance to Badaling Great Wall. Or, take Line 2 on the subway to Jishuitan and walk to Deshengmen bus terminus. From there, take Bus 880 to Badaling (Y12). Be warned: private taxis hang around the station and drivers will try to convince you that it's easier to go with them. It isn't. Stick to your guns and get on that bus.

■ **TIP→** **Most tours to Badaling will take you to the Thirteen Ming Tombs, as well. If you don't want a stop at the tombs—or at a tourist-trapping jade factory or herbal medicine center along the way—be sure to confirm the itinerary before booking.** ⊠ *Yanqing County* ✛ *70 km (43 miles) northwest of Beijing* ☎ *010/6912–1383* ⊕ *www.badaling.cn* ⌨ *Wall Y45; cable car Y80 one-way, Y100 round-trip* ☉ *Apr.–Oct., daily 6:30–6.30; Nov.–Mar., daily 7–6.*

Great Wall at Jinshanling. The Great Wall at Jinshanling is perhaps the least tamed of the restored Great Wall sections near Beijing, as well as the least visited. Besides being the starting point for a fantastic four-hour hike toward Simatai, it also stands as one of the few sections of the Great Wall on which overnight camping trips are available. A starry night here is gorgeous and unforgettable—go with a tour group such as Cycle China or Beijing Hikers. However, some have argued that unregulated tourism such as this goes against the efforts of others to preserve the wall, so tread carefully and leave nothing behind in order

7

Continued on page 200

THE GREAT WALL

For some people, the Great Wall is the main reason for a trip to China; for any visitor to Beijing, it's a must-see. Originally intended to keep foreigners out, the world's most famous wall has become the icon of an increasingly open nation. One of the country's most accessible attractions, the Great Wall promises both breathtaking scenery and cultural illumination.

Built by successive dynasties over two millennia, the Great Wall isn't one structure built at one time, but a series of defensive installations that shrank and grew. Especially vulnerable spots were more heavily fortified, while some mountainous regions were left un-walled altogether. The actual length of the wall remains a topic of considerable debate: at its longest, some estimates say the protective cordon spans 6,437 km (4,000 miles)—a distance wider than the United States. Although attacks, age, and pillaging (not to mention today's tourist invasion) have caused the crumbling of up to two-thirds of its length, new sections are being uncovered even today.

As kingdoms scrambled to protect themselves from marauding nomads, portions of wall cropped up, leading to a motley collection of northern borders. It was the first emperor of a unified China, Qin Shi-huang (circa 259–210 BC), founder of the Qin Dynasty, who linked these fortifications into a single network. By some accounts, Qin mustered nearly a million people, or one-fifth of China's workforce, to build this massive barricade, a mobilization that claimed countless lives and gave rise to many tragic folktales.

The Ming Dynasty fortified the wall like never before: for an estimated 5,000 km (3,107 miles), it stood 26 feet tall and 30 feet wide at its base. However, the wall failed to prevent the Manchu invasion that toppled the Ming in 1644. That historical failure hasn't tarnished the Great Wall's image, however. Although China once viewed it as a model of feudal oppression, the Great Wall is now touted as the national symbol. "Love China, Restore the Great Wall," declared Deng Xiaoping in 1984. Since then large sections have been repaired and opened to visitors, turning it also into a symbol of the tension between preservation and restoration in China.

AN ETERNAL WAIT

One legend concerns Lady Meng, whose husband was kidnapped on their wedding night and forced to work on the Great Wall. She traveled to the work site to await his return, believing her determination would bring him back. She waited so long that, in the end, she turned into a rock, which to this day stands at the head of the Great Wall in the beautiful seaside town of Qinhuangdao.

MATERIALS & TECHNIQUES

■ During the 2nd century BC, the wall was largely composed of packed earth and piled stone.

■ Some sections, like those in the Taklimakan Desert, were fortified with twigs, sand, and even rice (the jury's still out on whether workers' remains were used as well).

■ The more substantial brick-and-mortar ruins that wind across the mountains north of Beijing date from the Ming Dynasty (14th–17th centuries). Some Ming mortar kilns still exist in valleys around Beijing.

VISITING THE GREAT WALL

As a visitor to Beijing, you simply must set aside a day to visit one of the glorious Great Wall sites just outside the capital.

At Mutianyu in the mountains on a clear summer day

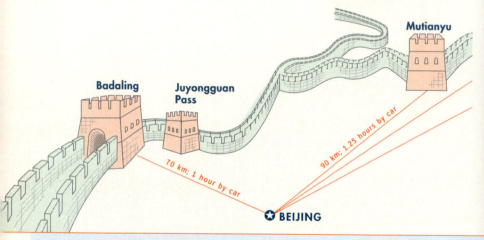

Mutianyu

Badaling

Juyongguan Pass

70 km; 1 hour by car

90 km; 1.25 hours by car

★ **BEIJING**

GREAT WALL SITES NEAR BEIJING

There are five Great Wall sites within relatively close proximity to the city of Beijing: depending on what you're looking for and how much time you have, there is one to fit your itinerary. Generally

Part of the Great Wall of China at Badaling

speaking, the farther you go from Beijing, the more rugged the terrain and the fewer tourists and hawkers you'll see. Badaling and Juyongguan are the most accessible sections of the Great Wall from Beijing, and these are where most of the tours go but there are tour options for all different kinds of Great Wall experiences. See the Great Wall Tours listings for some of our suggestions.

Badaling is about an hour-long drive from Beijing and is great for photo ops, with amazing postcard views.

Because it's easy to get to, though, there are often swarms of tourists, as well as lots of hawkers. The upside is that there are tourist-friendly facilities and there is better disability access here than elsewhere.

Juyongguan is also about an hour's drive from Beijing, and near Badaling. It has similarly impressive views and less crowds, but that's partly because the site has been heavily restored and feels a bit commercial.

If you're looking for a less-traveled section of the wall

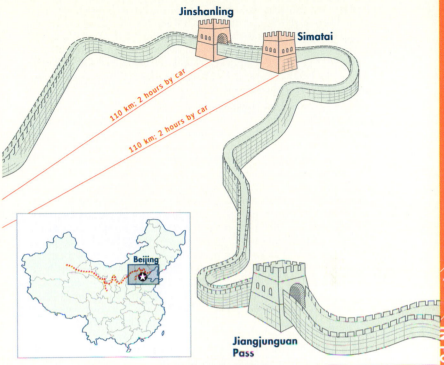

Jinshanling

Simatai

110 km; 2 hours by car

110 km; 2 hours by car

Beijing

Jiangjunguan Pass

that is still accessible from Beijing, head to fantastic **Mutianyu**. It's only slightly farther from Beijing than Badaling but significantly more spectacular. Although you'll see the occasional souvenir stand, it's much less crowded than Badaling, and you'll be able to enjoy more solitude, along with amazing views from the towers and wall. Mutianyu is definitely more about hiking than Badaling or Juyongguan. It's a strenuous hour's hike out of the parking lot, although there is a cable car that can

The Great Wall between Jinshan-lin and Simatai

take you up to the wall, from where there are additional trails.

Jinshanling is the most rustic and the least touristed section of the Wall that's

within easy proximity to Beijing. It's about a 2-hour drive from Beijing and most people come here on an overnight camping trip. This is an unforgettable experience if you have the time and like to camp.

Simatai is for adventure-seekers. It's remote and often precarious. It's also about a 2-hour drive from Beijing.

to reduce your impact. If you must take a souvenir, pack a piece of charcoal and paper to make rubbings of the bricks that still bear the stamp of the date they were made. The trip by car to Jinhshanling from central Beijing should cost around Y700 and take about two hours. By public transportation, take a train from Beijing North Train Station to Luanping and a local bus or taxi from there. Trains leave almost every hour until 8 pm. ✉ *Jinshanling ✚ 110 km (68 miles) northeast of Beijing* ☎ *031/4883–0222* 🖅 *Apr.–Oct. Y65, Nov.–Mar. Y55; overnight stays at campsite Y150* ⊙ *Daily 5–7.*

Great Wall at Juyongguan. Juyongguan is a quick, easygoing alternative for those not willing to blow a whole day traveling to Mutianyu or Jinshanling, or brave the more testing, unrestored sites such as Jiankou. It's the part of the wall that runs closest to Beijing and once guarded a crucial pass to the city, repelling hordes of Mongol and, latterly, Japanese invaders. The section also lies not far from Badaling, essentially acting as an overflow for its oversubscribed neighbor. It certainly loses nothing in the comparison, boasting similarly impressive views but with far less abrasive crowds. However, Juyongguan has been heavily restored and does feel a little sterile and commercial as a result. The main attraction here is the Cloud Platform (or "Crossing Street Tower"), which was built in 1342 during the Yuan Dynasty. In appearance, it now resembles a rather squat Arc de Triomphe. The three white Tibetan stupas that originally sat atop it were destroyed during the early Ming period, only to be replaced with a Buddhist Tai'an temple, which was later toppled by fire in 1702. Today, carvings on the inner portal depicting the Four Heavenly Kings (Buddhist gods who defend the four compass points) and some elegant script work make for fascinating viewing on the way up the pass. The trip by car from central Beijing to Juyongguan should cost around Y450 for the round trip and takes about an hour. By public transportation, take Line 13 on the subway to Longze. Exit the station and walk to the bus stop across the street to take Bus 58 (Y12) to Shahe; take bus 68 at the same stop to Juyongguan Gongjiaochang and walk to the wall from there. The trip takes about 2½ hours. ✉ *Juyongguan ✚ 59 km (37 miles) northwest of Beijing* ☎ *010/6977–1665* 🖅 *Apr.–Oct. Y45, Nov.–Mar. Y28* ⊙ *Apr.–Oct. daily 8–5; Nov.–Mar. daily 8:30–4:30.*

Great Wall at Mutianyu. Only slightly farther from downtown Beijing than Badaling, the Great Wall at Mutianyu is more spectacular and, despite the occasional annoyances of souvenir stands, significantly less crowded. This long section of wall, first built during the Northern Qi Dynasty (6th century) and restored and rebuilt throughout history, can offer a less busy Great Wall experience, with unforgettable views of towers winding across mountains and woodlands. On a clear day, you'll swear you can see the deserts of Mongolia in the distance.

The lowest point on the wall is a strenuous one-hour climb above the parking lot. As an alternative, you can take a cable car on a breathtaking ride to the highest restored section, from which several hiking trails descend. Take a gorgeous 1½-hour walk east to reach another cable car that returns to the same parking lot. Mutianyu is also known for its toboggan run—the perfect way to end a long hike.

The trip by car from central Beijing to Mutianyu should cost around Y600 and it takes about an hour. By public transportation, take bus 936 from Dongzhimen to Huairou bus stop. From there take a minibus to Mutianyu (Y25–Y30) or hire a taxi to take you there and back (about Y100–Y150 round-trip).

■ TIP➜ **For those taking a car, the road from Huairou, a suburb of Beijing, to Mutianyu follows a river upstream and is lined with restaurants selling fresh trout. In addition, Hongluo Temple is a short drive from the bottom of the mountain.** ⊠ *Huairou County* ✛ *90 km (56 miles) northeast of Beijing* ☎ *010/6162–6022* ✉ *Apr.–Oct. Y25; cable car Y80 one-way, Y100 round-trip* ⊗ *Apr.–Oct., daily 8–5; Nov.–Mar., daily 8:30–4:30.*

Great Wall at Simatai (司马台长城 *Sīmǎtái chángchéng*). Remote and largely unrestored, this section of the Great Wall is ideal if you're seeking adventure. Near the frontier garrison at Gubeikou, the wall traverses towering peaks and hangs precariously above cliffs. Be prepared for no-handrails hiking, tough climbs, and unparalleled vistas.

The first 10 watchtowers are currently accessible to visitors, and the hike to the top and back is just under two hours. Alternatively, a cable car takes you two-thirds of the way up; from there it's a steep 30-minute climb to the summit.

The trip by car from central Beijing to Simitai costs about Y800 and takes about two hours. By public transportation, take the 980 or 980快 (fast bus) from Dongzhimen bus stop to Miyun, getting off at Gulou. Cross the road to the opposite bus station and transfer to Bus 51 or 38 toward Simatai and get off at Gubeikou Water Town (or Gubeikou Shuizhen). Follow directions to the ticket hall where you can pick up your pre-booked online tickets for the wall.

■ TIP➜ **It's necessary to reserve a ticket online using a Chinese mobile number, to which a ticket code will be sent (your hotel or a travel agency can help with these arrangements).** ⊠ *Near Miyun, Miyun County* ✛ *120 km (75 miles) northeast of Beijing* ☎ *010/8100–9999* ⊕ *www.wtown.com* ✉ *Y40 (Y110 including Gubeikou Water Town); cable car, Y80 one-way, Y120 round-trip* ⊗ *Apr.–Oct., daily 9–6; Nov.–Mar., daily 9–5.*

THIRTEEN MING TOMBS (明十三陵 MÍNG SHÍSĀNLÍNG)

48 km (30 miles) north of Beijing.

A narrow valley just north of Changping is the final resting place for 13 of the Ming Dynasty's 16 emperors (the first Ming emperor was buried in Nanjing; the burial site of the second one is unknown; and the seventh Ming emperor was dethroned and buried in an ordinary tomb in northwestern Beijing). Ming monarchs once journeyed here each year to kowtow before their clan forefathers and make offerings to their memory. These days, few visitors can claim royal descent, but the area's vast scale and imperial grandeur do convey the importance attached to ancestor worship in ancient China. A leisurely stroll down the Sacred Way, inspecting the series of charming larger-than-life statues of imperial officials and animals, is a wonderful experience. Many visitors combine a stop here with an excursion to the Badaling section of the Great Wall, which is found off the same expressway.

Zhaoling. Allow ample time for a hike or drive northwest from Changling to the six fenced-off **unrestored tombs,** a short distance farther up the valley. Here crumbling walls conceal vast courtyards shaded by pine trees. At each tomb a stone altar rests beneath a stele tower and burial mound. In some cases the wall that circles the burial chamber is accessible on steep stone stairways that ascend from either side of the altar. At the valley's terminus (about 5 km [3 miles] northwest of Changling), the Zhaoling Tomb rests beside a traditional walled village that's well worth exploring.

Picnics amid the ruins have been a favorite weekend activity among Beijingers for nearly a century; if you picnic here, be sure to carry out all trash. ⊠ *Changping District* ✉ *Apr.–Oct. Y35; Nov.–Mar. Y25* ⏰ *Apr.–Oct., daily 8:30–5:30; Nov.–Mar., daily 8:30–5.*

THE WESTERN TEMPLES

20–70 km (12–43 miles) west of Beijing.

Some of China's most spectacular temples and other monuments are on wooded hillsides west of Beijing. Here you'll discover magnificent murals at Fahai Temple, about an hour's drive from the center, and Jietai, an ancient Buddhist site nearby. Tian Yi Mu is not a temple but the elaborate tomb of one of the high-ranking eunuchs who once played a vital role in affairs of state. Yunju Temple is best known for its mind-boggling collection of 14,278 minutely carved Buddhist tablets. While all these sights are in the western suburbs of Beijing, you will probably want to approach them as three separate excursions: Fahai Temple and Tian Yi Mu on one; Jietai Temple and nearby Tanzhe Temple on another; and Yunju Temple on a third. If traveling by taxi or private car, you could work visits to Fahai Temple, Tian Yi Mu, and Jietai and Tanzhe temples into one full day.

Fahai Temple (法海寺 *Fǎhǎi sì*). The stunning works of Buddhist mural art at Fahai Temple, 20 km (12 miles) west of the central city, are among the most underappreciated sights in Beijing. Li Tong, a favored eunuch in the court of Emperor Zhengtong (1436–49), donated funds to construct Fahai Temple in 1443. The project was highly ambitious: Li Tong invited only celebrated imperial and court painters to decorate the temple. As a result, the murals in the only surviving chamber of that period, Daxiongbaodian (the Mahavira Hall), are considered the finest examples of Buddhist mural art from the Ming Dynasty. Sadly, statues of various Buddhas and one of Li Tong himself were destroyed during China's Cultural Revolution.

The most famous of the nine murals in Mahavira Hall is a large-scale triptych featuring Guanyin (the Bodhisattva of Compassion) and Wenshu (the Bodhisattva of Marvelous Virtue and Gentle Majesty)

BEIDAIHE & YESANPO

Beidaihe (北戴河 *Běidàihé*). Chairman Mao and the party's favorite spot for sand, sun, and seafood, Beidaihe (250 km [170 miles] northeast of Beijing) is one of China's few beach resorts (though it's definitely no Bali). This crowded spot is just 2½ hours by train from Beijing Station. Nearly every building in town has been converted to a hotel, and every restaurant has tanks of pick-your-own seafood lining the street. ⊠ *West of Beidaihe District, Qinhuangdao.*

Yesanpo (野三坡 *Yěsān pō*). Yesanpo (150 km [90 miles] northeast of Beijing) is a sleepy village between Beijing and neighboring Hebei province, nestled in a national park of the same name. Go here if you're craving a slower-paced scene and some outdoor fun. The accommodations aren't first class, but there are plenty of opportunities for boating, hiking, horseback riding, and other outdoor activities. Several trains leave from Beijing West Station daily for the two-hour ride. Yesanpo is also known for its whole barbecued lamb. Traditionally, locals have houses with extra rooms for guests, and owners will strive to make your stay as comfortable as possible. A clean room with two beds and an air conditioner should run you no more than Y150. There are also a few hotels on the main street by the train station. Train 6437 leaves Beijing West Station at 5:29 pm and arrives at 8:29 pm. Return train 6438 leaves at 9:35 am daily ⊠ *Yesanpo.*

7

in the center, and Poxian (the Buddha of Universal Virtue) on either side. The depiction of Guanyin follows the theme of "moon in water," which compares the Buddhist belief in the illusoriness of the material world to the reflection of the moon in the water. Typically painted with Guanyin are her legendary mount Jin Sun and her assistant Shancai Tongzi. Wenshu is often presented with a lion, symbolic of the bodhisattva's wisdom and strength of will, while Poxian is shown near a six-tusked elephant, each tusk representing one of the qualities that leads to enlightenment. On the opposite wall is the *Sovereign Sakra and Brahma* mural, with a panoply of characters from the Buddhist canon.

The murals were painted during the time of the European Renaissance, and though the subject matter is traditional, there are comparable experiments in perspective taking place in the depiction of the figures, as compared with examples from earlier dynasties. Also of note is a highly unusual decorative technique; many contours in the hall's murals, particularly on jewelry, armor, and weapons, have been set in bold relief by the application of fine gold threads.

The temple grounds are also beautiful, but of overriding interest are the murals themselves. Visitors stumble through the dark temple with rented flashlights (free with your ticket). Viewing the murals in this way, it's easy to imagine oneself as a sort of modern-day Indiana Jones unraveling a story of the Buddha as depicted in ancient murals of unrivaled beauty. Fahai Temple is only a short taxi ride from Beijing's Pingguoyuan subway station. ⊠ *Moshikou Lu, Shijingshan District, Beijing* ✥ *Take an approximately Y19 taxi ride from Pinguoyuan subway station directly to the temple* ☎ *010/8871–3975* 📠 *Y20 (Y100 including Buddhist murals)* 🕐 *Daily 9–4.*

Tian Yi Mu (北京宦官文化陈列馆田义幕 *Tiányì mù*). Eunuchs have played a vital role throughout Chinese history, frequently holding great sway over the affairs of state. Their importance, often overlooked, is celebrated in the **Beijing Eunuch Culture Exhibition Hall** and the tomb of the most powerful eunuch of all, **Tian Yi** (1534–1605). Tian Yi was only nine when he was voluntarily castrated and sent into the service of the Ming emperor Jiajing. During the next 63 years of his life he served three rulers and rose to one of the highest ranks in the land. By the time he died, there were more than 20,000 eunuchs in imperial service. Thanks to their access to private areas of the palace, they became invaluable as go-betweens for senior officials seeking gossip or the royal ear, and such was Tian Yi's influence. It's said that upon his death The Forbidden City fell silent for three days.

Though not as magnificent as the Thirteen Ming Tombs, the final resting place of Tian Yi befits a man of high social status. Of special note are the intricate stone carvings around the base of the central burial mound. The four smaller tombs on either side belong to other eunuchs who wished to pay tribute to Tian Yi by being buried in the same compound.

The small exhibition hall at the front of the tomb complex contains the world's only "eunuch museum" and offers some interesting background (albeit mostly in Mandarin), particularly on China's last eunuch, Sun Yaoting (1902–96). It's worth visiting, if only to see the rather gruesome mummified remains of one castrato that holds center stage—you can still make out the hairs on his chin. Another equally squirm-inducing sight is the eye-watering collection of castration equipment; keep a look out for the ancient Chinese character meaning "to castrate," which resembles two knives, one inverted, side by side. The hall and tomb are a five-minute walk from Fahai Temple; just ask people the way to Tian Yi Mu. ✉ *80 Moshikou Lu, Shijingshan District, Beijing* ☎ *010/8872–4148* 📠 *Y8* 🕐 *Daily 9–3:30.*

Jietai Temple (戒台寺 *Jiètái sì*). The four main halls of one of China's most famous ancient Buddhist sites occupy terraces on a gentle slope up to Ma'an Shan (Saddle Hill), 35 km (22 miles) west of Beijing. Built in AD 622, the temple has been used for the ordination of Buddhist novices since the Liao Dynasty. The temple complex expanded over the centuries and grew to its current scale in a major renovation conducted by devotees during the Qing Dynasty (1644–1912). The temple buildings, plus three magnificent bronze Buddhas in the Mahavira Hall, date from this period. There's also a huge potbellied Maitreya Buddha carved from the roots of what must have been a truly enormous tree. To the right of this hall, just above twin pagodas, is the Ordination Terrace, a platform built of white marble and topped with a massive bronze statue of Shakyamuni Buddha seated on a lotus flower. Tranquil courtyards, where ornate stelae and well-kept gardens bask beneath a scholar tree and other ancient pines, add to the temple's beauty. Many modern devotees from Beijing visit the temple on weekends. Getting to Jietai and the nearby Tanzhe Temple is easy using public transportation. Take subway

Line 1 to its westernmost station, Pingguoyuan. From there, take the No. 931 public bus to either temple—it leaves every half hour and the ride takes about 70 minutes. A taxi from Pingguoyuan to Jietai Temple should be Y50 to Y60; the bus fare is Y6. ⊠ *Mentougou County, Beijing* ☏ *010/6980–6611* 💳 *Y45* 🕐 *Daily 8:30–5.*

NEARBY

Tanzhe Temple (潭柘寺 *Tánzhè sì*). A Buddhist complex nestled in a grove of *zhe* (cudrania) trees near Jietai Temple was established around AD 400 and once home to more than 500 monks. Tanzhe was heavily damaged during the Cultural Revolution. It's since been restored, but if you look closely at some of the huge stone tablets, or *bei*, littered around the site you'll see that many of the inscriptions have been destroyed. The complex makes an ideal side trip from Jietai Temple or Marco Polo Bridge. ⊠ *Mentougou County, Beijing* ⊕ *10 km (6 miles) northeast of Jietai Temple* ☏ *010/6086–2500* 💳 *Y55* 🕐 *Summer, daily 7:30–5; winter, daily 7:30–4:30.*

Yunju Temple (云居寺 *Yúnjū sì*). To protect the Buddhist canon from destruction by Taoist emperors, the devout Tang-era monk Jing Wan carved Buddhist scriptures into stone slabs that he hid in sealed caves in the cliffs of a mountain. Jing Wan spent 30 years creating these tablets until his death in AD 637; his disciples continued his work for the next millennium into the 17th century, thereby compiling one of the most extensive Buddhist libraries in the world, a mind-boggling collection of 14,278 minutely carved Buddhist tablets. A small pagoda at the center of the temple complex commemorates the remarkable monk. Although the tablets were originally stored inside Shijing Mountain behind the temple, they're now housed in rooms built along the temple's southern perimeter.

Four central prayer halls, arranged along the hillside above the main gate, contain impressive Ming-era bronze Buddhas. The last in this row, the Dabei Hall, displays the spectacular *Thousand-Armed Avalokiteshvara*. This 13-foot-tall bronze sculpture—which actually has 24 arms and five heads and stands in a giant lotus flower—is believed to embody boundless compassion. A group of pagodas, led by the 98-foot-tall Northern Pagoda, is all that remains of the original Tang complex. These pagodas are remarkable for their Buddhist reliefs and ornamental patterns. Heavily damaged during the Japanese occupation and again by Maoist radicals in the 1960s, the temple complex remains under renovation.

Yunju Temple is 70 km (43 miles) southwest of central Beijing. By bus, take no. 917 from Tianqiao Long-distance Bus Station to Liangxiang Ximen, then change to Fangshan bus Nos. 12, 19, 31 to Yun Ju Si. ⊠ *Off Fangshan Lu, Nanshangle Xiang, Fangshan County, Beijing* ☏ *010/6138–9612* 💳 *Y40* 🕐 *Daily 8:30–4.*

7

The Eastern Qing Tombs are the most expansive burial grounds in China.

EASTERN QING TOMBS
(清东陵 QĪNGDŌNGLÍNG)

125 km (78 miles) east of Beijing.

Modeled on the Thirteen Ming Tombs, the mausoleum complex at Zunhua, known as the Eastern Qing Tombs, replicate the Ming walkways, walled tomb complexes, and subterranean burial chambers. But they're even more extravagant in their scale and grandeur, and far less touristy.

These imposing ruins contain the remains of five emperors, 14 empresses, and 136 imperial concubines, all laid to rest in a broad valley chosen by Emperor Shunzhi (1638–61) while on a hunting expedition. By the Qing's collapse in 1911, the tomb complex covered some 18 square miles (46 square km) of farmland and forested hillside, making it the most expansive burial ground in all China.

The Eastern Qing Tombs are in much better repair than their older Ming counterparts—and considerably less crowded. Although several of the tomb complexes have undergone extensive renovation, none is overdone. Peeling paint, grassy courtyards, and numerous stone bridges and pathways convey a sense of the area's original grandeur. Often visitors are so few that you may feel as if you've stumbled upon an ancient ruin unknown beyond the valley's farming villages.

The tombs are a two- to three-hour drive from the capital and are surrounded by dramatic rural scenery, making this trip one of the best full-day excursions outside Beijing. Consider bringing a bedsheet, a bottle of wine, and boxed lunches, as the grounds are ideal for a picnic.

Fodor's Choice **Yuling** (裕陵 *Yùlíng*). Of the nine tombs open to the public, Yuling is not to be missed. This is the resting place of the Qing Dynasty's most powerful sovereign, Emperor Qianlong (1711–99), who ruled China for 59 years. Beyond the outer courtyards, Qianlong's burial chamber is accessible from inside Stela Hall, where an entry tunnel descends some 65 feet (20 meters) into the ground and ends at the first of three elaborately carved marble gates. Beyond, exquisite carvings of Buddhist images and sutras rendered in Tibetan adorn the tomb's walls and ceiling. Qianlong was laid to rest, along with his empress and two concubines, in the third and final marble vault, amid priceless offerings looted by warlords early in the 20th century. ⊠ *Hebei province, Zunhua County, Malanguan* ☎ *0315/694–0888* ✉ *Y152 (with rest of tombs)* ⊘ *Daily 8:30–5.*

> **THE LOCALS**
>
> The attention foreign travelers receive in rural China may seem overwhelming, but it's usually good-natured and the best response is politeness. Locals can be extremely kind (Confucius said: "To have friends come from afar, isn't that happiness?"), inviting you to their homes for tea, a meal, or even to stay the night. If you wish to turn them down, do so politely, but taking them up on their hospitality can be extremely rewarding. A gift of a small quantity of fruit or a bottle of *baijiu* (a Chinese spirit distilled from sorghum) is always appreciated.

Fodor's Choice **Dingdongling** (定东陵 *Dìngdōnglíng*). The most elaborate of the Qing tombs was built for the infamous Empress Dowager Cixi (1835–1908). Known for her failure to halt Western-imperialist encroachment, Cixi once spent funds allotted to strengthen China's navy on a traditional stone boat for the lake at the Summer Palace. Her burial compound, reputed to have cost 72 tons of silver, is the most elaborate (if not the largest) at the Eastern Qing Tombs. Many of its stone carvings are considered significant because the phoenix, which symbolizes the female, is level with, or even above, the imperial (male) dragon—a feature ordered, no doubt, by the empress herself. A peripheral hall paneled in gold leaf displays some of the luxuries amassed by Cixi and her entourage, including embroidered gowns, jewelry, imported cigarettes, and even a coat for one of her dogs. In a bow to tourist kitsch, the compound's main hall contains a wax statue of Cixi sitting Buddha-like on a lotus petal flanked by a chambermaid and a eunuch. ⊠ *Hebei province, Zunhua County, Malanguan* ☎ *0315/694–0888* ✉ *Y152 (with rest of tombs)* ⊘ *Daily 8:30–5.*

7

CHENGDE

4 hrs (230 km [140 miles]) by train northeast of Beijing; 7 hrs (470 km [291 miles]) by train southwest of Shenyang.

An increasingly common stop on the China tour circuit, some visitors regard Chengde as one of the highlights of their trip. It had been just another village until the 18th century, when Qing Dynasty Emperor Kangxi stumbled upon it during a hunting trip. With the Wulie River gurgling through and the Yanshan Mountains providing an impressive

EIGHT OUTER MONASTERIES

On the eastern and northern slopes of the Mountain Resort, this collection of temples offers a powerful insight into Chengde's role as not just a royal getaway, but as a political arena. Each temple was built to reflect the architectural style of a different minority, so when meetings with rival border groups took place, they provided handy diplomatic currency (the large Tibetan influence was for the benefit of the Mongols, who were devout Lamaists).

Of the dozen monasteries originally built during the Qing Dynasty, only eight survive today in good condition (two were destroyed, two are now dilapidated). Just a few are open to the public. Buses Nos. 6 and 10 take visitors from the Mountain Resort to the eastern and northern temples respectively. If you're strapped for time prioritize the Temple of Potaraka Doctrine, which is a stunning replica of Tibet's Potala Palace, and the Temple of Universal Peace, which is still in use by monks today. The other temples include the Temple of Universal Happiness, Anyuan Temple, and Puren Temple.

backdrop, Chengde was deemed an ideal spot to establish a summer retreat where the Emperor could escape the heat of the capital and indulge in hunting and fishing. Now it is a UNESCO World Heritage Site, home to the magnificent Mountain Resort. It's best to visit in summer or early autumn, as some tourist facilities close in the off-season.

GETTING HERE AND AROUND

TRAIN TRAVEL

Most travelers take the K7711 direct train from Beijing, departing from Beijing Main Rail Station. It is by far the fastest train of the day, departing at 7:56 am and arriving in Chengde at 12:31 pm. Chengde is on a northern rail line between Beijing and Shenyang, and the journey from the capital takes 4½ hours.

TAXI TRAVEL

Chengde is a small city, so you shouldn't have to pay more than Y15 to get from the city center out to the temples.

SAFETY AND PRECAUTIONS

Like most Chinese cities, Chengde is a very safe place to explore. Violent crime is extremely rare, but petty theft can be a problem. Keep a close eye on your personal belongings in crowded places.

TIMING

Chengde is a small city, and most of the main attractions are bunched northeast of the Mountain Resort, so one or two full days should be enough time to see the sights. That said, the Mountain Resort is huge, and could easily take up a full day. If you want to do any hiking in the surrounding countryside, plan on three full days.

TOURS

All hotels in Chengde run tours covering the main sights, at least during the high season. An English-speaking guide costs around Y100.

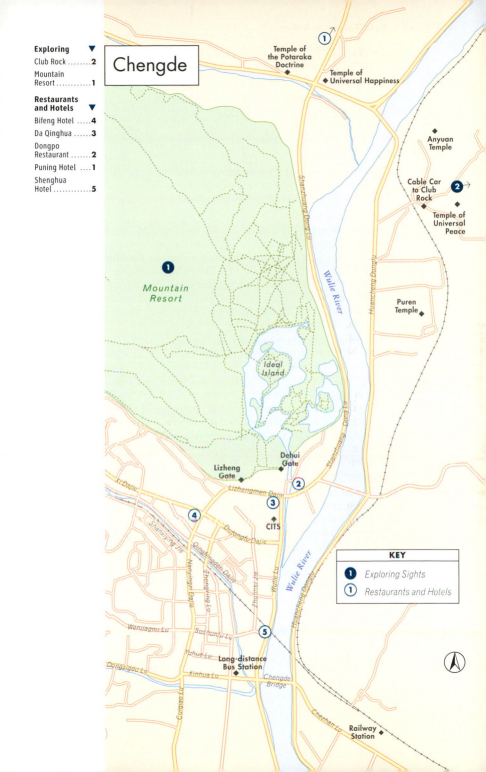

Chengde

Temple of
the Potaraka
Doctrine

Temple of
Universal Happiness

Anyuan
Temple

Cable Car
to Club
Rock

Temple of
Universal
Peace

Puren
Temple

Mountain
Resort

Ideal
Island

Shanzhuang Dong Lu

Wulie River

Huancheng Donglu

Dehui
Gate

Lizheng
Gate

Lizhengmen Dajie

Dujongfu Dajie

CITS

Shanxiying Jie

Qingchengdon Dajie

Zhonghua Lu

Nanyingzi Dajie

Wulie Lu

Zhulinsi Jie

Huancheng Donglu

Wulie River

Wenjiagou Lu

Sushuntu Lu

Yuhua Lu

Xinhua Lu

Dongzigou Lu

Cuimao Lu

Long-distance
Bus Station

Chengde
Bridge

Chezhan Lu

Railway
Station

KEY

1 *Exploring Sights*

1 *Restaurants and Hotels*

ESSENTIALS

Medical Assistance **Chengde Chinese-Western Hospital** ✉ *12 Xi Da Jie* ☎ *0314/202–2222.*

Train Contact **Chengde Train Station** ✉ *Chezhan Lu.*

Visitor and Tour Info **Chengde CITS** ✉ *Yun Shan Lu* ☎ *0314/2061848.*

EXPLORING

Don't waste your energy wandering around the city itself. The massive scale of the Mountain Resort, twice as large as Beijing's Summer Palace, means you will be doing plenty of walking.

TOP ATTRACTIONS

Fodor'sChoice
★

Mountain Resort (避暑山庄 *Bìshǔ Shānzhuāng*). Moved by Chengde's lush mountains, cool weather, and plentiful game—along with a desire to enjoy the first two while shooting arrows at the latter—Emperor Kangxi ordered construction of the first palaces of the Mountain Resort in 1703. Within a decade, what was previously just a simple village had dozens of ornate temples, pagodas, and spectacular gardens spread out across 1,500 acres. By the end of the 18th century nearly 100 imperial structures filled the town.

The result was more than just a smaller version of the Summer Palace, however. Besides luxurious quarters for the emperor and his court, great palaces and temples were completed to house visiting dignitaries and to impress them with the grandeur of the Chinese empire. The location was useful, as Chengde lay far enough away from Beijing to host talks with rivals groups who wouldn't otherwise set foot in the capital. From the interconnected palaces, each built in a different architectural style, to the replicas of famous temples representing different Chinese religions, everything about the resort was designed to reflect China's diversity. In retrospect, it was as much a Qing statement of intent as it was a holiday home.

Today the palace (a UNESCO World Heritage Site) and the surrounding landscape of lakes, meadows, and forests make for an engaging stroll. The mountains in the northern half of the park and giant pagoda in the center afford beutiful panoramas. The resort is also home to the largest imperial garden in China. Even during peak season (April to October) it rarely feels crowded. ✉ *Center of town* ☎ *0314/2029771* 💳 *Apr.–Oct. Y120; Nov.–Mar. Y90* 🕐 *Apr.–Oct., daily 7–5; Nov.–Mar., daily 7:00–4:30.*

WORTH NOTING

Club Rock (棒槌峰 *Bàngchuí Fēng*). A cable-car ride and a 30-minute hike lead from Pule Temple up to a phallic protrusion that spawned a local legend: if the rock should fall, so will the virility of local men. 💳 *Y50* 🕐 *Daily 8–5.*

WHERE TO EAT

Given Chengde's role as a royal hunting ground, it's no surprise that the local specialty is wild game. Spiced deer meat sold in clusters for Y5 and pheasant-and-mushroom–stuffed dumplings can be sampled at the visitor-friendly shops on the street south of the Summer Resort.

$ ✕ **Da Qinghua.** Overlooking Lizheng Gate, this cheerful place with a
CHINESE   rustic wooden exterior is a good choice if you want to sample local dishes. Try the specialty: homemade dumplings filled with pheasant and local mushrooms. The picture menu helps, as the staff does not speak English. Look for the dragons on the building's exterior. ⑤ *Average main: Y80* ✉ *Shan Zhuang Lu* ☎ *0314/2036–2222* ▭ *No credit cards.*

$ ✕ **Dongpo Restaurant** (东坡饭庄 *Dōngpō Fànzhuāng*). With one branch
SICHUAN   near Dehui Gate (east of Lizheng Gate) and two others around town, Dongpo serves hearty Sichuan fare. There's no English menu, but classics like *gongbao jiding* (chicken with peanuts) and *niurou chao tudou* (beef and potatoes) are available. ⑤ *Average main: Y80* ✉ *Shanzhuang Dong Lu* ☎ *0314/208–1886.*

WHERE TO STAY

$ 🏨 **Bifeng Hotel.** Although not fit for an emperor and not much to look at
HOTEL   from the outside, this city-center choice is clean and comfortable inside. **Pros:** central location; decent home cooking in the restaurant. **Cons:** a bit scruffy; no Western breakfast. ⑤ *Rooms from: Y170* ✉ *Dehui Building, 9 Huoshenmiao, Tower B* ☎ *0314/205–0668* ⤶ *71 rooms.*

$ 🏨 **Puning Hotel.** Location is everything, as they say, and the historic set-
HOTEL   ting, adjoining Puning Temple, and a pleasant courtyard place it high above the other options in the center of the city. **Pros:** convenient location; easy access to sights; vegetarian dining options. **Cons:** indifferent service; small rooms. ⑤ *Rooms from: Y320* ✉ *West Courtyard of Puning Temple, Puning Lu* ☎ *0314/205–8888* ⤶ *100 rooms* ⑩ *Breakfast.*

$ 🏨 **Shenghua Hotel** (盛华大酒店 *Shènghuá dàjiǔdiàn*). At 14 stories tall,
HOTEL   this silver tower of glass and steel soars above the city, and beyond the rather dark reception area the rooms have wide windows letting in lots of natural light. **Pros:** tasty restaurant; reliable service; near bus and train stations. **Cons:** a bit far from the main sights. ⑤ *Rooms from: Y430* ✉ *22 Wulie Lu* ☎ *0314/227–1000* ⊕ *www.shenghuahotel.com* ⤶ *111 rooms* ⑩ *Breakfast.*

NIGHTLIFE AND PERFORMING ARTS

The main shopping street, Nanyingzi Dajie (parallel to Wuli River), is a good place to stroll in the evening, when a night market stretches all the way down the street. Many of the vendors sell antiques and fun knickknacks.

CHINESE VOCABULARY

CHINESE VOCABULARY

CHINESE	ENGLISH EQUIVALENT	CHINESE	ENGLISH EQUIVALENT

CONSONANTS

CHINESE	ENGLISH EQUIVALENT	CHINESE	ENGLISH EQUIVALENT
b	**b**oat	p	**p**ass
m	**m**ouse	f	**f**lag
d	**d**ock	t	**t**ongue
n	**n**est	l	**l**ife
g	**g**oat	k	**k**eep
h	**h**ouse	j	and **y**et
q	**ch**icken	x	**sh**ort
zh	ju**dge**	ch	chur**ch**
sh	**sh**eep	r*	**r**ead
z	see**ds**	c	do**ts**
s	**s**eed		

VOWELS

CHINESE	ENGLISH EQUIVALENT	CHINESE	ENGLISH EQUIVALENT
ü	**y**ou	ia	**ya**rd
üe	y**ou + e**	ian	**yen**
a	f**a**ther	iang	**young**
ai	k**i**te	ie	**yet**
ao	n**ow**	o	**a**ll
e	**ea**rn	ou	**go**
ei	d**ay**	u	w**oo**d
er	c**ur**ve	ua	**wa**ft
i	**yie**ld	uo	**wa**ll
i (after z, c, s, zh, ch, sh)	thunde**r**		

WORD ORDER

The basic Chinese sentence structure is the same as in English, following the pattern of subject-verb-object:

He took my pen.   Tā ná le wǒ de bě.

s   v   o   s   v   o

NOUNS

There are no articles in Chinese, although there are many "counters," which are used when a certain number of a given noun is specified. Various attributes of a noun—such as size, shape, or use—determine which counter is used with that noun. Chinese does not distinguish between singular and plural.

a pen   yìzhī bǐ

a book   yìběn shū

VERBS

Chinese verbs are not conjugated, and they do not have tenses. Instead, a system of word order, word repetition, and the addition of a number of adverbs serves to indicate the tense of a verb, whether the verb is a suggestion or an order, or even whether the verb is part of a question. Tāzài ná wǒ de bǐ. (He is taking my pen.) Tā ná le wǒ de bǐ. (He took my pen.) Tā you méi you ná wǒ de bǐ? (Did he take my pen?) Tā yào ná wǒ de bǐ. (He will take my pen.)

TONES

In English, intonation patterns can indicate whether a sentence is a statement (He's hungry.), a question (He's hungry?), or an exclamation (He's hungry!). In Chinese, words have a particular tone value, and these tones are important in determining the meaning of a word. Observe the meanings of the following examples, each said with one of the four tones found in standard Chinese: mā (high, steady tone): mother; má (rising tone, like a question): fiber; mǎ (dipping tone): horse; and mà (dropping tone): swear.

PHRASES

You don't need to master the entire Chinese language to spend a week in China, but taking charge of a few key phrases in the language can aid you in just getting by.

COMMON GREETINGS

Hello/Good morning	Nǐ hǎo/Zǎoshàng hǎo
Good evening	Wǎnshàng hǎo
Good-bye	Zàijiàn
Title for a married woman or an older unmarried woman	Tàitai/Fūrén
Title for a young and unmarried woman	Xiǎojiě
Title for a man	Xiānshēng
How are you?	Nǐ hǎo ma?
Fine, thanks. And you?	Hěn hǎo. Xièxiè. Nǐ ne?
What is your name?	Nǐ jiào shénme míngzi?
My name is . . .	Wǒ jiào . . .
Nice to meet you	Hěn gāoxìng rènshì nǐ.
I'll see you later.	Huítóu jiàn.

POLITE EXPRESSIONS

Please	Qǐng.
Thank you	Xièxiè.
Thank you very much.	Duōxiè.
You're welcome.	Búkèqi.
Yes, thank you.	Shì de, xièxiè.
No, thank you.	Bù, xièxiè.
I beg your pardon.	Qǐng yuánliàng.
I'm sorry.	Hěn baòqiàn.
Pardon me.	Dùibùqǐ.
That's okay.	Méi shénme.
It doesn't matter.	Méi guānxi.
Do you speak English?	Nǐ shuō Yīngyǔ ma?
Yes.	Shì de.
No.	Bù.
Maybe.	Bù yī dìng.
I can speak a little.	Wǒ néng shūo yī diǎnr.
I understand a little.	Wǒ dǒng yì diǎnr.
I don't understand.	Wǒ bù dǒng.
I don't speak Chinese very well.	Wǒ Zhōngwén shūo de bù haǒ.
Would you repeat that, please?	Qǐng zài shūo yíbiàn?
I don't know.	Wǒ bù zhīdaò.
No problem.	Méi wèntí.
It's my pleasure.	Méi guānxi.

NEEDS AND QUESTION WORDS

I'd like . . .	Wǒ xiǎng . . .
I need . . .	Wǒ xūyào . . .
What would you like?	Nǐ yaò shénme?
Please bring me . . .	Qǐng gěi wǒ . . .
I'm looking for . . .	Wǒ zài zhǎo . . .
I'm hungry.	Wǒ è le.

I'm thirsty.	Wǒ kǐukě.
It's important.	Hěn zhòngyào.
It's urgent.	Hěn jǐnjí.
How?	Zěnmeyàng?
How much?	Duōshǎo?
How many?	Duōshǎo gè?
Which?	Nǎ yí gè?
What?	Shénme?
What kind of?	Shénme yàng de?
Who?	Shuí?
Where?	Nǎli?
When?	Shénme shíhòu?
What does this mean?	Zhè shì shénme yìsi?
What does that mean?	Nà shì shénme yìsi?
How do you say . . . in Chinese?	. . . yòng Zhōngwén zěnme shūo?

AT THE AIRPORT

Where is . . .	. . . zài nǎr?
customs?	Hǎiguān
passport control?	Hùzhào jiǎnyàn
the information booth?	Wènxùntái
the ticketing counter?	Shòupiàochù
the baggage claim?	Xínglǐchù
the ground transportation?	Dìmìan jiāotōng
Is there a bus service	Yǒu qù chéng lǐ de gōnggòng
to the city?	qìchē ma?
Where are . . .	. . . zài nǎr?
the international departures?	Guójì hángbēn chūfě diǎn
the international arrivals?	Guójì hángbēn dàodá diǎn.
What is your nationality?	Nǐ shì něi guó rén?
I am an American.	Wǒ shì Měiguó rén.
I am Canadian.	Wǒ shì Jiānádà rén.

AT THE HOTEL, RESERVING A ROOM

I would like a room . . .	Wǒ yào yí ge fángjiān.
for one person	yìjiān dānrén fáng
for two people	yìjiān shuāngrén fáng
for tonight	jīntiān wǎnshàng
for two nights	liǎng gè wǎnshàng
for a week	yí ge xīngqī
Do you have a different room?	Nǐ hái yǒu biéde fángjiān ma?
with a bath	dài yùshì de fángjiān
with a shower	dài línyù de fángjiān
with a toilet	dài cèsuǐ de fángjiān
with air-conditioning	yǒu kōngtiáo de fángjiān
How much is it?	Duōshǎo qián?
My bill, please.	Qǐng jiézhàng.

AT THE RESTAURANT

Where can we find a good restaurant?	Zài nǎr kěyǐ zhǎodào yìjiě hǎo cānguǎn?
We'd like a(n) . . . restaurant.	Wǒmen xiǎng qù yì gè . . . cānguǎn.
elegant	gāo jí
fast-food	kuàicān
inexpensive	piányì de
seafood	hǎixiān
vegetarian	sùshí
Café	kāfeī diàn
A table for two	Liǎng wèi
Waiter, a menu please.	Fúwùyuán, qǐng gěi wǒmen càidān.
The wine list, please.	Qǐng gěi wǒmen jiǔdān.
Appetizers	Kāiwèi cài
Main course	Zhǔ cài
Dessert	Tiándiǎn

What would you like?	Nǐ yào shénme cài?
What would you like to drink?	Nǐ yào shénme yǐnliào?
Can you recommend a good wine?	Nǐ néng tūijiàn yí ge hǎo jiǔ ma?
Wine, please.	Qǐng lǎi diǎn jiǔ.
Beer, please.	Qǐng lǎi diǎn píjiǔ.
I didn't order this.	Wǐ méiyǒu diǎn zhè gè.
That's all, thanks.	Jiù zhèxie, xièxiè.
The check, please.	Qǐng jiézhàng.
Cheers!/Bottoms Up!	Gānbēi!
To your health!	Zhù nǐ shēntì jiànkāng.

OUT ON THE TOWN

Where can I find . . .	Nǎr yǒu . . .
an art museum?	yìshù bówùguǎn?
a museum of natural history?	zìránlìshǐ bówùguǎn?
a history museum?	lìshǐ bówuguǎn?
a gallery?	huàláng?
interesting architecture?	yǐuqù de jiànzhùwù?
a church?	jiàotáng?
the zoo?	dòngwùyuán?
I'd like . . .	Wǒ xiǎng . . .
to see a play.	kàn xì.
to see a movie.	kàn diànyǐng.
to see a concert.	qù yīnyuèhuì.
to see the opera.	kàn gējù.
to go sightseeing.	qù guānguāng.
to go on a bike ride.	qí zìxíngchē.

SHOPPING

Where is the best place to go shopping for . . .	Mǎi . . . zuì hǎo qù nǎr?
clothes?	yīfu
food?	shíwù

souvenirs?	jìniànpǐn
furniture?	jīajù
fabric?	bùliào
antiques?	gǔdǐng
books?	shūjí
sporting goods?	yùndòng wùpǐn
electronics?	diànqì
computers?	diànnǎo

DIRECTIONS

Excuse me. Where is . . .	Duìbùqǐ . . . zài nǎr?
the bus stop?	Qìchēzhàn
the subway station?	Dìtiězhàn
the rest room?	Xǐshǐujiān
the taxi stand?	Chūzū chēzhàn
the nearest bank?	Zùijìn de yínháng
the hotel?	Lǚ guǎn
To the right	Zài yòubiān.
To the left.	Zài zuǐbiān.
Straight ahead.	Wǎng qián zhízǐu.
It's near here.	Jìuzài zhè fùjìn.
Go back.	Wǎng húi zǐu.
Next to . . .	Jǐnkào . . .

TIME

What time is it?	Xiànzài jǐdiǎn?
It is noon.	Zhōngwǔ.
It is midnight.	Bànyè.
It is 9:00 a.m.	Shàngwǔ jǐu diǎn.
It is 1:00 p.m.	Xiàwǔ yì diǎn.
It is 3 o'clock.	Sān diǎn (zhōng).
5:15	Wǔ diǎn shíwǔ fēn.
7:30	Qī diǎn sānshí (bàn).

9:45	Jǐu diǎn sìshíwǔ.
Now	Xiànzài
Later	Wǎn yì diǎnr
Immediately	Mǎshàng
Soon	Hěn kuài

DAYS OF THE WEEK

Monday	Xīngqī yī
Tuesday	Xīngqī èr
Wednesday	Xīngqī sān
Thursday	Xīngqī sì
Friday	Xīngqī wǔ
Saturday	Xīngqī lìu
Sunday	Xīngqī rì (tiān)

MODERN CONNECTIONS

Where can I find . . .	Zài nǎr kěyǐ shǐ yòng . . .
a telephone?	dìanhuà?
a fax machine?	chuánzhēnjī?
an Internet connection?	guójì wǎnglù?
How do I call the United States?	Gěi Měiguó dǎ diànhuà zěnme dǎ?
I need . . .	Wǒ xūyào . . .
a fax sent.	fā chuánzhēn.
a hookup to the Internet.	yǔ guójì wǎnglù liánjiē.
a computer.	diànnǎo.
a package sent overnight.	liányè bǎ bāoguǐ jìchū.
some copies made.	fùyìn yìxiē wénjiàn.

EMERGENCIES AND SAFETY

Help!	Jìumìng a!
Fire!	Jìuhuǐ a!
I need a doctor.	Wǒ yào kàn yīshēng.
Call an ambulance!	Mǎshàng jiào jìuhùchē!
What happened?	Fashēng le shénme shì?

I am/My wife is/My husband is/	Wǒ/Wǒ qīzi/Wǒ Zhàngfu/
My friend is/Someone is . . . very sick.	Wǒ péngyǒu/Yǒu rén . . .
having a heart attack.	bìng de hěn lìhài.
choking.	yēzhù le.
losing consciousness.	yūndǎo le.
about to vomit.	yào ǒutùwù le.
having a seizure.	yòu fābìng le.
stuck.	bèi kǎ zhù le.
I can't breathe.	Wǒ bù néng hūxī.
I tripped and fell.	Wǒ bàn dǎo le.
I cut myself.	Wǒ gē shěng le.
I drank too much.	Wǒ jiǔ hē de tài duō le.
I don't know.	Wǒ bù zhīdào.
I've injured my . . .	Wǒ de . . . shòushěng le.
head	tóu
neck	bózi
back	bèi
arm	gē bèi
leg	tuǐ
foot	jiǎo
eye(s)	yǎnjīng
I've been robbed.	Wǒ bèi qiǎng le.

NUMBERS

0	Líng
1	Yī
2	Èr
3	Sān
4	Sì
5	Wǔ
6	Liù
7	Qī

8	Bā
9	Jiǔ
10	Shí
11	Shíyī
12	Shí'èr
13	Shísān
14	Shísì
15	Shíwǔ
16	Shíliù
17	Shíqī
18	Shíbā
19	Shíjiǔ
20	Èrshí
21	Èrshíyī
22	Èrshí'èr
23	Èrshísān
30	Sānshí
40	Sìshí
50	Wǔshí
60	Liùshí
70	Qīshí
80	Bāshí
90	Jiǔshí
100	Yìbǎi
1,000	Yìqiān
1,100	Yìqiān
2,000	Yìqiān
10,000	Yíwàn
100,000	Shíwàn
1,000,000	Bǎiwàn

TRAVEL SMART BEIJING

GETTING HERE AND AROUND

▊ GETTING ORIENTED

Beijing has exploded over the past few decades, thanks to China's economic boom. Whole neighborhoods have been demolished, constructed, or "renovated," and the relentless march toward modernity has caused some controversy. Old neighborhoods such as Gulou's much-loved *hutong*s (narrow lanes), near the Drum and Bell towers in north-central Beijing, are being eyed by developers. Old-timers can barely recognize many sections of the city, and maps go out of date almost overnight. It's a good idea to get the latest bilingual version on arrival.

The city's five concentric ring roads look like a target, with the Forbidden City in the bull's-eye. Note that, oddly, there is no First Ring Road; this is commonly thought to have been the original tramline that circled the Forbidden City until it was disbanded in the 1950s. The Second Ring Road follows the line of the old city walls, and consequently many of the stops have the suffix "men" (meaning "gate"). The circular subway Line 2 runs below it. The Third Ring Road passes through part of Beijing's Central Business District (CBD) and links up with the Airport Expressway.

The three remaining ring roads have equally unimaginative names (Fourth, Fifth, Sixth). Along the center of the north Fourth Ring Road is Olympic Park, where you'll find the impressive National Stadium (the "Bird's Nest") and the National Aquatics Center (the "Water Cube"). If you're sticking to central Beijing, these roads won't be much use, though fare-hungry taxi drivers would love you to believe otherwise.

Beijing's traffic can be a nightmare, especially at rush hour when the gridlock extends from the center of the city all the way out to the Fourth Ring Road. With the opening of a number of new subway lines and several more expected to follow by 2016, the subway is a good way to escape the bumper-to-bumper traffic. The Airport Express Line (20 minutes from the airport to the Dongzhimen subway stop northeast of the city center) has proven to be a boon. Also a great success is the city's electronic fare system, where all rides cost a very reasonable Y2.

The city's wide thoroughfares are laid out on a grid system, with roads running north–south or east–west. These compass points often make up part of the street name, so *bei* (north), *dong* (east), *nan* (south), *xi* (west), and *zhong* (middle) are useful words to know. Networks of ancient lanes and alleys known as hutongs run between these main streets.

Beijing's most important thoroughfare runs east–west along the northern edge of Tiananmen Square. Generally known as Chang'an Jie, or the "Avenue of Heavenly Peace," it actually changes names several times along its length (as do many other major streets).

▊ AIR TRAVEL

Beijing is one of China's three major international hubs, along with Shanghai and Hong Kong. The number of nonstop flights to Beijing has been steadily increasing, with a few new nonstop flights added every month. You can catch a nonstop flight here from New York (13¾ hours), Chicago (13½ hours), Washington, D.C. (14 hours), Los Angeles (13 hours), Sydney (11½ hours), and London (11 hours). Besides state-run stalwart Air China, carriers such as Hainan Airlines, China Southern, and China Eastern all have nonstop flights. Multiple-stop flights from other cities generally stop in Tokyo, Seoul, Hong Kong, or Vancouver.

Airlines and Airports Airline and Airport Links.com. Airline and Airport Links.com has links to many of the world's airlines and airports. ⊕ *www.airlineandairportlinks.com.*

Airline Security Issues Transportation Security Administration. The TSA has answers for almost every question that might come up. ⊕ *www.tsa.gov.*

AIRLINE TICKETS

A number of Chinese cities are included in the One World Alliance's Visit Asia Pass, including major destinations like Beijing, Shanghai, and Hong Kong as well as interior stops such as Xi'an, Chengdu, Xiamen, Nanjing, Kunming, and Wuhan. Cities are grouped into zones, and there is a flat rate for each zone. Inquire through American Airlines, Cathay Pacific, or any other One World member. It won't be the cheapest way to get around, but you'll be flying on some of the world's best airlines.

If you are flying into Asia on a SkyTeam airline (Delta, for example) you're eligible to purchase a Go Greater China Pass. It allows travel to nearly 150 destinations, and prices are based on a zone system. You'll have to book directly with a Sky Team airlines (such as China Eastern or China Southern) to get the discounted fares.

The Star Alliance's China Airpass is a good choice if you plan to stop in multiple destinations within China (including Macao and Hong Kong). With one ticket you can choose from more than 70 different locations, though the ticket is only good for three to 10 individual flights on Air China or Shenzhen Airlines. The catch? Chinese domestic flight schedules can be changed or canceled at a moment's notice.

Air Pass Info China Airpass ☏ *800/241–6522* ⊕ *www.staralliance.com/en/fares/airpasses/china-airpass.* **Go Greater China** ☏ *800/221–1212* ⊕ *www.skyteam.biz/en/travel-offers/go-china.* **Visit Asia Pass** ☏ *800/433-7300* ⊕ *www.oneworld.com/flights/single-continent-fares/visit-asia.*

AIRPORTS

The efficient Beijing Capital International Airport (PEK) is 27 km (17 miles) northeast of the city center. The three terminals are connected by walkways and a tram system: T1 serves mainly domestic flights, while T2 and T3 serve both domestic and international flights. If you can't find your flight on the departure board, check that you're in the correct terminal. The best advice is to check with the airport website before heading to the airport, as you'll need to let your taxi driver know which terminal you need.

Clearing customs and immigration can take a while, depending on how busy the airport is. Make sure you arrive at least two hours before your scheduled flight time. Be sure to fill out the departure card before the immigration check or you'll have to leave the line, fill out the card, and start all over.

There is an uninspiring transit lounge for T1 and T2 in which to while away the hours. T3's waiting area is a bit more comfortable. Both Chinese and Western-style fast-food outlets are available if you hunt around, but they are expensive for what you get. If you've got a long stopover, consider buying a package from one of the Plaza Premium Traveler's Lounges, near Gate 11 in T2 and Gate E13 in T3. Both have comfortable armchairs, Internet access, newspapers, and a buffet.

While wandering the airport, someone may approach you offering to carry your luggage, or even just to give you directions. Be aware that this "helpful" stranger will almost certainly expect payment.

Airport Information Beijing Capital International Airport ☏ *010/96158* ⊕ *www.bcia.com.cn.*

GROUND TRANSPORTATION

The easiest way to get from the airport to Beijing is by taxi. Most major hotels have representatives at the airport who can arrange a car or minivan. When departing from Beijing, prebook airport transport through your hotel.

When you arrive in Beijing, head for the clearly labeled taxi line just outside the terminal, beyond a small covered parking area. The (usually long) line moves quickly. Ignore offers from touts trying to coax you away from the line—they're privateers looking to rip you off. At the head of the line, a dispatcher will give you your taxi's number, useful in case of complaints or forgotten luggage. Insist that your driver use the meters, and do not negotiate a fare. If the driver is unwilling to comply, feel free to change taxis.

The initial fare is Y13—good for 3 km (2 miles)—with Y2.3 for each additional kilometer. A trip to the center of Beijing costs around Y80. In light traffic it takes about 30 minutes to reach the city center; during rush hour expect the trip to take an hour. After 11 pm, taxis impose a 20% late-night surcharge. A Y10 toll is added to fares when you're headed to the airport.

Another option for getting downtown is the Airport Express Subway Line, which departs from T2 and T3 and stops at Sanyuanqiao (northeast Third Ring Road) and Dongzhimen (northeast Second Ring Road) subway stations. The trip takes 20 minutes and costs Y25.

Air-conditioned airport shuttle buses are the cheapest way of getting into town. There are six numbered routes, all of which leave from outside the arrivals area. Tickets, which cost Y15 to Y24, are available from the ticket booth just inside the arrival halls. Departures are every 15 to 30 minutes. There's a detailed route map on the airport website.

FLIGHTS

Air China, a member of the Star Alliance, is the country's flagship carrier. It operates nonstop flights from Beijing to various North American and European cities. China Southern is the major carrier for domestic routes. Like all Chinese carriers, it's a regional subsidiary of the Civil Aviation Administration of China.

Buy tickets in the United States through airline websites or travel agencies. It's worth contacting a Chinese travel agency like China International Travel Service (CITS) to compare prices, as these can

> ### LUCKY NUMBERS
>
> Sichuan Airlines bought the number 28/8888–8888 for 2.33 million yuan ($280,723), making it the most expensive telephone number in the world. The number eight (*ba* in Chinese) is considered lucky in China, as it sounds similar to *fa*, the first character in the phrase *facai*, which means "to gain wealth."

vary substantially. If you're in China and want to book flights to other cities in the country, the websites ⊕ *www.ctrip.com* and ⊕ *www.elong.com* are excellent options. Flights though this website are often much cheaper than if you book them through a foreign website.

The service on most Chinese airlines is more on par with low-cost American airlines than with big international carriers—be prepared for limited legroom, iffy food, and possibly no personal video monitors. More important, always arrive at least two hours before departure, as chronic overbooking means latecomers lose their seats.

▎ BUS TRAVEL

TO AND FROM BEIJING

China has plenty of long-distance buses with air-conditioning and movies (whether you want them or not). Buying tickets can be complicated if you don't speak Chinese, so it's best to have your hotel concierge or a travel agent make arrangements. Better yet, consider taking a train or plane.

Buses depart from the city's several long-distance bus stations. The main ones are: Dongzhimen (Northeast); Muxiyuan (at Haihutun in the south); Beijiao, also called Dewai (North); and Majuan or Guangqumen (East).

Bus Information Beijiao ✉ *A30 Huayan Beili, Chaoyang District* ☎ *010/8284–6760.* **Dongzhimen** ✉ *45 Dongzhimenwai Xiejie, Dongcheng District* ☎ *010/6467–1346.* **Majuan**

✉ *22 Guangqumenwai Dajie, Chaoyang District* ☎ *010/6771–7620.* **Muxiyuan** ✉ *16 Nanyuan, Fengtai District* ☎ *010/6726–7149.*

WITHIN BEIJING

Unless you know Beijing well, public buses aren't the best choice for getting around. There are hundreds of routes, which are hot and crowded in summer and cold and crowded in winter. Just getting on and off can be, quite literally, a fight.

The Beijing Public Transportation Corporation is the city's largest bus service provider. Routes 1 to 199 are regular city buses and cost a flat fare of Y1. Routes in the 200s only run at night, costing Y1. Routes 300 to 799 go from downtown Beijing to suburban areas, and fares (starting at Y1) depend on how far you're going—have your destination written in Chinese. The newer air-conditioned buses in the 800s and 900s start at Y2 and increase depending on distance.

If you bought an IC card for the subway, you can use it on buses. Most buses allow you to scan your card as you board. On the suburban buses you'll scan as you board and as you depart, calculating the fare. For buses that go even farther afield, there is a conductor onboard who will take your fare or scan your card.

Contact Beijing Public Transportation Corporation ✉ *29 Lianhuachi Xili, Fengtai District* ☎ *010/6396–0008* ⊕ *www.bjbus.com.*

■ CAR TRAVEL

You won't be able to rent a car in Beijing because neither U.S. nor international licenses are recognized in China. This restriction should be cause for relief, as city traffic is terrible. If you want to get around by car, put yourself in the experienced hands of a local driver and sit back and relax.

The quickest way to hire a car and driver is to flag down a taxi and hire it for the day. After some negotiating, expect to pay between around Y600 and Y700. Most hotels can make arrangements for you, though they often charge you double that rate—you can probably guess who gets the difference. Most drivers do not speak English, so it's a good idea to have your destination and hotel name written down in Chinese.

Another alternative is American car-rental agency Avis, which includes mandatory chauffeurs as part of all rental packages—although this can also be very expensive, with chauffeurs alone costing Y235 per hour.

Contact Avis ☎ *400/882–1119* ⊕ *www.avis.cn.*

■ SUBWAY TRAVEL

Beijing's quick and efficient subway system is an excellent way to get about town. After operating for years with only two lines, the network is growing exponentially, with eight lines servicing the inner city, a further eight heading out into the suburbs, and several more due to open over the next few years.

Lines 1 and the newly expanded Line 6 run east–west across the city, stopping at tourist destinations such as Tiananmen Square and Beihai Park. Line 2 runs under the Second Ring Road, making it a good way to circle the city center. North–south Line 5 gives access to the Lama Temple and Temple of Heaven. Line 8 runs through the Olympic Village all the way down to Gulou, and Line 10 loops past such destinations as Sanlitun and the antiques market at Panjiayuan. In the west and south, Line 4 stops at the Summer Palace and also Beijing South station. The Airport Line connects the Dongzhimen interchange with the airport—now a 20-minute jaunt for Y25. The remaining lines are mainly used by commuters and are less useful for sightseeing.

Subway stations are marked by blue signs with a "D" (for *ditie*, or subway) in a circle. Signs are not always obvious, so be prepared to hunt around for entrances or ask directions; *Ditie zhan zai nar?* (Where's the subway station?) is a useful phrase, but sometimes simply saying *ditie* with an inquiring look may get you better results.

Stations are usually clean and safe, as are trains. Navigating the subway is very straightforward: station names are clearly displayed in Chinese and pinyin, and there are maps in each station. Once on board, each stop is clearly announced on a loudspeaker in Chinese and English.

■ TAXI TRAVEL

Taxis are the most comfortable way to get around. Be aware that they tend to disappear during inclement weather, and rush-hour traffic can be infuriating. There's a Y13 charge for the first 3 km (2 miles) and Y2.3 per kilometer thereafter. After 11 pm the initial charge rises to Y14 and there's a 20% surcharge per additional kilometer.

Drivers usually know the terrain well, but most don't speak English; make sure to have your destination written down in Chinese. (Keep a card with the name of your hotel on it for the return trip.) Hotel doormen can help you tell the driver where you're going. It's a good idea to study a map and have some idea where you are, as some drivers will take you for a ride—a much longer one—if they think they can get away with it.

Contacts Taxi Booking Service
☎ *010/96103 in English.*

■ TRAIN TRAVEL

China's enormous rail network is one of the world's busiest. Trains are usually safe and run strictly to schedule. Although there are certain intricacies to buying tickets, once you've got one, trips are generally hassle-free. Beijing is a major rail hub. Services to the rest of China leave from its four huge stations. The Trans-Siberian Railway leaves from Beijing Zhan, the main station. Trains to Hong Kong and to areas in the west

and south of China leave from Beijing Xi Zhan (West). Most Z-series trains (nonstop luxury service) use these two stations. Lesser lines headed north and east leave from Beijing Bei Zhan (North) and Beijing Dong Zhan (East). C- and D-series trains (intercity nonstop rail) mostly use Beijing Nan Zhan (South).

China's high-speed rail network is rapidly becoming one of the longest in the world, and new routes are debuting every year. Journeys that used to be overnight affairs, such as Beijing to Xi'an or Shanghai, now take around five hours. Smooth rides and few delays make rail travel a tempting alternative to domestic flights. You can buy most tickets 10 days in advance (remember to bring your passport); two to three days ahead is usually enough time, except around the three national holidays—Chinese New Year (two days in mid-January to February, depending on the lunar calendar), Labor Day (May 1), and National Day (October 1)—when tickets sell out weeks in advance.

The cheapest tickets are found at the stations, and there are ticket offices for foreigners staffed with English speakers at Beijing Zhan (first floor) and Beijing Xi Zhan (second floor). Most travel agents, including CITS, can book tickets for a small surcharge (Y20 to Y50), saving you the hassle of going to the station. Tickets can be bought from ticket offices around the city for a Y5 fee. You can also buy tickets for slow trains through online retailers like China Train Ticket, and they'll deliver the tickets to your hotel.

Trains are always crowded, but you are guaranteed your designated seat, though not always the overhead luggage rack. Note that theft on trains is increasing; on overnight trains, sleep with your valuables or else keep them on the inside of the bunk. Overpriced dining cars serve meals that are often inedible, so you'd do better to make use of the massive thermoses of boiled water in each compartment or the taps in the carriage section and take along your own noodles or instant soup, as the locals do.

You can find out just about everything about Chinese train travel at Seat 61's fabulous website. China Highlights has a searchable online timetable for major train routes. The tour operator Travel China Guide has an English-language website that can help you figure out train schedules and fares.

Information Beijing Bei Zhan ✉ *Xizhimen, Xicheng District* ☏ *010/5182–6623.* **Beijing Nan Zhan** ✉ *12 Yongdingmenwai Dajie, Chongwen District* ☏ *010/5183–6272.* **Beijing Xi Zhan** ✉ *118 Lianhuachi Donglu, Fengtai District* ☏ *010/6321–6253.* **Beijing Zhan** ✉ *A13 Maojiawang Hutong, east side of Dongbianmen Gate, Dongcheng District* ☏ *010/5101–9999.* **China Highlights** ☏ *800/268–2918* ⊕ *www.chinahighlights. com/china-trains/index.htm.* **Seat 61** ⊕ *www. seat61.com/china.htm.* **Travel China Guide** ☏ *800/315–3949* ⊕ *www.travelchinaguide. com/china-trains/index.htm.*

BIG TRAIN RIDES

Taking the Trans-Siberian railway is a serious undertaking. The two weekly services cover the 8,050 km (5,000 miles) between Moscow and Beijing. The Trans-Manchurian is a Russian train that goes through northeast China, whereas the Trans-Mongolian is a Chinese train that goes through the Great Wall and crosses the Gobi Desert. Both have first-class compartments with four berths (Y3,522), or luxury two-berth compartments (Y5,674), one-way. Keep in mind that you will have to obtain all the necessary visas before embarking on your journey.

ESSENTIALS

▪ COMMUNICATIONS

INTERNET

Beijing is a very Internet-friendly place for travelers with laptops. Most mid-range to high-end hotels have in-room Wi-Fi access, but you might have to pay extra for it. Most hotels have a computer with Internet access that you can use for a fee.

When you're out and about, coffee chains like Starbucks are good places to find Wi-Fi connections. Internet cafés are ubiquitous (look for signs reading 网吧); new ones open and close all the time, so ask your hotel for a recommendation. Prices vary considerably. Near the northern university districts you could pay as little as Y2 to Y3 per hour; slicker downtown places could cost 10 times that.

⚠ **Remember that there is strict government control of the Internet in China. Google and Gmail are accessible, if tooth-grindingly slow. It's impossible to access some news sites and blogs without using a virtual private network (VPN), which circumnavigates the government's attempts to block.**

PHONES

The country code for China is 86; the city code for Beijing is 010 (omit the first "0"), and the city code for Shanghai is 21. To call China from the United States or Canada, dial the international access code (011), followed by the country code (86), the area or city code, and the eight-digit phone number.

Numbers beginning with 800 within China are toll-free. Note that a call from China to a toll-free number in the United States or Hong Kong is a full-tariff international call.

CALLING WITHIN CHINA

The Chinese phone system is cheap and efficient. You can make local and long-distance calls from your hotel or any public phone on the street. Some pay phones accept coins, but it's easier to buy an IC calling card, available at convenience stores and newsstands. Local calls are generally free from landlines, though your hotel might charge a nominal rate. Long-distance rates in China are very low. Calling from your hotel room is a viable option, as hotels can only add a 15% service charge.

Beijing's city code is 010, and Beijing phone numbers have eight digits. When calling within the city, you can drop the city code. In general, city codes appear written with a 0 in front of them; if not, you need to add this when calling another city within China.

For directory assistance, dial 114 (Chinese), or 2689–0114 (for help in English, though you may not get through). If you want information for other cities, dial the city code followed by 114 (note that this is considered a long-distance call). For example, if you're in Beijing and need directory assistance for a Shanghai number, dial 021–114. The operators do not speak English, so if you don't speak Chinese you're best off asking your hotel for help.

Contacts Weather ☎ *400/6000–121.*

CALLING OUTSIDE CHINA

To make an international call from within China, dial 00 (the international access code within China) and then the country code, area code, and phone number. The country code for the United States is 1.

International direct dialing is available at all hotels, post offices, shopping centers, and airports. By international standards the prices aren't unreasonable, but it's vastly cheaper to use a long-distance calling card, known as an IP card. The rates also beat AT&T, MCI, and Sprint hands down.

CALLING CARDS

Calling cards are a key part of the Chinese phone system. There are two kinds: the IC card for local and domestic long-distance calls using a pay phone; and the IP card for international calls from any phone. You can buy both at post offices, convenience stores, and street vendors.

IC cards come in values of Y20, Y50, and Y100 and can be used in any pay phone with a card slot—most Beijing pay phones have them. Local calls using them cost around Y0.30 a minute, and less on weekends and after 6 pm.

To use IP cards, you first dial a local access number, then press 2 for English instructions. This is often free from hotels, however at public phones you need an IC card to dial the access number. You then enter a card number and PIN, and finally the phone number complete with international dial codes. Minutes from both cards are deducted at the same time. There are countless different card brands; China Unicom is one that's usually reliable. IP cards come with values of Y20, Y30, Y50, and Y100; however, the going rate is much less, so bargain vendors down.

CELL PHONES

If you have a multiband phone and your service provider uses the world-standard GSM network (as do AT&T, T-Mobile, and Verizon), you can probably use your phone abroad. Roaming fees can be steep, however: 99¢ a minute is considered reasonable. And overseas you normally pay the toll charges for incoming calls. It's almost always cheaper to send a text message than to make a call, since text messages have a very low set fee (often less than 5¢).

If you just want to make local calls, consider buying a new SIM card (note that your provider may have to unlock your phone for you to use a different SIM card) and a prepaid service plan in the destination. You'll then have a local number and can make local calls at local rates. If your trip is extensive, you could also simply buy a new cell phone in your destination, as the initial cost will be offset over time.

TIP→ If you travel internationally frequently, save one of your old cell phones or buy a cheap one on the Internet; ask your cell-phone company to unlock it for you, and take it with you as a travel phone, buying a new SIM card with pay-as-you-go service in each destination.

If you have a GSM phone, pick up a local SIM card (*sim ka*) from any branch of China Mobile or China Unicom. You'll be presented with a list of possible phone numbers, with varying prices—an "unlucky" phone number (one with lots of 4s) could be as cheap as Y50, whereas an auspicious one (full of 8s) could fetch Y300 or more. You then buy prepaid cards to charge minutes onto your SIM—do this straightaway, as you need credit to receive calls. Local calls to landlines cost Y0.25 a minute, and to cell phones, Y0.60. International calls from cell phones are very expensive. Remember to bring an adapter for your phone charger. You can also buy cheap handsets from China Mobile. If you're planning to stay even a couple of days this is probably cheaper than renting a phone.

Beijing Limo rents cell phones, which they can deliver to your hotel or at the airport. Renting a handset starts at $5 a day, and you buy a prepaid package with a certain amount of call time; prices start at $49. Beijing Impression travel agency rents handsets at similar rates, and you buy a regular prepaid card for calls. For that money, you may as well buy your own pay-as-you-go cell phone once you arrive (the cheapest Nokia handset goes for around Y220). Cell phone shops are plentiful, though you may need an interpreter to help you deal with the people behind the counter and to reset the language.

Contacts Beijing Impression ☎ 010/6400–0300 ⊕ www.beijingimpression.cn. **Beijing Limo** ☎ 010/6546–1588 ⊕ www.beijinglimo.com/english. **Cellular Abroad** ☎ 800/287–5072 ⊕ www.cellularabroad.com. **China Mobile** ☎ 10086 English-language assistance ⊕ www.chinamobileltd.com. **China Unicom** ☎ 010/116–114 English-language assistance

⊕ www.chinaunicom.com. **Planet Fone**
☎ 888/988–4777 ⊕ www.planetfone.com.

CUSTOMS AND DUTIES

Except for the usual prohibitions against narcotics, explosives, plant and animal materials, firearms, and ammunition, you can bring anything into China that you plan to take away with you. GPS equipment, cameras, video recorders, laptops, and the like should pose no problems. However, China is very sensitive about printed matter deemed seditious, such as religious, pornographic, and political items, especially articles, books, and pictures on Tibet. All the same, small amounts of English-language reading matter aren't generally a problem. Customs officials are for the most part easygoing, and visitors are rarely searched. It's not necessary to fill in customs declaration forms, but if you carry in a large amount of cash, say several thousand dollars, you should declare it upon arrival.

On leaving, you're not allowed to take out any antiquities dating to before 1795. Antiques from between 1795 and 1949 must have an official red seal attached.

U.S. Information U.S. Customs and Border Protection ☎ 877/227–5511 ⊕ www.cbp.gov.

ELECTRICITY

The electrical current in China is 220 volts, 50 cycles alternating current (AC), so most American appliances can't be used without a transformer. A universal adapter is especially useful in China, as wall outlets come in a bewildering variety of configurations: two- and three-pronged round plugs, as well as two-pronged flat sockets.

Consider making a small investment in a universal adapter, which has several types of plugs in one lightweight, compact unit. Most laptops and cell-phone chargers are dual voltage (i.e., they operate equally well on 110 and 220 volts), so require only an adapter. These days the same

is true of small appliances such as hair dryers. Always check labels and manufacturer instructions to be sure. Don't use 110-volt outlets marked "for shavers only" for high-wattage appliances such as hair dryers.

Contacts Steve Kropla's Help for World Traveler's. Steve Kropla's Help for World Traveler's has information on electrical and telephone plugs around the world. ⊕ www. kropla.com. **Walkabout Travel Gear.** Walkabout Travel Gear has a good coverage of electricity under "adapters." ☎ 800/852–7085 ⊕ www.walkabouttravelgear.com.

EMERGENCIES

The best place to head in a medical emergency is the Beijing United Family Health Center, which has 24-hour emergency services. International SOS is another clinic with a good reputation; it can arrange Medivac. For over-the-counter medicines, Watsons pharmacies can be found all over the city, including in most large shopping centers.

Beijing has different numbers for each emergency service, though staff members often don't speak English. If in doubt, call the U.S. embassy first: staff members are available 24 hours a day to help handle emergencies and facilitate communication with local agencies.

Emergency Contacts Fire ☎ 119. **Police** ☎ 110. **Medical Emergency** ☎ 120. **Traffic Accident** ☎ 122. **U.S. Embassy** ✉ 55 Anjialou Lu, Chaoyang District ☎ 010/8531–4000 🖷 010/8531–3300 ⊕ beijing.usembassy-china. org.cn.

Hospitals and Clinics Beijing United Family Hospital and Clinics ✉ 2 Jiangtai Lu, Chaoyang District ☎ 010/5927–7000, 010/5927–7120 emergencies ⊕ www.ufh.com. cn/en. **China-Japan Friendship Hospital** ✉ Ying Hua Dong Jie, Heping Li ☎ 010/6422–2952, 010/6428–2297 ⊕ english.zryhyy. cn. **Hong Kong International Medical Clinic** ✉ Hong Kong Macau Center–Swissotel, 2 Chaoyangmen Bei Da Jie, 9th fl., Chaoyang

LOCAL DO'S AND TABOOS

GREETINGS

Chinese people aren't very touchy-feely with one another, even less so with strangers. Keep bear hugs and cheek kissing for your next European trip and stick to handshakes.

Always use a person's title and surname until they invite you to do otherwise.

RULES AND RULE BREAKING

By and large, the Chinese are a rule-abiding bunch. Follow their lead and avoid doing anything signs advise against.

Beijing is a crowded city, and pushing, nudging, and line jumping are commonplace. It may be hard to accept, but it has become the norm, so avoid reacting (even verbally) if you're accidentally shoved.

OUT ON THE TOWN

It's a great honor to be invited to someone's house, so explain at length if you can't go. Arrive punctually with a small gift for the hosts; remove your shoes outside if you see other guests doing so.

Tea, served in all Chinese restaurants, is a common drink at mealtimes, though many locals only accompany their food with soup.

Smoking is one of China's greatest vices. No-smoking sections in restaurants are becoming more prevalent, but people light up anywhere they think they can get away with it.

Holding hands in public is fine, but keep passionate embraces for the hotel room.

DOING BUSINESS

Time is of the essence when doing business in Beijing. Make appointments well in advance and be extremely punctual.

Chinese people have a keen sense of hierarchy in the office: the senior member should lead proceedings. Respect silences in conversation and don't hurry things or interrupt.

Suits are the norm in China, regardless of the outside temperature. Women should avoid plunging necklines, overly short skirts, or very high heels.

When entertaining, local businesspeople may insist on paying: after a protest, accept.

Business cards are a big deal: not having one is a bad move. If possible, have yours printed in English on one side and Chinese on the other (your hotel can often arrange this). Proffer your card with both hands and receive the other person's in the same way.

Many gifts, including clocks and cutting implements, are considered unlucky in China. Food—especially presented in a showy basket—is always a good gift choice, as are imported spirits.

LANGUAGE

Learn a little of the local language. You need not strive for fluency; even just mastering a few basic words and terms is bound to make chatting with the locals more rewarding.

Everyone in Beijing speaks Putonghua ("the common language") as the national language of China is known. It's written using ideograms, or characters; in the 1950s the government also introduced a phonetic writing system that uses the Roman alphabet. Known as pinyin, it's widely used to label public buildings and station names. Even if you don't speak or read Chinese, you can easily compare pinyin names with a map, but be warned: written pinyin is lost on taxi drivers, so always come prepared with your destination written in Chinese characters.

District ☏ 010/6553–2288 ⊕ www.hkclinic.
com. **International Medical Center Beijing**
✉ Beijing Lufthansa Center, 50 Liangmaqiao
Lu, Room 106, Chaoyang District ☏ 010/6465–
1561 ⊕ www.imcclinics.com. **International
SOS** ✉ Kunsha Building, 16 Xinyuanli, Wing
1, Suite 105, Chaoyang District ☏ 010/6462–
9112 Clinic, 010/6462–9100 24-hour hotline
⊕ www.internationalsos.com. **Peking Union
Medical College Hospital** ✉ 1 Shui Fu Yuan,
Dongcheng District ☏ 010/6529–5284 ⊕ www.
pumch.cn.

Pharmacies Watsons ✉ Holiday Inn Lido
Hotel, Jichang Lu, Chaoyang District ✉ Sanli-
tun Village South, 19 Sanlitun Lu, Chaoyang
District ⊕ www.watsons.com.cn.

▮ HEALTH

The most common types of illnesses are
caused by contaminated food and water.
Drink only bottled, boiled, or purified
water; don't drink from public fountains
or beverages with ice. Tap water in Beijing is safe for brushing teeth, but you're
better off buying bottled water to drink.
Make sure food has been thoroughly
cooked and is served to you fresh and hot.
If you have problems, mild cases of traveler's diarrhea may respond to Imodium
(known generically as loperamide) or
Pepto-Bismol. Be sure to drink plenty of
fluids; if you can't keep fluids down, seek
medical help immediately.

Infectious diseases can be airborne or
passed via mosquitoes and ticks and
through direct or indirect physical contact with animals or people. Some, including Norwalk-like viruses that affect your
digestive tract, can be passed along
through contaminated food. Condoms
can help prevent most sexually transmit-
ted diseases, but they aren't absolutely
reliable and their quality varies from
country to country. China is notorious for
fake condoms, so it might be best to bring
your own from home or get them from a
health clinic. Speak with your physician
or check the Centers for Disease Control and Prevention or the World Health

Organization websites for health alerts,
particularly if you're pregnant, traveling
with children, or have a chronic illness.

SPECIFIC ISSUES IN BEIJING

Pneumonia and influenza are common
among travelers returning from China—
talk to your doctor about inoculations
before you leave. If you need to buy pre-
scription drugs, use pharmacies of reputable private hospitals.

OVER-THE-COUNTER REMEDIES

Most pharmacies carry over-the-counter
Western medicines and traditional Chinese medicines. By and large, you need
to ask for the generic name of the drug
you're looking for, not a brand name.

SHOTS AND MEDICATIONS

No immunizations are required for entry
into China, but it's a good idea to be
immunized against typhoid and hepatitis
A and B before traveling to Beijing; also
a good idea is to get routine shots for tet-
anus-diphtheria and measles. In winter, a
flu vaccination is also smart.

**Health Warnings National Centers for
Disease Control and Prevention** (CDC).
☏ 800/232-4636 ⊕ www.cdc.gov/travel.
World Health Organization (WHO). ⊕ www.
who.int.

▮ HOURS OF OPERATION

Most offices are open between 9 and 6 on
weekdays; most museums keep roughly
the same hours six or seven days a week.
Everything in China grinds to a halt for
the first two or three days of Chinese New
Year (sometime in mid-January through
February, depending on the lunar calendar), and opening hours are often reduced
for the rest of that season.

Banks and government offices are open
weekdays 9 to 5, although some close
for lunch (sometime between noon and
2). Bank branches and CTS tour desks
in hotels often keep longer hours and
are usually open Saturday (and occasionally even Sunday) mornings. Many hotel

currency-exchange desks remain open 24 hours.

Pharmacies are open daily from 8:30 or 9 am to 6 or 7 pm. Some large pharmacies stay open until 9 pm or even later.

Shops and department stores are generally open daily 9 to 9; some stores in popular tourist areas stay open even later during peak season.

HOLIDAYS

National holidays include New Year's Day (January 1); Chinese New Year (mid-January/through February); Tomb-Sweeping Day (April 5); International Labor Day (May 1); Dragon Boat Festival (late May/early June); anniversary of the founding of the Communist Party of China (July 1); anniversary of the founding of the Chinese People's Liberation Army (August 1); Mid-Autumn Festival (mid- to late September), and National Day (October 1).

▮ MAIL

International mail from China is reliable. Airmail letters to any place in the world should take five to 14 days. Express Mail Service (EMS) is available to many international destinations. Letters within Beijing arrive the next day, and mail to the rest of China takes a day or two longer. Domestic mail can be subject to search, so don't send sensitive materials, such as religious or political literature, as you might cause the recipient trouble.

Service is more reliable if you mail letters from post offices rather than mailboxes. Buy envelopes here, too, as there are standardized sizes in China. You need to glue stamps onto envelopes, as they're not self-adhesive. Most post offices are open daily between 8 and 7. Your hotel can usually send letters for you, too.

You can use the Roman alphabet to write an address. Do not use red ink, which has a negative connotation. You must also include a six-digit zip code for mail within China. The Beijing municipality is assigned the zip code 100000, and each neighboring county starts with 10. For example, the code for Fangshan, to the immediate southwest of Beijing proper, is 102400.

Sending airmail postcards costs Y4.20 and letters Y5.50 to Y6.50.

Main Branches International Post and Telecommunications Office ⊠ Jianguomenwai Dajie, Yabao Lu, Chaoyang District ☎ 010/6512-8114 ⊕ vip.fesco.com.cn/bipto/en.htm.

SHIPPING PACKAGES

It's easy to ship packages home from China. Take what you want to send *unpacked* to the post office—everything will be sewn up officially into satisfying linen-bound packages, a service that costs a few yuan. You have to fill in lengthy forms, and enclosing a photocopy of receipts for the goods inside isn't a bad idea, as they may be opened by customs along the line. Large antiques stores often offer reliable shipping services that take care of customs in China. Large international courier services like DHL, Federal Express, and UPS have offices around Beijing.

Express Services DHL ⊠ 45 Xinyuan Jie, Chaoyang District ☎ 800/810-8000, 010/5860-1076 ⊕ www.cn.dhl.com. **FedEx** ⊠ 3/F, Golden Land Building, 32 Liangmaqiao Lu, Chaoyang District ☎ 010/6464-8855, 800-/988-1888 ⊕ www.fedex.com/cn_english. **UPS** ⊠ China World Trade Center, Bldg. 1, 1 Jianguomenwai Dajie, Chaoyang District ☎ 800/820-8388 ⊕ www.ups.com.

▮ MONEY

The best places to convert your dollars into yuan are at your hotel's front desk or a branch of a major bank, such as Bank of China, CITIC, or HSBC. All these operate with standardized government rates—anything cheaper is illegal, and thus risky. You need to present your passport to change money.

Although credit cards are widespread in China, for day-to-day transactions cash is definitely king. Getting change for larger notes can be a problem in small shops and taxis, so try to stock up on 10s and 20s when you change money.

ATMS AND BANKS

Your own bank will probably charge a fee for using ATMs abroad; the foreign bank you use may also charge a fee. Nevertheless, you'll usually get a better rate of exchange at an ATM than you will at a currency-exchange office or even when changing money in a bank. And extracting funds as you need them is a safer option than carrying around a large amount of cash.

Among the Chinese banks, your best bets for ATMs are Bank of China and ICBC. That said, machines frequently refuse to give cash for mysterious reasons. Move on and try another. Citibank and HSBC have lots of branches in Beijing, and accept all major cards. On-screen instructions appear automatically in English. Be sure to check all bills that you receive from the ATM; sometimes fake notes find their way into the system and it can be a nightmare to get the bank to exchange for real ones—especially if you leave the premises.

CREDIT CARDS

It's a good idea to inform your credit-card company before you travel, especially if you're going abroad and don't travel internationally very often. Otherwise, the credit-card company might put a hold on your card owing to unusual activity—not a good thing halfway through your trip. Record all your credit-card numbers—as well as the phone numbers to call if your cards are lost or stolen—in a safe place, so you're prepared should something go wrong. Both MasterCard and Visa have general numbers you can call (collect if you're abroad) if your card is lost, but you're better off calling the number of your issuing bank, since MasterCard and Visa usually just transfer you to your bank; your bank's number is usually printed on your card.

If you plan to use your credit card for cash advances, you'll need to apply for a PIN at least two weeks before your trip. Although it's usually cheaper (and safer) to use a credit card abroad for large purchases (so you can cancel payments or be reimbursed if there's a problem), note that some credit-card companies *and* the banks that issue them add substantial percentages to all foreign transactions, whether they're in a foreign currency or not. Check on these fees before leaving home, so there won't be any surprises when you get the bill.

■TIP→ **Before you charge something, ask the merchant whether or not he or she plans to do a dynamic currency conversion (DCC). In such a transaction the credit-card processor (shop, restaurant, or hotel, not Visa or MasterCard) converts the currency and charges you in dollars. In most cases you'll pay the merchant a 3% fee for this service in addition to any credit-card company and issuing-bank foreign-transaction surcharges.**

Dynamic currency conversion programs are becoming increasingly widespread. Merchants who participate in them are supposed to ask whether you want to be charged in dollars or the local currency, but they don't always do so. And even if they do offer you a choice, they may well avoid mentioning the additional surcharges. The good news is that you *do* have a choice. And if this practice really gets your goat, you can avoid it entirely thanks to American Express; with its cards, DCC simply isn't an option.

In Beijing, American Express, MasterCard, and Visa are accepted at most major hotels and a growing number of upmarket stores and restaurants. Diners Club is accepted at many hotels and some restaurants.

Reporting Lost Cards American Express
☎ 800/528–4800 in the U.S., 336/393–1111 collect from abroad ⊕ www.americanexpress. com. **Diners Club** ☎ 800/234–6377 in the U.S., 514/881–3735 collect from abroad

⊕ www.dinersclub.com. **MasterCard**
☎ 800/627–8372 in the U.S., 636/722–7111
collect from abroad ⊕ www.mastercard.com.
Visa ☎ 800/847–2911 in the U.S., 410/581–
9994 collect from abroad ⊕ www.visa.com.

CURRENCY AND EXCHANGE

The Chinese currency is officially called the yuan (Y), and is also known as *renminbi* (RMB), or "People's Money." You may also hear it called *kuai*, an informal expression like "buck." After being pegged to the dollar at around Y8 for years, it was allowed to float within a small range starting in 2005. It was held firm again until mid-2010 when it was allowed to float again. As of this writing, the conversion was Y6.24 to $1.

Both old and new styles of bills circulate simultaneously in China, and many denominations have both coins and bills. The Bank of China issues bills in denominations of 1 (green), 5 (purple), 10 (turquoise), 20 (brown), 50 (blue-green), and 100 (red) yuan. There are Y1 coins, too. The yuan subdivides into 10-cent units called *jiao* or *mao*; these come in bills and coins of 1, 2, and 5. The smallest denomination is the *fen,* which comes in coins (and occasionally tiny notes) of 1, 2, and 5; these are largely useless in day-to-day exchanges. Counterfeiting is rife here, and even small stores inspect notes with ultraviolet lamps. Change can also be a problem—don't expect much success paying for a Y3 purchase with a Y100 note, for example.

Exchange rates in China are fixed by the government daily, so they're the same in banks, department stores, and at your hotel's exchange desk, which often has the added advantage of being open 24 hours a day. A passport is required. Hold on to your exchange receipt, which you need to convert your extra yuan back into dollars.

▌ PACKING

Most Chinese people dress for comfort, and you can do the same. There's little risk of offending people with your dress, no matter how casual. Sturdy, comfortable, closed-toe walking shoes are a must. Summers are dusty and hot, so lightweight slacks, shorts, and short-sleeve shirts are great options. A light raincoat is useful in spring and fall. Come winter, thermal long underwear is a lifesaver. An overcoat, scarf, hat, and gloves will help keep icy winds at bay. That said, in Beijing you can arrive unprepared: the city is a shopper's paradise. If you can't fit a bulky jacket in your suitcase, buy a cheap one upon arrival. Scarves, gloves, and hats are also cheap and easy to find.

Carry packets of tissues and antibacterial hand wipes with you—toilet paper isn't common in Chinese public restrooms. A small flashlight with extra batteries is also useful. Chinese pharmacies can be limited, so take adequate stocks if you're picky about lotions and potions. Beijing is quite dry, so moisturizer is a must. Choice is also limited for feminine-hygiene products, so bring along extra or pay outrageous prices in the expat supermarkets.

If you're planning a longer trip or will be using local guides, bring a few items from your home country as gifts, such as candy, T-shirts, and small cosmetic items like lipstick and nail polish.

■TIP➔ **If you're a U.S. citizen traveling abroad, consider registering online with the State Department (⊕ step.state.gov), so the government will know to look for you should a crisis occur in the country you're visiting.**

PASSPORTS AND VISAS

All U.S. citizens, even infants, need a valid passport with a tourist visa stamped in it to enter China (except for Hong Kong, where you only need a valid passport). Getting a tourist visa (known as an "L" visa) in the United States is straightforward, but be sure to check the Chinese embassy website to make sure you're bringing the correct documents. Visa regulations sometimes change on short notice. Standard visas are for single-entry stays of up to 30 days and are valid for

90 days from the day of issue (*not* the day of entry), so don't get your visa too far in advance. Costs range from $140 for a tourist visa issued within two to three working days to $170 for a same-day service. CIBT Visas is a fast, efficient processer of all types of China visa requests.

As of 2013, U.S. travelers (and those of 44 other countries) transiting through Beijing Capital Airport and Shanghai's Hongqiao and Pudong airports can now stay for up to 72 hours visa-free, so long as you have proof of an onward ticket to a third country. Signs at the international arrivals area of the airport will direct you toward the appropriate channels.

Travel agents in Hong Kong can also issue visas to visit mainland China. ■**TIP→ The visa application will ask your occupation. The Chinese authorities don't look favorably upon those who work in publishing or the media. People in these professions routinely give their occupation as "teacher."**

Under no circumstances should you overstay your visa. To extend your visa, go to the Division of the Entry and Exit of Aliens of the Beijing Municipal Public Security Bureau a week before your visa expires. The office is also known as the Foreigner's Police; it's open weekdays 8 am to noon and 1:30 pm to 4 pm. Under normal circumstances it's generally no problem to get a month's extension on a tourist visa, but the rules change often. Bring your passport and a registration of temporary residency from your hotel. Keep in mind that you'll need to leave your passport there for five to seven days, so get a receipt and always keep a photocopy of your passport on you. If you're trying to extend a business visa, you'll need the above items as well as a letter from the business that originally invited you to China.

Information CIBT Visas ☎ *800/929–2428* ⊕ *cibtvisas.com/china-visa.php.*

In the U.S. Consulate General of the People's Republic of China ⊠ *520 12th Ave.,* *New York, New York, USA* ☎ *212/244–9456,* *212/244–9392* ⊕ *www.nyconsulate.prchina.org.* **Embassy of the People's Republic of China, Washington** ⊠ *2201 Wisconsin Ave. NW, Suite 110, Washington, District of Columbia, USA* ☎ *202/337–1956* ⊕ *www.china-embassy.org.*

Visa Extensions Beijing Municipal Public Security Bureau Division of the Entry and Exit of Aliens ⊠ *2 Andingmen Dong Dajie, Dongcheng District* ☎ *010/8401–5300, 010/8402–0101.*

■ RESTROOMS

Public restrooms abound in Beijing—the street, parks, restaurants, department stores, and major tourist attractions are all likely locations. Some charge a small fee (usually less than Y1), and seldom provide Western-style facilities or private booths. Instead, expect squat toilets, open troughs, and rusty spigots; "wc" signs at intersections point the way to these facilities. Toilet paper or tissues and antibacterial hand wipes are good things to have in your day pack. The restrooms in the newest shopping plazas, fast-food outlets, and deluxe restaurants catering to foreigners are generally on a par with American restrooms.

Find a Loo The Bathroom Diaries. The Bathroom Diaries is flush with unsanitized info on restrooms the world over—each one located, reviewed, and rated. ⊕ *www.* *thebathroomdiaries.com.*

■ SAFETY

There is little violent crime against tourists in China, partly because the penalties are severe for those who are caught—China's yearly death-sentence tolls run into the thousands. Single women can move about Beijing without too much hassle. Handbag snatching and pickpocketing do occur in markets and on crowded buses or trains—keep an eye open and your money safe and you should have no problems. Use the lockbox in your hotel room to store any valuables. You should always carry either your passport or a photocopy of the information page and the visa page of your passport with you for identification purposes.

Beijing is full of people looking to make a quick buck. The most common scam involves people persuading you to go with them for a tea ceremony, which is often so pleasant that you don't smell a rat until several hundred dollars appear on your credit-card bill. "Art students" who pressure you into buying work is another common scam. The same rules that apply to hostess bars worldwide are also true in Beijing. Avoiding such scams is as easy as refusing *all* unsolicited services—be it from taxi or pedicab drivers, tour guides, or potential "friends."

Beijing traffic is as manic as it looks, and survival of the fittest (or the biggest) is the main rule. Crossing streets can be an extreme sport. Drivers rarely give pedestrians the right-of-way and don't even look for pedestrians when making a right turn on a red light. Cyclists have less power but are just as aggressive.

Beijing's severely polluted air can bring on, or aggravate, respiratory problems. If you're a sufferer, take the cue from locals, who wear special pollution masks, or a scarf or bandanna as protection.

■ TIP→ Distribute your cash, credit cards, IDs, and other valuables between a deep front pocket, an inside jacket or vest pocket, and a hidden money pouch. Don't reach for the money pouch once you're in public.

Safety Transportation Security Administration (TSA). ☎ 866/289–9673 ⊕ www.tsa.gov.

■ TAXES

There is no sales tax in China. All hotels charge a 5% tax, and larger international hotels also add a 10% to 15% service fee. Some restaurants charge a 10% service fee.

■ TIME

Beijing is 8 hours ahead of London, 13 hours ahead of New York, 14 hours ahead of Chicago, and 16 hours ahead of Los Angeles. There's no daylight saving time, so subtract an hour in summer.

Time Zones Timeanddate.com. Timeanddate. com can help you figure out the correct time anywhere in the world. ⊕ www.timeanddate. com/worldclock.

■ TIPPING

Tipping is a tricky issue in China. It's officially forbidden by the government, and locals simply don't do it. In general, follow their lead without qualms. Nevertheless, the practice is beginning to catch on, especially among tour guides, who often expect Y10 a day. You don't need to tip in restaurants or in taxis—many drivers insist on handing over your change, however small.

■ TOURS

SPECIAL-INTEREST TOURS

Bespoke Beijing offers personalized tours, and WildChina leads distinctive, ecologically sensitive journeys all over China. Stretch-a-Leg Travel specializes in small group tours of Beijing's side streets and off-the-beaten-track sights by expert guides.

Contacts Bespoke Beijing ⊠ B510, 107 Dongsi Bei Dajie, Dongcheng District ☎ 010/6400–0133 ✍ info@bespoke-beijing. com ⊕ www.bespoke-beijing.com ⊗ Daily 9–5. Stretch-A-Leg Travel ⊠ 2 Qian'gulouyuan, Jiaodaokou, Dongcheng District ☎ 010/6401–8933 ✍ info@stretchaleg.com ⊕ www. stretchalegtravel.com ⊗ Weekdays 10–6. WildChina ⊠ Oriental Place, 9 East Dongfang Lu, Room 803, Chaoyang District ☎ 010/6465–6602, 888/902–8808 in the U.S. ✍ info@ wildchina.com ⊕ www.wildchina.com ⊗ Weekdays 9–6.

BIKING

Cycle China offers plenty of cycling trips in and around Beijing and beyond, such as the Great Wall. You can hire bikes from them, or take your own. Bike China Adventures organizes trips of varying length and difficulty all over China.

Contacts Bike China Adventures ☎ 800/818–1778 ⊕ www.bikechina.com. **Cycle China** ✉ 12 Jingshan Dong Jie, Dongcheng District ☎ 139/1188–6524 ⊕ www.cyclechina. com ⊙ Daily 9–6.

CULTURE

Local guides are often creative when it comes to showing you history and culture, so having an expert with you can make a big difference. Learning is the focus of Smithsonian Journeys' small-group tours, which are led by university professors. China experts also lead National Geographic Expeditions trips, but all that knowledge doesn't come cheap. The China Culture Center is a wonderful resource for tours, classes, lectures, and other events in Beijing. The China Guide is a Beijing-based, American-managed travel agency offering tours that do *not* make shopping detours.

Contacts China Culture Center ✉ 21 Liangmaqiao Rd., inside the Drive-in Movie Theater Park, Chaoyang District ☎ 010/6432–9341, 010/8420-0671 weekends ⊕ www. chinaculturecenter.org. **The China Guide** ✉ Building 7-1, Jianguomenwai Waijiaogongyu Diplomatic Compound, 8th Floor, Room 81 ☎ 010/8532–1860 ⊘ book@ thechinaguide.com ⊕ www.thechinaguide.com ⊙ Weekdays 10–6. **National Geographic Expeditions** ☎ 888/966-8687 ⊕ www. nationalgeographicexpeditions.com. **Smithsonian Journeys** ☎ 855/330–1542 in the U.S. ⊕ www.smithsonianjourneys.org.

CULINARY

Intrepid Travel is an Australian company offering foodie tours with market visits, cooking demonstrations, and plenty of good eats. Imperial Tours combines sightseeing with lectures, cooking demonstrations, and lots of five-star dining.

Contacts Imperial Tours ✉ 2-2004 Wanguocheng, 1 Xiangheyuan Lu, Dongcheng District ☎ 888/888–1970 in the U.S., 010/8440–7162 in China ⊕ www.imperialtours.net. **Intrepid Travel** ☎ 800/970–7299 in the U.S. ⊕ www. intrepidtravel.com.

HIKING

Beijing Hikers offer multiple hikes and camping stays on and around the Great Wall, They always make sure to leave no rubbish behind, unlike many other companies.

Contacts Beijing Hikers ✉ 10 Jiuxianqiao Zhong Lu, Building A, Suite 4012, Chaoyang District ☎ 010/6432–2786 ⊕ www. beijinghikers.com ⊙ Weekdays 9–6.

■ VISITOR INFORMATION

For general information, including advice on tours, insurance, and safety, call, or visit China National Tourist Office's website, as well as the website run by the Beijing Tourism Administration (BTA). **■ TIP➔** The BTA maintains a 24-hour hotline for tourist inquiries and complaints, with operators fluent in English. BTA also runs Beijing Tourist Information Centers, whose staff can help you with free maps and directions in Beijing.

The two best-known Chinese travel agencies are China International Travel Service (CITS) and China Travel Service (CTS), both under the same government ministry. Although they have some tourist information, they are businesses, so don't expect endless resources if you're not booking through them.

Tourist Information Beijing Tourism Administration ☎ 010/8353–1111 ⊘ visit-beijingeng@163.com ⊕ english.visitbeijing. com.cn. **Beijing Travel Hotline** ☎ 010/12301 ⊕ english.visitbeijing.com.cn. **BTG International Travel and Tours** ✉ Beijing Tourism Building, 28 Jianguomenwai Dajie, Chaoyang District ☎ 400–010–0808 ⊕ www.btgtravel. com.cn. **China International Travel Service** ☎ 010/6522–2991 in China, 626/568–8993 in the U.S. ⊕ www.cits.net. **China Travel Service**

📠 *400/811-6666 in China, 800/899–8618 in the U.S.* ⊕ *www.ctsho.com.*

ONLINE TRAVEL TOOLS

All About Beijing **Beijing Expat.** Beijing Expat has pages and pages of advice and listings from foreigners living in Beijing. ⊕ *beijing.asiaxpat.com.* **Beijing International.** This is a comprehensive, if slightly dry, guide to the city. ⊕ *www.ebeijing.gov.cn.* **China Digital Times.** This excellent Berkeley-run site tracks China-related news and culture. ⊕ *www.chinadigitaltimes.net.*

Business **Caixin.** This is the English-language website for the popular business and economic publication. ⊕ *english.caixin.com.* **China Daily.** This popular newspaper's website has a large business section. ⊕ *www.chinadaily.com.cn.*

Global Times. The best of the local newspapers has lots of business coverage. ⊕ *www.globaltimes.cn.*

Culture and Entertainment **The Beijinger.** A weekly newsletter lets you know what's going on in the city. ⊕ *www.thebeijinger.com.* **Chinese Culture.** This detailed database has information on Chinese art, literature, film, and history. ⊕ *www.chinaculture.org.* **Smart Beijing.** This website has extensive listings, reviews, and offbeat articles on life in the city. ⊕ *www.smartbeijing.com.* **Time Out Beijing.** The popular magazine provides a great overview of all the major cultural events in the city. ⊕ *www.timeoutbeijing.com.*

INDEX

PHOTO CREDITS

Front cover: JDHeaton/age fotostock [Forbidden City]. 1, Boaz Rottem / age fotostock. 2-3, TAO IMAGES / age fotostock. 5, lu linsheng/iStockphoto. Chapter 1: Experience Beijing: 8-9, SuperStock/ age fotostock. 10, Artifan/Shutterstock. 11 (left), Hotel G Beijing. 11 (right), DK.samco/Shutterstock. 12, Brian Jeffery Beggerly/Flickr. 13 (left), Fan Ping/Shutterstock. 13 (right), Wikimedia Commons. 16 (left), Ivan Walsh/Flickr. 16 (top center), Chris Ronneseth/iStockphoto. 16, (bottom right), Jonathan Larsen/Shutterstock. 16 (top right), Ivan Walsh/ Flickr. 17 (top left), zhang bo/iStockphoto. 17 (bottom left), fotohunter/Shutterstock. 17 (right), claudio zaccherini/Shutterstock. 18, Holly Peabody, Fodors. com member. 19, Frans Schalekamp, Fodors.com member. 20, China National Tourist Office. 21 (left), Honza Soukup/Flickr. 21 (right), claudio zaccherini/Shutterstock. 23 (left), yxm2008/Shutterstock. 23 (right), bbobo, Fodors.com member. 25 (left), Eastimages/Shutterstock. 25 (right), gary718/Shutterstock. 26, Johann 'Jo' Guzman, Fodors.com member. 27, Steve Slawsky. 28, Gretchen Winters, Fodors. com member. 29, huang shengchun/iStockphoto. 32, Stefano Tronci/Shutterstock. 33, qing-qing/Shutterstock. 34 (left), Kowloonese/Wikimedia Commons. 34 (top right), Daniel Shichman & Yael Tauger/ Wikimedia Commons. 34 (bottom right), Wikipedia.org. 35 (left), Hung Chung Chih/Shutterstock. 35 (right), rodho/Shutterstock. 36 (left), Chinneeb/ Wikimedia Commons. 36 (top right), B_cool/Wikimedia Commons. 36 (bottom right), Imperial Painter/Wikimedia Commons. 37 (left), Wikimedia Commons. 37 (top right), Joe Brandt/iStockphoto. 37 (bottom right), 38 (all), and 39 (top left), Public Domain, via Wikimedia Commons. 39 (bottom left), ImagineChina. 39 (right), tomislav domes/Flickr. 40, Jarno Gonzalez/iStockphoto. Chapter 2: Exploring: 41, TAO IMAGES / age fotostock. 42, fotohunter/Shutterstock. 44, lu linsheng/iStockphoto. 45 (top), TAO IMAGES / age fotostock. 45 (bottom), Bob Balestri/iStockphoto. 46, Lance Lee | AsiaPhoto.com/iStockphoto. 47 (left), Jiping Lai/iStockphoto. 47 (top right), May Wong/Flickr. 47 (right, 2nd from top), William Perry/iStockphoto. 47 (right, 3rd from top), bing liu/iStockphoto. 47 (bottom right), William Perry/iStockphoto. 48 (top), Helena Lovincic/iStockphoto. 48 (bottom left and right), Wikipedia. 49 (top), rehoboth foto/Shutterstock. 49 (bottom left and right), Wikipedia. 50, Alexander Savin/Flickr. 53, shalunishka/Shutterstock. 54, claudio zaccherini/Shutterstock. 56, TAO IMAGES / age fotostock. 59, P. Narayan / age fotostock. 61, claudio zaccherini/Shutterstock. 63, claudio zaccherini/Shutterstock. 64, Jose Fuste Raga / age fotostock. 66. Lim Yong Hian/Shutterstock. 69, TAO IMAGES / age fotostock. 71, JTB Photo / age fotostock. 73, TAO IMAGES / age fotostock. 75, sanglei slei/iStockphoto. 77, William Ju/Shutterstock. 78, FRILET Patrick / age fotostock. 80, Sylvain Grandadam / age fotostock. 83 and 85, Daderot/Wikimedia Commons. 86, View Stock/age fotostock. 88, TAO IMAGES / age fotostock. Chapter 3: Where to Eat: 91, TAO IMAGES / age fotostock. 92, Frans Schalekamp, Fodors.com member. 100, beggs/Flickr. 101, FOTOSEARCH RM / age fotostock. 102 (bottom), Fotoos-VanRobin/Wikimedia Commons. 102 (top), Chubykin Arkady/Shutterstock. 103 (left), ImagineChina. 103 (top right), hywit dimyadi/iStockphoto. 103 (bottom right), Maria Ly/Flickr. 104 (bottom), Hannamariah/Shutterstock. 104 (top), zkruger/iStockphoto. 105 (top left), Ritesh Man Tamrakar/Wikimedia Commons. 105 (center left), Rjanag/ Wikimedia Commons. 105 (bottom left), Craig Lovell / Eagle Visions Photography / Alamy. 105 (right), Cephas Picture Library / Alamy. 106 (top left), Eneri LLC/iStockphoto. 106 (bottom left), Man Haan Chung/iStockphoto. 106 (top right), Holger Gogolin/iStockphoto. 106 (bottom right), Eneri LLC/ iStockphoto. 114 Fumio Okada / age fotostock. 117, Thomas Roetting / age fotostock. 122, patrick frilet / age fotostock. Chapter 4: Where to Stay: 131, The Ritz-Carlton Beijing, Financial Street. 132, Hotel G Beijing. Chapter 5: Shopping: 153, Oote Boe / age fotostock. 154, fi repile/Flickr. 157, Renaud Visage / age fotostock. 162, TAO IMAGES / age fotostock. 165, Christian Kober / age fotostock. 168, TAO IMAGES / age fotostock. Chapter 6: Nightlife and Performing Arts: 171, Peter Adams / age fotostock. 172, PhotoTalk/iStockphoto. 179, Werner Bachmeier / age fotostock. 181, TAO IMAGES / age fotostock. 182-83, Sylvain Grandadam / age fotostock. Chapter 7: Best Side Trips: 187, Sylvain Grandadam / age fotostock. 188, dspiel, Fodors.com member. 190, Hung Chung Chih/Shutterstock. 194, Luoxubin | Dreamstime.com. 195, Wikipedia. 196-97, Liu Jianmin/age fotostock. 198 (top), Eugenia Kim/iStockphoto. 198 (bottom), Alan Crawford/iStockphoto. 199, Chris Ronneseth/iStockphoto. 206, JTB Photo / age fotostock. 211, richliy/Shutterstock. Back cover (from left to right): cozyta/Shutterstock; jaume/Shutterstock; Holly Peabody, Fodors.com member. Spine: testing/Shutterstock.

About Our Writers: All photos are courtesy of the writers except for the following: Kit Gillet, courtesy of Jonah Kessel.

NOTES

NOTES

NOTES

NOTES

NOTES